Co-Occurring Disorders

Integrated Assessment and Treatment of
Substance Use and Mental Disorders

By Charles Atkins, MD

"This book is wonderful. I plan to adopt it as a textbook for my MSW Co-Occurring Disorder Program."

-- **Jaak Rakfeldt, Ph.D.**, Co-Occurring Disorder Cohort Program, MSW Coordinator, Southern Connecticut State Unviersity Professor

"So much valuable information in a user friendly manner, clinicians as well as others will find this book useful in their practice. This resource is a powerful tool and I am especially proud of the way he connects issues related to gender and trauma."

-- **Colette Anderson, LCSW, CEO**
The Connecticut Women's Consortium

"A clear, concise and straightforward and up to date text on co-occurring disorders has been glaringly lacking in the Behavioral Health Field. Co-Occurring Disorders: The Integrated Assessment and Treatment of Substance Use and Mental Disorders offers students and clinicians at all levels a comprehensive view of the challenges of treating those with a co-occurring mental health and substance use disorder. Written in plain language, Atkins provides a clinical road map beginning with an outline of key issues and ending with treatment planning. Atkins also does what most don't and that is to stress the importance of peer support, natural supports and self-help. Co-Occurring Disorders: The Integrated Assessment and Treatment of Substance Use and Mental Disorders is an important addition to any educator's and clinician's bookshelf."

--**Eileen M. Russo, MA, LADC**, Assistant Professor,
Drug and Alcohol Recovery Counselor Program,
Gateway Community College, New Haven, CT

Published by
PESI Publishing & Media
PESI, Inc
3839 White Ave
Eau Claire, WI 54703

Cover: Amy Rubenzer
Layout: Bookmasters
Edited by: Bookmasters

ISBN: 978-1-936128-54-9

Printed in the United States of America

Library of Congress Cataloging-in-Publication Data

Atkins, Charles, author.
    Co-occurring disorders : integrated assessment and treatment of substance
use and mental disorders / by Charles Atkins.
        p. ; cm.
    Includes bibliographical references and index.
    ISBN 978-1-936128-54-9 (pbk. : alk. paper) — ISBN 1-936128-54-3 (pbk. : alk. paper)
I. Title.
    [DNLM: 1. Substance-Related Disorders—complications.   2. Substance-Related
Disorders—therapy.   3. Mental Disorders—complications.   4. Mental Disorders—
therapy.   5. Psychotherapy—methods. WM 270]
    RC564
    616.86—dc23   2014036016

PESI
Publishing
& Media
www.pesipublishing.com

Books by Charles Atkins

NON-FICTION

The Bipolar Disorder Answer Book
The Alzheimer's Answer Book

FICTION

The Portrait
Risk Factor
Cadaver's Ball
The Prodigy
Ashes Ashes
Mother's Milk
Go to Hell
Vultures at Twilight
Best Place to Die
Done to Death

YOUNG ADULTS FICTION WRITING AS CALEB JAMES

Haffling

To librarians extraordinaire Linda Spadaccini and Lynn Sabol

Table of Contents

Acknowledgments

I wish to express my gratitude for all of those who helped me develop this book. In particular Eileen Russo, Colette Anderson, Aili Arisco, Steve Jayson, Karen Kangas, Steven Southwick, Lauren Doninger, Martha Schmitz, Lynn Zinno, Carol Genova, Marie Johnston, Lori Sobel, Thomas Reinhardt, Doreen Elnitsky, Laura Nesta, Cheryl Planten, Sheila Zimmerman, Jason Schwarz, Pam Kieras, Karen Savage, Diane Passander, Bob Taylor, Susan Hayward, Elizabeth Fitzgerald, Linda Jackson, and Michael Olson. So much of this book originates in work I did with my wonderful colleagues and clients at Waterbury Hospital's West Main Behavioral Health and Community Mental Health Affiliates (CMHA) in New Britain, CT. We learn so much from each other, and experience is our greatest teacher.

About the Author

Photo: Bobby Miller

Charles Atkins, MD is a board-certified psychiatrist, published author, clinical trainer, and the Chief Medical Officer for Community Mental Health Affiliates, LLC (CMHA) in New Britain, Connecticut.

He has written both non-fiction and fiction, including books on Bipolar Disorder, and Alzheimer's Disease. His recent novels include the Barrett Conyors forensic thriller series and The Strauss and Campbell Connecticut cozies. His first young adult novel—HAFFLING—was published in 2013 under the pen name, Caleb James.

Dr. Atkins has written hundreds of articles, columns, and shorts stories for professional and popular magazines, newspapers, and journals. He is a member of the Yale volunteer clinical faculty. He's been a regular contributor to the American Medical Association's *American Medical News*, a consultant to the Reader's Digest Medical Breakthrough series, and his work has appeared in publications ranging from *The Journal of the American Medical Association (JAMA)* to *Writer's Digest Magazine*. He's been twice featured in the *New York Times*, as well as many other publications.

Introduction

More than 8 million Americans meet the criteria for having at least one co-occurring substance use and mental disorder. This represents a large and diverse group of people, from a top executive with obsessive-compulsive disorder, who drinks more than a pint of hard liquor a day to a homeless woman who smokes cannabis heavily and has been in and out of psychiatric hospitals with a diagnosis of schizophrenia. With this vast spectrum of people affected with co-occurring disorders, and the almost endless number of diagnostic combinations, it is easy to see how the assessment and overall treatment must be custom fit to the person and their real-life circumstances. Strategies to help the homeless woman with schizophrenia will totally miss the mark with the germ phobic executive who drinks heavily to quiet his intrusive obsessive thoughts, and vice versa.

Studies that look at particular pieces of this co-occurring matrix are still in their infancy. But on balance, the research shows that integrated treatment (i.e., treatment that addresses both the substance use and mental disorders) leads to better outcomes for both. For this reason, I've undertaken to write this book to give clinicians an overview on how to both assess co-occurring disorders and to develop effective treatment with their specific clients.

The how and why someone develops co-occurring substance use and mental health disorders makes sense. We are the sum of our experiences and upbringing, genetics, epigenetics, family history, lifestyle, and temperament. Perhaps someone got into trouble with drugs as a way of medicating crippling anxiety and depression. For a person with attention deficit disorder, perhaps they began to abuse their prescribed stimulants (Ritalin, Adderall, etc.) or discovered cocaine helped them calm down and focus. Maybe someone got hooked on prescription pain pills following a medical problem, or maybe they just liked the high, or perhaps they were part of a social group where substance use was the norm and things got out of hand.

For some, the drugs came first and serious psychiatric symptoms followed. New research has shown that for certain people, taking drugs can be like pressing the ON button to serious mental illnesses, such as schizophrenia. In other cases, things got bad following a traumatic event. For many with no history of mental illness, trauma—experiencing or witnessing life-threatening circumstances (war, sexual assault, prison, natural or human-made disasters, such as 9/11)—can leave us changed. There is no more frightening an experience than to find that one day your mind, which you thought was under your control, is now playing horrible and frightening tricks that can include vivid flashbacks and re-experiencing horrific events.

When people are in pain, physical or emotional, they want relief, even if temporary. When someone with overwhelming anxiety and panic attacks discovers the calming effects of alcohol, it's easy to see how returning to the bottle becomes a daily habit. Likewise, the soothing and euphoric effects of opioids—from pain pills to heroin—can quickly change from an occasional indulgence to an enslaving addiction, where going even a few hours or a day without a pill or the next hit of dope leads to unbearable symptoms of withdrawal.

I sometimes use the metaphor that treating co-occurring disorders is like assembling a Thanksgiving meal, where you're firing—literally—on all burners. Some things must be carefully watched lest they get ruined, while other dishes can simmer on the back of the stove. The front burner items must be immediately tended to, including active withdrawal syndromes, suicidality, homelessness, serious legal issues, child-safety concerns, and dangerous behaviors. Once those issues are safely managed, or at least not about to boil over, the focus shifts to less pressing, but still serious, issues, such as an untreated or inadequately treated depression or anxiety disorder.

The goals of this book are to give you, the reader, both the framework for constructing treatment and the tools with which to do it. It is written for the clinician but is also accessible for people in recovery, their families, and their loved ones.

- The first part of the book explores key topics in working with people with co-occurring mental illness and substance use disorders. This section includes how to conduct a comprehensive and ongoing assessment, clarify diagnoses, and establish and understand the person's goals and level of motivation (both to change the substance use behavior and to work on mental health problems). The first several chapters lay down a step-by-step process of constructing the problem/need list, establishing goals, and mapping out treatment.

- The second portion of this book goes through the major classes of mental disorders. Each chapter utilizes case studies to demonstrate the tight connections between particular disorders and the ways substance use problems develop and co-occur. Each chapter includes specific therapeutic approaches, as well as the importance of wellness regimens (attention to health, diet, exercise, relationships, meaningful activities, spirituality, etc.), and the use of medications, when indicated.

- The final section covers topics related to specific substances, such as alcohol withdrawal, opioid replacement therapies, misuse of over-the-counter medications, substances obtained through the Internet, and so forth. Therapies approved by the Food and Drug Administration (FDA) for particular drugs will be reviewed, along with other "off label" and alternative treatments and the evidence—or lack thereof—to support their efficacy.

- References and resources specific to each chapter, and appendix for state drug monitoring programs and state agencies, are included at the back of the book.

For myself, I find working with people who have co-occurring mental and substance use disorders to be highly gratifying. People can, and do, transform their lives, and it's a wonderful thing to be a part of that transformation.

SECTION I

Getting Started

CHAPTER 1

The Co-Occurring Basics: Overview, Terms, and Key Concepts

Overview

Historical Perspective

Key Concepts and Definitions

> Recovery
>
> Co-Occurring Disorders (COD)
>
> "No Wrong Door" Policy
>
> Person-Centered
>
> Cultural Competence
>
> Trauma Informed
>
> Gender- and Sexual-Orientation Sensitivity
>
> The Quadrants of Care
>
> Stages of Treatment
>
> Sequential, Parallel, and Integrated Treatment
>
> Integration of Behavioral Health and Substance Use Services
> with Primary Care: The Patient-Centered Medical Home (PCMH)

Understanding Behavioral Health Diagnoses and the DSM-5

OVERVIEW

The 2012 National Survey on Drug Use and Health (NSDUH) reports that 43.7 million Americans older than 18 have at least one mental illness (18.6% of the population), 17 million (6.5%) people are heavy alcohol users, and 23.7 million (9.2%) have used illicit drugs in the past month. Among those 43.7 million people with mental illness, roughly 8.4 million (19.7%) also have problems with drugs or alcohol. Among those with more serious mental illness this percentage is higher (27.3%). These numbers contrast starkly with the 6.4 percent of the general population reported to have a substance use disorder. Finally, for those individuals with co-occurring substance use and mental disorders, nearly 50 percent (46.3%) will receive some substance use and/or mental health treatment within the year.

3

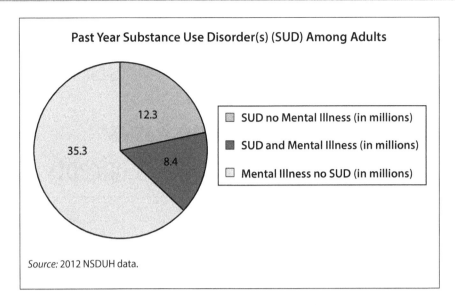

Past Year Substance Use Disorder(s) (SUD) Among Adults

- 12.3
- 35.3
- 8.4

- ☐ SUD no Mental Illness (in millions)
- ■ SUD and Mental Illness (in millions)
- ☐ Mental Illness no SUD (in millions)

Source: 2012 NSDUH data.

For behavioral health clinicians, the question has become not, "Did you use drugs?" but "What drugs did you use? And why?" For the substance abuse counselor, the question is, "Did you use drugs to get high, to be social, or was it—at least in part—to medicate away painful emotions, memories, or others symptoms of mental health problems?"

The scope and magnitude of co-occurring disorders (COD) include the following:

- More than 8 million Americans have COD in any given year.
- Mental illness rates in people seeking substance abuse treatment range from 50% to 75%.
- Substance use disorders are found in 50% of people seeking mental health services.
- People with COD are far more likely to require hospitalization than people with either just a mental illness or a substance use disorder.
- Across mental health diagnoses, people who have co-occurring substance use disorders have worse outcomes, including more hospitalizations, lower quality of life, more physical health problems and more psychiatric diagnoses.
- Higher rates of serious suicidal thinking, suicide plans, and suicide attempts are seen in people with co-occurring disorders.
- Rates of illicit substance use are higher, for all substances, among people with mental illness.

HISTORICAL PERSPECTIVE

The mid- to late-twentieth century saw a movement away from the long-term hospitalization of people with serious mental illnesses, such as schizophrenia, bipolar disorder, and severe depression. Many of these individuals had spent much of their lives in institutionalized settings. Although efforts at deinstitutionalization were deemed humanitarian, and the emphasis was placed on "least-restrictive settings," the transition into the community was not a smooth one.

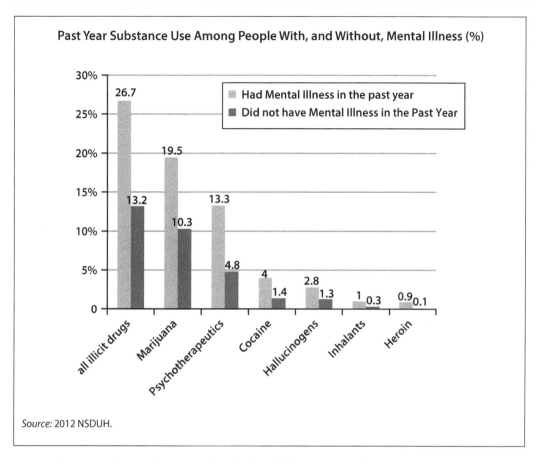

Past Year Substance Use Among People With, and Without, Mental Illness (%)

Source: 2012 NSDUH.

As large state hospitals emptied and closed, their prior residents experienced high rates of homelessness, exposure to violence, increased rates of serious infections (HIV and hepatitis), arrests and legal problems, and use of drugs and alcohol. At the same time younger individuals with serious mental illness, for whom these long-term hospitalizations were no longer an option, came to the attention of researchers. In particular, a growing awareness focused on younger people with mental illness turning to drugs and alcohol.

In the late 1980s the terms *dual diagnosis* and *co-occurring* emerged to describe individuals who had both serious mental illness and substance use disorders. What also became clear was that services for substance use disorders and mental illness were not linked and had exclusionary criteria that created barriers. The norm was for a substance abuse treatment program to exclude people with a history of significant mental illness, and mental health providers were reluctant to work with people who were actively using drugs or alcohol.

By the 1990s, growing concern and clinical literature began linking the problems of substance use disorders and mental illness. Clearly, the risks associated with co-occurring disorders were real and ranged from increased rates of hospitalization, homelessness, poverty, arrests, violence and traumatization, HIV and hepatitis infection, and poor overall psychosocial functioning. What emerged, initially in working with people with more serious mental illness and co-occurring substance use disorders, was the concept of integrated treatment. Early studies and efforts to integrate treatment showed improved outcomes, with decreased rates of relapse and hospitalization, and improved quality of life.

In the past three decades, greater attention has surrounded the issues of co-occurring disorders (COD). In 2005 the Center for Substance Abuse Treatment (CSAT), a part of the Substance Abuse Mental Health Service Administration (SAMHSA) released a treatment improvement protocol (TIP 42) that both explored the scope of the issue and urged clinicians, programs, and mental health and substance abuse systems to move toward increasingly integrated approaches to working with people with co-occurring disorders.

In TIP 42, as well as in other publications since, there is an acknowledgment that any discussion of co-occurring disorders involves a vast matrix of people and diagnoses. What has been carefully studied is only the tip of the iceberg. The overall field of integrated behavioral health and substance use treatment is still in its infancy.

For researchers, the task is a daunting one. Co-occurring disorders by definition imply multiple variables, which make for challenging research questions such as whether a medication or therapy work with a certain group of people who have a certain psychiatric diagnosis <u>and</u> a particular substance use disorder. Because of this complexity, relatively few studies have looked at specific medications and therapies in people with co-occurring disorders. For instance, little is known about the specific benefits of any FDA-approved antipsychotic medication for people who have both schizophrenia and a cocaine or alcohol use disorder, or which medication might be the best choice for a person with a panic disorder who also has an alcohol use disorder.

On the plus side, a growing body of research examines specific psychosocial and psychotherapeutic approaches for people with specific co-occurring disorders, such as treatments for trauma survivors who also have substance use disorders. So even though the research and empirical evidence are important, they lag behind what clinicians and people with co-occurring disorders need to construct effective and realistic recovery and treatment plans.

It all comes down to the individual who wants to change, what they present with, their strengths, and the challenges they face. What may work for the tax attorney who drinks too much and has a panic disorder, may be the wrong approach for the woman living in a shelter with bipolar disorder, hepatitis, and a severe cocaine problem, or the adolescent with attention deficit disorder who has just been arrested for selling his stimulants to buy heroin.

As the principles of integrated treatment take root, the challenge has been, and continues to be, creating services and treatments that meet the needs of people with COD. Those challenges have been pushed further in the past several years with the recognition that overall health outcomes are poor for people with COD and that access to primary medical care is often inadequate, especially for those with serious mental illness. These challenges and the efforts to meet them have led to the next wave of integrated treatment and the birth of exciting new services, such as the person-centered behavioral health medical home.

KEY CONCEPTS AND DEFINITIONS

Recovery

The use of the term *recovery* has a long history founded in the substance abuse self-help movement (AA, NA, etc.). In the past, recovery was often equated to time abstaining from drugs and/or alcohol: "I've been in recovery for ten years now." More recently, *recovery* has been promoted as an overarching goal for all behavioral health and substance use problems. Although the following guidelines, which emphasize respect, hope, meaning, and autonomy, may seem like common sense, the notion of recovery from mental disorders is a relatively new one. It replaces a prior attitude that mental disorders, especially serious ones, were chronic conditions for which true recovery was not possible. Embedded in that older belief was a paternalistic approach to individuals with mental disorders, "They're not responsible for their actions, so we need to take care of them." This attitude resulted in a system in which the rights and civil liberties of people with mental disorders were given little importance. It was standard practice, up until the early 1980s, for people with serious mental illness to find themselves involuntarily hospitalized for extended periods of time, with little or no due process. Just having a diagnosis of schizophrenia could result in a person being locked away in a state hospital for months, years, and even decades.

In 2013, the Substance Abuse Mental Health Service Administration (SAMHSA) published a working definition of recovery, along with four dimensions, and ten guiding principles.

- SAMHSA's working definition of recovery: "A process of change through which individuals improve their health and wellness, live a self-directed life, and strive to reach their full potential."
- Four dimensions of recovery:
    1. Health—Attending to physical, mental, and substance use disorders and symptoms
    2. Home—Safe and stable housing
    3. Purpose—A full and meaningful life, including work, volunteerism, hobbies, family, and the ability to participate fully in society
    4. Community—Nurturing of social connections that provide support, friendship, and love
- Ten guiding principles of recovery:
    1. Recovery emerges from hope.
    2. Recovery is person-driven.
    3. Recovery occurs via many pathways.
    4. Recovery is holistic.
    5. Recovery is supported by peers and allies.
    6. Recovery is supported through relationship and social networks.
    7. Recovery is culturally based and influenced.
    8. Recovery is supported by addressing trauma.
    9. Recovery involves individual, family, and community strengths and responsibility.
    10. Recovery is based on respect.

Co-Occurring Disorders (COD)

For the purposes of this book, co-occurring disorders are those that involve one or more non-nicotine substance use disorder and one or more mental disorder. Specific disorders are based on criteria in the DSM-5 (the current standard diagnostic system in use at the time of this book's publication).

"No Wrong Door" Policy

The "no wrong door" policy signaled a major change in the focus of working with people with COD. It means that wherever a person first presents, or pursues treatment, the entirety of what they need will be addressed. If a particular program, clinical practice, or agency is unable to meet all of that person's particular needs, referrals and linkages will be made.

Beyond this initial point, "no wrong door" begins to address the importance of integrating all phases of the assessment process and, where possible and practical, treatment. That is, in a predominately substance abuse program, it's now the expected standard of care to carefully screen for mental disorders, and the same holds true for assessing substance use problems and histories in people presenting for mental health services.

Person-Centered

Person-centered treatment can be summed up with a slogan taken from the grassroots Harm Reduction movement: "Meet the person where they're at." Person-centered treatment, as an overarching philosophy and approach to treatment, cues the clinician to focus on the individual, what they want and what they want to change now (level of motivation/stage of change). Embedded within person-centered treatment are the following principles:

- Empowerment for the person seeking treatment/supporting self-efficacy
- Treatment goals and intervention based on a thorough understanding of the person in treatment, not a "cookie cutter" treatment (What does this person want? What are their goals?)
- Nonjudgmental approaches on the part of clinicians
- Recognition and validation of all positive change
- Identification of the individual's strengths
- An understanding of the person's entire social, religious, and cultural context

Cultural Competence

Throughout the assessment and treatment process attention needs to be paid to the entirety of the person in treatment, including specific issues of ethnicity, race, country of origin, primary language, gender, gender identity/expression, faith, spiritual practices, sexual orientation, and identification with specific groups. The culturally competent clinician maintains an openness and willingness to learn from clients, and to try and understand their perspectives, free from stereotypes and assumptions.

For programs and agencies, achieving and enhancing cultural competence might include trainings and in-services regarding particular groups, the hiring of multicultural and bilingual staff at all levels of the organization, including leadership, access to interpreter services, teletypewriting devices for the deaf (TTD/TTY), brochures and forms available in multiple languages, and attending to the choice of artwork in waiting areas and clinician offices.

Trauma Informed

People with COD have rates of trauma and PTSD far higher than the general population. Trauma-informed services are those that provide the following:

- Actively assess histories of trauma (see Chapter 2) in all clients.
- Avoid re-traumatization and retriggering in the process of therapy.
- Provide a safe and healing treatment environment.
- Support a person's natural coping skills, while helping them develop and enhance their ability to recover from the effects of trauma.
- Support the person's sense of self-efficacy and empowerment.
- Where appropriate, consider gender-specific groups. This approach is strongly recommended in trauma and trauma/substance use disorder group therapies.

Gender and Sexual-Orientation Sensitivity

Part of the process of recovery involves rigorous honesty with oneself about deeply personal matters, including disclosure of personal information to both one's therapist and possibly to other group members. Being able to disclose such personal matters requires a degree of trust and comfort that can be fostered by attending to issues related to gender and sexuality.

Some important things to consider include:

- Being able to frankly and accurately offer nonjudgmental counseling to women of child-bearing age regarding their reproductive health as it relates to their substance use, mental disorder(s), and medications they may be prescribed. Depending on their circumstances these issues might include:
    - Careful selection of medication for women who are contemplating getting pregnant or are currently pregnant
    - Guidance and liaison with a woman's OB/gyn when she is pregnant
    - Attention to the woman's preferences regarding pregnancy and breastfeeding
    - Clear information about the relative risks and benefits of various treatments, such as whether it's better for her to remain on opioid maintenance therapy through the course of her pregnancy (see Chapter 18)
    - Helping women with serious mood disorders, such as bipolar disorder, which is associated with high rates of severe third-trimester and postpartum mood episodes, to enhance their chances of having a stable mood throughout their pregnancy and postpartum period
- Understanding the specific concerns of individuals who are GLBTQ (gay, lesbian, bisexual, transgendered, or questioning), and how these concerns might be affected in various treatment settings. Being able to disclose—"come out"—about sexual orientation and/or gender identity/expression in any situation is a highly personal, and at times, stressful decision. Disclosures need to be met in a nonjudgmental and openly accepting manner. This level of acceptance cannot be assumed, especially in group settings. Just

as gender-specific groups will make sense in particular areas, having groups targeted for GLBTQ people can lessen one source of treatment-related anxiety.

The Quadrants of Care

People with co-occurring disorders represent a tremendously large and heterogeneous group. They range from people with mild bouts of anxiety and depression who also meet criteria for mild alcohol use disorder, to people with severe and persistent psychotic symptoms or disabling panic and anxiety who have multiple severe substance use disorders. These differences, along with other variables such as personal preference and resources will guide every step of the treatment process. Services and treatments appropriate for one person, would be far too intrusive, and frankly unnecessary for another. On account of this vast heterogeneity, it's sometimes helpful to think of people in terms of the severity of each of their co-occurring disorders.

Developed in the 1990s, the quadrants of care is one way to conceptualize large groups of people with COD based on the relative severity of their mental health and substance use problems, not their specific diagnoses. The intent was to identify groups of people and the likely levels of care and resources they might require. It was particularly useful when thinking about systems and the allocation of substance use and mental health resources.

Quadrant I. Mild substance use/Mild mental illness

Quadrant II. Mild substance use/Severe mental illness

Quadrant III. Severe substance use/Mild mental illness

Quadrant IV. Severe substance use/Severe mental illness

On the next page The Four Quadrants grid, where S stands for substance use disorder and M stands for mental disorder, provides some typical resources and levels of care for people in each of the quadrants. A lowercase letter indicates a lesser degree of severity and acuity (can be addressed as an outpatient, might or might not require medication), and a capital letters refers to a more long-standing and severe problem (might require inpatient resources, medication, specialized therapies).

Although using these broad categories can be helpful, it is important to remember that as people improve, or relapse, they change quadrants. That is, someone with schizophrenia and severe alcohol-use disorder (quadrant IV) might initially require an inpatient co-occurring admission when they are acutely psychotic and in alcohol withdrawal. After obtaining and maintaining abstinence from alcohol and achieving good symptom control of their psychiatric illness, they would require much less restrictive and intrusive treatment interventions (quadrant II or possibly quadrant I).

Evolution and Revision of the Four Quadrants: In reality, the four quadrant system as it was initially configured is not widely used today. However, the underlying basic principle of characterizing the relative severity of the substance use and mental illness components is an important one when trying to match treatment, including the level of care and clinical setting, to the person. Additionally, some state mental health and substance abuse systems continue to use the four quadrant classifications when considering eligibility for resources (such as admission to state hospitals and state-operated substance use programs).

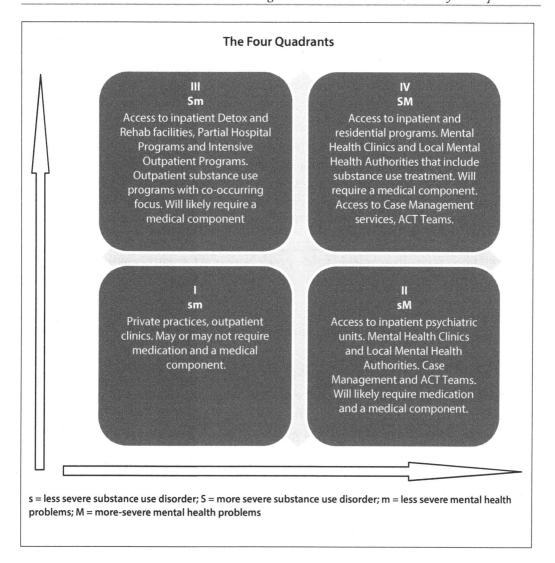

The Four Quadrants

III
Sm

Access to inpatient Detox and Rehab facilities, Partial Hospital Programs and Intensive Outpatient Programs. Outpatient substance use programs with co-occurring focus. Will likely require a medical component

IV
SM

Access to inpatient and residential programs. Mental Health Clinics and Local Mental Health Authorities that include substance use treatment. Will require a medical component. Access to Case Management services, ACT Teams.

I
sm

Private practices, outpatient clinics. May or may not require medication and a medical component.

II
sM

Access to inpatient psychiatric units. Mental Health Clinics and Local Mental Health Authorities. Case Management and ACT Teams. Will likely require medication and a medical component.

s = less severe substance use disorder; S = more severe substance use disorder; m = less severe mental health problems; M = more-severe mental health problems

The underlying principle of the four quadrant system and others like it continues to be of use because it gets the assessing clinician to focus on the relative severity of the different pieces of a person's co-occurring presentation. It starts the process of trying to match treatment and specific interventions to an actual person with specific needs.

A more-recent usage of the four quadrant approach has been put forward by the National Council for Community Behavioral Healthcare, when looking at where to locate, or co-locate, medical services (primary care) for people with mental and substance use disorders. This issue has become increasingly relevant with the burgeoning expansion of the patient-centered medical home model, where the expectation is that an individual can have all of their health needs, including issues with mental health and substance use, addressed in a single setting and/or well-coordinated system. In this reworking of the four quadrant system, the substance use disorder and the psychiatric disorders are lumped together, and characterized as more severe or less severe, and they are then matched with more or less severe medical disorders and needs.

Quadrant I: This category is for people with lower severity of both behavioral health and primary health care needs. People in this category could likely have their needs met in a typical primary care setting with access to coordinated behavioral health and psychiatric consultation. Behavioral health and substance use screenings would be included in the overall assessment.

Quadrant II: For this population with higher severity behavioral health and lower severity primary health care needs, a full spectrum of behavioral health and substance use services needs to be available. One model for service delivery might include an embedded primary care physician and/or primary care APRN in a more predominately behavioral health clinic or behavioral health person-centered medical home.

Quadrant III: This quadrant would include people with lower severity behavioral health and substance use problems and higher severity health issues. This population will require access to coordinated medical services, including access to specialty medical, surgical, and in-home services. Similar to quadrant I, behavioral health assessment will be included in the overall processes, with the availability of behavioral health consultation.

Quadrant IV: This category is for people with both higher severity behavioral health/substance use needs and physical health needs. One model for service delivery would be a person-centered medical home within a behavioral health setting. A full spectrum of both medical and behavioral health services would be included, including access to specialty medical/surgical services.

Stages of Treatment: The stages of treatment derive from the stages of change model (see Chapter 4) developed by DiClemente and Prochaska. The stages of treatment provide a model by which a person becomes involved in and progresses through treatment. Each stage involves a particular goal that needs to be met prior to moving on.

Engagement. The engagement phase of treatment involves the initial steps in which an individual connects with a therapist or treatment program. Engagement strategies can be generated by the person seeking treatment or by a clinician or agency looking to try and offer services to an individual in need. During this stage of treatment the client may or may not be interested in addressing problem substance use. The goal of the engagement stage is for the client to become connected to some form of treatment/therapist. Engagement strategies can include:

- Screening phone calls by a person wanting to get information about programs
- Calls to 211 info line
- Searching available services via the Internet
- Outreach by agencies to people with mental illness and substance use disorders, to let them know about available services, including homeless outreach and the use of peer engagement specialists
- Attending an open 12-step meeting (AA, NA, Dual Diagnosis in Recovery, etc.)

Persuasion: Persuasion relates to the stage of treatment in which a therapeutic relationship is established and the person begins to explore goals they might have around their mental health and substance use. For the clinician, this part of treatment includes an explanation of the benefits of treatment, and the clients are persuaded to address problem behaviors. In one sense, it can be thought of as the sales pitch: "I can see that you're living in a type of hell. What if I told you that this particular treatment can get you out of there? Would you be interested?"

Specific persuasion strategies might include:

• Motivational interviewing (see Chapter 4) to help the person review the pros and cons of various risk behaviors related to their substance use and mental illness, and to begin establishing goals

• Intervention strategies, such as a family coming together to express worry and concern to a specific family member with substance use and mental health problems, and requesting that they engage in treatment

• Education about recommended therapies, including public service announcement, fliers, websites, and so forth

Active Treatment: Active treatment includes a broad range of strategies all employed in the interest of helping the person in recovery advance toward individual goals and eliminate the use of harmful substances. The list of potential treatments and interventions is long, and will be tailored to the person's specific needs. Common forms of active treatment include:

• Group and individual psychotherapies

• Education around substance use and mental disorders

• Medications targeting specific disorders and symptoms

• The use of peer supports and mutual self-help groups such as 12-step

• Development of positive support systems, including family, friends, and faith communities

• Wellness strategies, such as getting adequate, and regular, exercise, good nutrition, and nurturing positive relationships and meaningful activities, including work and hobbies

• Attending to active medical issues and obtaining follow-up as needed

Relapse Prevention: In the relapse prevention stage of treatment the client has achieved abstinence from harmful substances, and the goal is to prevent relapse. On the mental health side of the co-occurring equation, relapse prevention will include those strategies, treatments, and possibly medications that help the individual remain in remission from significant psychiatric symptomatology. Beyond these aspects, relapse prevention is the stage of treatment where efforts are directed at ways to maintain and expand upon healthy habits, wellness, and recovery. Relapse preventions strategies might include:

• Ongoing involvement with mutual self-help, and taking on commitments, such as leading, or even starting a 12-step group

• Maintenance of healthy habits and attention to wellness

• Ongoing participation with necessary psychiatric treatment

• Ongoing attention to any medical issues

Sequential, Parallel, and Integrated Treatment

One way to conceptualize treatments and interventions is with the terms *sequential, parallel,* and *integrated.* Even though organizations such as the Substance Abuse and Mental Health Service Administration (SAMHSA) urge providers to find ways to effectively and more fully integrate treatment for co-occurring disorders, it is not always possible, practical, or even desirable to do so. However, using the concepts of sequential, parallel, and integrated treatment, it is possible to address all of the active problems and needs. It is useful to remember that these broad terms may be subject to overlap. So even when sequential (one problem at a time) treatment is provided, elements of integration are likely to occur. And even the most-integrated manual-driven therapies will include sessions and modules that focus on one of the major issues and then move on to the next.

Sequential Treatment and Interventions: These approaches address one of the major issues (substance use or mental illness) at a time. As an overall treatment philosophy, it embodies older approaches to the treatment of co-occurring disorders, where it was felt that the substance use problem needed to be fully treated before moving on to address any mental disorder. Historically this approach led to a segregation of services (different agencies, different settings) between those that focused on substance use disorders and those that focused on mental disorders.

Nowadays, there will be times, often when there is a pressing safety issue, where sequencing of treatment is both desirable and necessary. Sequential treatment can be provided in separate settings, or within a single agency, system, clinic, or private practice. Examples include:

- A woman in alcohol withdrawal, who is also depressed. Here, the most-pressing concern is to first treat her withdrawal and ensure it doesn't progress to delirium tremens (DTs).

- Someone who has a moderate or severe opioid use disorder and is going in and out of withdrawal on a daily basis, and is anxious and depressed. That person would likely benefit from treatment with opioid replacement therapy (Buprenorphine, Methadone) before mood and anxiety symptoms can be adequately addressed. It's likely that some, or even all, of the depression and anxiety may be withdrawal symptoms.

- A teen with bipolar disorder who is currently manic and engaged in high risk behaviors, but who is also smoking cannabis and drinking daily, may need an inpatient psychiatric hospitalization to treat the mania before the substance use problems can be addressed. Although here, with inpatient treatment, the alcohol and drug use will be curtailed in the supervised setting.

Parallel Treatment and Interventions: These types happen simultaneously, but often in different settings and with different providers. Examples include:

- A man with obsessive-compulsive disorder (OCD) and moderate alcohol use disorder in early remission, receiving Cognitive-Behavioral Therapy (CBT) for the OCD with a private therapist, possibly in combination with a prescribing psychiatrist or APRN, while simultaneously attending Alcoholics Anonymous.

- A woman with an opioid use disorder and schizophrenia might be enrolled in a Methadone or Buprenorphine program while obtaining psychiatric services from a local mental health authority, community mental health center, or clinic.

• A woman with posttraumatic stress disorder may attend a trauma-survivor's group while simultaneously attending a weekly relapse-prevention group for her alcohol use disorder.

Integrated Treatment for Co-Occurring Disorders. This approach can be conceptualized along a continuum of "how integrated?" Are all active issues addressed within a particular program, with a single therapist, or with specific therapies that target both/all problems?

Because of the interrelatedness of substance use and mental disorders, it can at times be useful to conceptualize a person's presenting issues as a single non-DSM diagnosis such as "bipolar alcohol use disorder," "schizophrenia opioid use disorder," or "obsessive-compulsive alcohol use disorder." Although clearly not how one would document diagnoses, this approach can help clinicians and clients identify how the substance use impacts the mental illness, and vice versa. Additionally, by keeping the focus on all disorders, treatment can be individualized in meaningful ways. Despite the reality of few absolutes in the treatment of co-occurring disorders, one that appears to be consistent is that improvements in either the substance use or mental health problem typically lead to progress in addressing the other disorder.

Examples of integrated treatments include:

• Manual-driven therapies and adaptations of therapies that specifically target both the substance use and mental disorders, such as integrated group therapy (bipolar and SUDs, Chapter 11), dual diagnosis DBT (borderline personality disorder and SUDs, Chapter 15), integrated CBT (depression, PTSD, and SUDs, Chapters 10 and 13), and many others.

• Co-occurring partial hospital programs (PHP) and intensive outpatient programs (IOP) where groups and other interventions focus on both/all disorders through the course of the treatment day. Often emphasizing one more than the other depending on the group, for example, relapse prevention (substance use emphasis) versus a psycho education or managing illness group (mental disorder emphasis).

• Mutual self-help groups that focus on both substance use and mental health.

Integration of Behavioral Health and Substance Use Services with Primary Care: The Patient-Centered Medical Home (PCMH) or Behavioral Health Home

Even though this book focuses on the integration of mental health and substance abuse services, the current trend is toward a greater and more-comprehensive integration of all of a person's health care needs. This shift is embodied in the patient-centered medical home model (PCMH), sometimes referred to as a behavioral health home.

The PCMH model, which evolved from a collaboration of the American Academy of Family Physicians, the American College of Physicians, the American Academy of Pediatrics, and the American Osteopathic Association, emphasizes the delivery of high-quality evidence-based care through the use of well-coordinated teams in primary care settings.

Core components of the PCMH include:

• A personal physician or APRN with whom the patient can develop a relationship.

• A team approach, with a physician leader.

• Care management and care managers represent a movement away from episodic and acute care to a more long-term view of illness management. This approach is especially important when thinking about chronic disorders, whether psychiatric, substance use, or medical. The care manager (typically a nurse, but in some instances a social worker, psychologist, or other health care professional) works directly with the client and is part of the treatment team. Clinical functions of the care manager include:

o Maintain a connection and collaborative relationship with the patient.

o Provide education to the patient and the family.

o Monitor symptoms and communicate them to the physician/APRN and the team.

o Enhance and support self-efficacy and self-care.

o Problem solve with the patient to ensure maximization of adherence to the treatment plan.

• A whole-person (holistic) approach that includes all stages of life, attention to wellness and prevention strategies, in-home supports, community, family, and peer supports, and an overarching biopsychosocial approach.

• Coordinated care through the medical home that enables the person to access and obtain linkages to necessary specialty services, acute care when needed, labs, procedures, etc.

• Quality and safety with an emphasis on "best practices" and the use of evidence-based medicine.

• Enhanced access to care that may include open scheduling, where people are able to present for services without an appointment, clinic hours expanded to accommodate work schedules, on-site child care, and personal assistance in overcoming barriers to treatment, such as transportation.

• Reimbursement to the providers that reflects the added value of the PCMH.

UNDERSTANDING BEHAVIORAL HEALTH DIAGNOSES AND THE DSM-5

The current system of diagnoses in the United States is the American Psychiatric Association's *Diagnostic and Statistical Manual of Mental Disorders* (DSM-5™). This manual contains more than 300 diagnoses and the accompanying *International Classification of Disease*, 9th and 10th edition (ICD-9 and ICD-10) codes, which are used by all billing entities (insurance companies, The Centers for Medicare and Medicaid Services (CMS), hospitals, physicians' offices).

The DSM-5 utilizes clusters of symptoms that involve the patient's mood, perceptions, and thought processes (cognitions) and behaviors to define diagnoses. What elevates emotions, behaviors, and/or disturbance of thought to where they are labeled as abnormal and a disorder are that they cause significant impairment in the person's ability to function in one or more major aspects of their life (work, home, social, recreation) and/or they cause significant distress to the individual.

To complicate matters, tremendous overlap occurs between the disorders. People can often meet criteria for multiple disorders and/or their symptoms may not fit neatly into the diagnostic categories. In these instances, diagnoses such as "Other specified" or "Unspecified" may be appropriate.

It is important, then, to understand a key difference between the diagnosis of mental disorders and most other conditions in medicine. In behavioral science, diagnoses are currently based on a collection of symptoms experienced by the patient (anxiety, hearing voices, delusions, memory loss, suicidality, sadness, etc.), versus more-objective findings such as a tumor, infectious agents (bacteria, viruses) or abnormal physical symptoms (elevated blood pressure), abnormal lab values, and so forth.

This system has both merits and shortcomings, and its reliance on mostly subjective findings reflects the infancy in the understanding of the human brain, as well as its complexity. While spelling out how far behavioral science has come, and how far it still has to go, the DSM-5 does provide a common diagnostic language and conceptualization of mental disorders. Clinicians who work in behavioral health, substance use, and co-occurring arenas need to be familiar with its use.

The DSM-5 replaced the DSMIV-TR in May 2013. It includes both the ICD-9 and the ICD-10 codes, the latter are currently scheduled to go into effect in October 2015. Major changes in the new manual include:

- Elimination of the multiaxial diagnosis. All mental health and substance use diagnoses are now listed out in the same manner as other medical diagnoses.

- Elimination of the Global Assessment of Functioning scale. Clinicians are now encouraged to use other measures of functioning and disability, such as the World Health Organization's Disability Assessment Schedule version 2.0 (WHODAS 2.0).

- Several new diagnoses in the DSM-5 include disruptive mood dysregulation disorder, hoarding disorder, and binge eating disorder.

- Some diagnoses have been given new names; for example, substance abuse and dependence are now "substance use disorders" and are rated on a continuum of mild, moderate, and severe.

- Disorders have had criteria revised.

- An increased reliance on specifiers has been incorporated, such as with anxious distress, with mixed features, with rapid cycling, with panic attacks, and so on.

CHAPTER 2

The Comprehensive Assessment Part One: Personal, Psychiatric, Family, and Social Histories, and the Mental Status Examination

OVERVIEW

These next three chapters cover the process of getting to know the person who is accessing, or receiving, services (your patient/client). A thorough assessment includes a tremendous amount of data collection that starts at the first phone contact or visit and continues throughout treatment. It is important to remember that the process of clinical assessment, data collection, and synthesis, is continuous and always specific to the person in treatment and that person's goals.

    Beyond the generation of hundreds, if not thousands, of bits of information, the assessment process is where individuals in treatment get to tell their story, including how they might like it to change (their goals) and their level of motivation to make the changes happen.

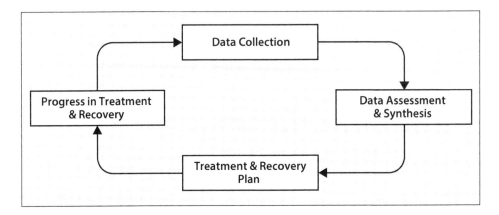

In working with people with co-occurring disorders, the challenge comes in trying to differentiate between symptoms best explained by the use of a substance versus those caused by an underlying psychiatric disorder, or even a medical one. It is the metaphor of trying to separate the forest and the trees. As clinicians, it is important to take in the information and not jump to conclusions about its meaning. A clinician needs to consider different possibilities, starting with the most common and moving to ones that are less likely, and generate hypotheses for what might be causing a particular symptom or syndrome. In medical lingo, this process is called generating a differential.

- Is the anxiety from an anxiety disorder or is it the anxiety seen in various states of withdrawal? Could it be both?
- Is someone manic or intoxicated with alcohol, PCP, stimulants, or a hallucinogen? Is the person manic and using alcohol to try and come down? Is the person manic and using other drugs as a symptom of the manic state (increased pleasure seeking activity)?
- Are the voices someone hears a symptom of schizophrenia or of alcohol withdrawal? Could they be caused by PCP or synthetic cannabis intoxication?
- Are an adolescent's intense mood swings and outburst of anger a result of normal adolescence, the start of bipolar disorder, intermittent opioid withdrawal from an addiction to pain medications, or a side effect of stimulants prescribed for ADHD?

Although broken up into three chapters, the comprehensive assessment of psychiatric and substance use symptoms and syndromes includes all aspects of a person's past and present history. Throughout the initial and ongoing assessments the clinician, along with the client, weighs all the information and uses it to clarify diagnoses, map out goals and objectives, and refine and assess treatment.

Throughout these chapters are a series of handouts that can either be completed by the person in treatment, completed collaboratively (the clinician and patient working on them together), or used as the basis for a structured interview (i.e., one where particular areas of information are addressed in a logical sequence). Taken in their totality, these chapters comprise a comprehensive and integrated assessment that addresses not only issues of mental health and substance use, but all areas of the person's life. Assessments of this nature are typical in agencies accredited by the Joint Commission, as well as the Commission on the Accreditation of Rehabilitation Facilities (CARF), and are the standard for facilities and practices that bill organizations such as the Centers for Medicare and Medicaid Services (CMS), and most insurance companies and HMOs.

PERSONAL/IDENTIFYING INFORMATION

Personal and identifying information includes the client's age, race, marital status, and other pieces of data the clinician wants included, such as the number of children, current living situation, and occupation. When presenting cases between clinicians, the identifying information becomes the opening line, for example, of "This is a 24-year-old never-married Caucasian father of two who presents with. . . ."

CHIEF COMPLAINT/PRESENTING PROBLEM

The chief complaint contains the stated reason your client or patient has presented.

- "I want to get clean."
- "I'm hearing voices that tell me to hurt myself."
- "My anxiety is through the roof."

Typically, although not always, the chief complaint is left in the person's own words. In some instances, the necessities of billing may require the chief complaint be replaced, or at least include, more clinical language.

- "I want to get clean." = Achieve abstinence
- "I'm hearing voices that tell me to kill myself." = Suicidal with command auditory hallucinations
- "My anxiety is through the roof. It's gotten to where I can't even leave the house." = Disabling anxiety and agoraphobia (fear of leaving the house)

HISTORY OF PRESENTING PROBLEM

This portion of the evaluation allows the patient to tell his or her story. It's where the clinician gets a sense of how the person is piecing together their current situation. How does the person think things got to where they are? What are the different factors, both positive and negative, that led to today's visit?

It is common for first visits—regardless of location—to involve some element of a crisis, where active stresses are contributing to the current difficulties.

Example: Mrs. Jones states that she's been feeling increasingly depressed and anxious for the past three weeks. It started when her hours were reduced at work, and she found herself unable to sleep at night, worrying about how she'd meet her mortgage and other financial responsibilities. She's also concerned about her increased use of alcohol, which has gone from 2–4 drinks per week, to consuming the better part of a 1.5-liter bottle of wine on a nightly basis. In the past two weeks she has begun to drink earlier in the day to calm her nerves, and she's noticed that her hands shake in the morning.

PSYCHIATRIC HISTORY

Obtaining a thorough psychiatric history at the start of treatment is crucial for understanding the client. As with the substance use history (see Chapter 3), it is best to have multiple sources of information (e.g., the patient, past records, family, etc.). You want to know about all past treatment, as well as when the person began to first notice a problem with mood, thoughts, and/or behavior.

Spending the time to obtain a thorough history is one of the best ways to decrease the likelihood of missed diagnoses and misdiagnoses. The clinician will learn about the individual's treatment preferences, past trials of medication, and other therapies that might, or might not, have been useful.

This point is also a logical place in the evaluation to determine whether the person has completed a psychiatric advance directive, or would like to do so.

Psychiatric advance directives are documents the person completes that describe personal preferences for treatment. These documents are most frequently filled out by individuals with a history of serious mental illness, who may have had multiple prior treatments, including inpatient admissions. Psychiatric advance directives may include the following elements:

- Specifics about the individual's symptoms and diagnoses, as well as what the individual might experience during a crisis
- Specifics about who the individual does, and does not, want contacted and involved with his or her treatment (informed consent)
- Whether the individual has designated another person to make healthcare decisions on the individual's behalf, should the individual be unable to do so
- Specifics concerning preferred medications
- Preferred facilities
- Strategies that work best for the individual should that person be emotionally or behaviorally out of control

A useful resource that explains psychiatric advance directives, including a state-by-state guide, is the National Resource Center on Psychiatric Advance Directives (NRC.PAD) at www. nrc-pad.org/.

FAMILY PSYCHIATRIC HISTORY

As with substance use disorders, most psychiatric disorders have a genetic component. If mood disorders (depression, bipolar), anxiety disorders, or psychotic disorders (schizophrenia) run in a person's family, the likelihood of developing a disorder is increased. This risk increases the closer the relative is to the person and if multiple relatives are affected.

Handout 1 can be completed by the patient, collaboratively with the patient, and/or used as a structured interview by the clinician.

HANDOUT 1
PSYCHIATRIC AND FAMILY PSYCHIATRIC HISTORY

Please complete all questions thoroughly. If you require further space, write on the back and/or use additional pages.

1. How old were you when you first had any interaction with a mental health professional?

   a. Why did you see this clinician?

2. When you were a child or teenager, were you ever diagnosed with a mental disorder, including attention deficit?

   a. How old were you at the time?

   b. Did you take medications for this problem?

3. Have you ever been in outpatient psychiatric treatment or counseling? (If yes, complete question 4; if no, skip to question 5.)

4. Please list all past outpatient psychiatric or behavioral health or counseling treatments. If you can't remember the specifics, give as much detail as you recall.

Who you saw	Age at the time	Reason for going	Was it helpful?	Type(s) of treatment. (individual, group, or family therapy; medication; other)

5. Have you ever had psychological testing? If so, when and by whom?
   a. If yes, do you have a copy of the test results?

6. Have you ever been admitted to a psychiatric hospital/ward? (If yes, complete question 7; if no skip to question 8. Do not include inpatient detoxification and rehabilitation stays here.)

7. Psychiatric admissions:

Name of facility	Your age at the time (or dates)	Reason for admission	Length of admission	Type(s) of treatment received	Was it helpful?

8. Have you ever been prescribed psychiatric medication(s)? (If no, skip to question 11.)

9. Are you currently on any psychiatric medications? (If yes, please fill out the following table.)

Name of medication	Dose	Prescriber	Reason for taking it	Is it helping?	Do you have problems (side effects, adverse reactions) with it?

10. Medication history: Please list all psychiatric medications you have taken in the past.

Name of medication	Your age (or dates) when you were taking it	Reason(s) it was prescribed	Dose(s)	Was it helpful?	Reason(s) it was stopped

11. Who in your family has a psychiatric history or disorder(s)? If you think someone has a psychiatric problem, but it's never been treated or diagnosed, describe what you think the problem is.

Family member	Diagnosis/Problem	Treatment history, if any

12. Has anyone in your family ever attempted or committed suicide? (If yes, please give details.)

13. Do you have a completed psychiatric advance directive? (A written document that describes your personal preferences for treatment, including who in your life you'd like to be involved in treatment, and what works best for you in crisis situations.)

14. Would you like the opportunity to create a psychiatric advance directive?

15. What other information regarding your psychiatric history do you think is important for your clinician to know?

SOCIAL HISTORY

People are formed and shaped by their genetics, how and where they were raised, their religious and cultural beliefs, sexual orientation, and the sum of their life's experiences. And like a good story, you want to know how things started, how they progressed, and how they got to the present point.

Having a thorough understanding of someone's upbringing and background provides important clues into that person's current situation, aspirations, and difficulties. Often in the course of obtaining a person's story and family and personal history—how they did in school, what major losses they might have suffered at an early age—one discovers the origins of various mental health and substance use problems. Likewise, family and cultural attitudes and practices can help clinicians understand their patients' frame of reference.

- "Everyone in my family uses drugs and drinks. I just thought that was normal."
- "Things went downhill when Dad left. Mom started drinking, and I was just angry all the time."
- "I was fine until everyone in my family dropped dead. I started to get panic attacks, and the only thing that helped was booze."
- "I could never sit still in school. I was always getting into trouble."
- "In my religion, we don't believe in psychiatry."

As with the previous handout, Handout 2 can be completed by the person in treatment, collaboratively, or used as the basis for a structured interview.

Handout 2
Personal History

Please complete all questions thoroughly. If you require further space, feel free to write on the back and/or use additional pages.

1. Where were you born and raised?

2. How many times did you move before age 18?

3. Describe your parents' relationship?

4. If your parents got divorced or separated, how old were you at the time?
   a. Who did you live with?

5. Describe your relationship with your mother.

6. Describe your relationship with your father.

7. How many brothers and sisters do/did you have?
   a. Where do you come in the birth order (i.e., oldest, youngest, in the middle)?
   b. Describe your relationship(s) with your siblings.

8. How did you do in school?
   a. Did you get in trouble in school (suspensions, detentions)?
   b. How far did you go in school (highest grade completed and degree(s) obtained)?
   c. If you dropped out, why did this happen?
   d. If you attended college or trade school, what was your major?

9. Your sexual orientation is _____.
   (heterosexual/straight, homosexual/gay, bisexual, transgender, questioning, other)

10. How old were you when you had your first romantic relationship?
    a. Describe your history of intimate relationships.
    b. Have you been married?
    c. How many times have you been married?

TRAUMA HISTORY

Trauma, the experience of being in or witnessing life-threatening or catastrophic situations, can leave people changed. It is an area of behavioral science in which particular disorders become tied to life events, such as with posttraumatic stress disorder and acute stress reactions.

In the assessment phases of treatment, it is important to understand a person's experience of having been victimized, abused, and/or assaulted (physically and/or sexually). As a child, did the person experience physical, sexual, and/or emotional abuse or neglect? Were there other adverse childhood experiences, such as living with a parent or caregiver who was frequently drunk or high? Did the person go through devastating natural or human-made events—floods, hurricanes, tornadoes, fires? Have they witnessed others, especially people they're close to, be assaulted, or killed? Has someone been involved in gang violence? Has someone been exposed to armed conflicts, either as a civilian or member of the military?

In addition to a history of past discrete traumatic experiences, such as a sexual assault or history of combat-related duty, it is also important to assess for a history of recurrent and ongoing trauma (sociocultural trauma). This type of trauma might include bullying at school or the workplace (including sexual harassment), expressed racism or homophobia, or living in a setting that includes an ongoing threat of violence or terrorism. For some, conditions of poverty, malnourishment, and unstable/unsafe housing may also overwhelm a person's ability to cope.

Our responses to traumatic events, which will be discussed further in Chapter 13, can vary from intense fear, helplessness, and anxiety, to uncontrollable surges of anger and rage, often with increased reliance on alcohol and substances of abuse. Other defenses that help people cope can include an emotional numbness and sense of walling out the memories for the event(s). Because of this tendency, especially in the early phases of treatment, the clinician needs to exercise great sensitivity so as not to unnecessarily open emotional wounds (retraumatization).

Screening questions, and how the client responds, will begin to lay the groundwork for how this material will be explored and treated. If the person describes a significant history of trauma, it would be reasonable to also have them complete a more thorough assessment tool, such as the PTSD checklist (PCL-5) available from the National Center for PTSD (www.ptsd.va.gov).

Trauma Screening Questions

1. As a child, did you experience anything you would consider emotional abuse or neglect?
2. As a child, did you experience any physical abuse?
   a. Bullying at school or home (by other siblings, relatives)?
3. As a child or adult, have you ever been physically assaulted?
4. As a child or adult, have you ever been in situations where you were coerced or forced into any kind of sexual act?
5. As a child or adult, have you directly (not through the media) witnessed or been involved in a natural or human-made disaster (fire, tornado, life-threatening flood, etc.)?
6. Have you been in a war zone, either as a combatant or civilian?
7. As a child or adult, have you ever felt overwhelmed by other life experiences, such as poverty, having inadequate food, or living in unsafe/unstable conditions?

8. Do you currently experience any symptoms that you believe are a result of the trauma you experienced?
    a. Nightmares?
    b. Panic attacks?
    c. Behavioral outbursts (rage attacks)?
    d. Flashbacks?
    e. Situations (people, places, things) you avoid for fear they will trigger symptoms?

LEGAL HISTORY

Both substance use disorders, as well as some symptomatic mental disorders, are associated with high rates of arrests and legal problems. It is an unfortunate truth that more than 1 million people with serious mental illness in this country are currently incarcerated. Prior arrests, periods of incarceration, and felony records are important pieces of information that can have a direct bearing on the person's treatment as well as potential barriers to his or her life goals. A prime example, is that once a person has a felony record, that person's ability to apply for certain jobs and live in various housing settings may be hampered. Also, incarceration is associated with high rates of stress-related mental disorders, such as PTSD.

Getting an accurate legal history often involves the use of multiple informants (sources of information), because individuals may be reluctant to divulge prior and current legal problems. Many states maintain searchable databases for prior offenses, as well as lists of registered sex offenders. If a person currently has a probation or parole officer, then it is important for the clinician to get permission at the start of treatment in order to be able to communicate with that individual.

When obtaining the legal history, a matter-of-fact and nonjudgmental stance is best. At times, a person's legal status may be the driving motivator for treatment. This can range from court-mandated treatment, to the advice of an attorney in the setting of pending legal problems, such as a driving under the influence (DUI/DWI) arrest. It is important to know this from the outset, and to not assume that someone will disclose this information.

At a minimum you would like to know the following:

1. Do you have any current legal problems or involvement?
2. Have you ever had a DUI/DWI? If yes, ask how many, and get the details. Was time served?
    If a DUI/DWI case is pending, get the specifics and what the expected legal outcomes might be—suspension of license, jail time, mandated treatment.
3. Have you ever been arrested?
4. How many times have you been arrested?
5. What were you charged with?
    a. Do you have any felonies on your record? (If yes, get the details. It's important to know when the last one was, and if the person is attempting to have his or her record expunged.)
    b. Have you ever been charged with a sex crime? (If yes, get the details, and ascertain whether the person is currently on a registered sex offender list.)

6. Have you ever been incarcerated?
7. How many times have you been incarcerated?
    a. How long were you incarcerated?
    b. Were you in the general population or a specialized (behavioral health) unit?
    c. How much time of your original sentence did you serve?
8. Are you currently on probation or parole?
    a. Who is your probation or parole officer?
    b. Are you willing to sign a release of information so we can communicate with your probation or parole officer?

THE MENTAL STATUS EVALUATION

The mental status evaluation can be thought of as similar—or as an extension—to a physical examination. With this evaluation, a systematic review of a person's thought processes, observable behaviors, and emotional state is conducted. A mental status evaluation consists of standard components, but they need not be obtained in a particular order.

Any abnormal findings in the course of the mental status exam should be noted and explored. Again, it is important to observe and record areas of strength and areas where the person may struggle. But in the overall assessment phase, it is best to keep an open mind and not jump to conclusions about the causes of any particular symptom. For instance, if the person seems generally together, but shows significant problems with tasks involving memory and concentration, that could be an indicator of a dementia (neurocognitive disorder), such as Alzheimer's Disease. It might also be a symptom of an attention deficit disorder, or part of a hypomanic bipolar state, where the person's thoughts are moving so rapidly they struggle to focus and remember things you've just told them, or it could be the anxiety of the assessment itself.

Elements of the Mental Status Exam

1. General appearance: How does the person look, act, and smell?
    a. Clothing: Are they dressed appropriately for the weather, time of year, and their socioeconomic status? Are his/her clothes clean and in good repair?
    b. Personal hygiene: Is the person groomed? Notice tattoos and piercings. Does the person appear to have a sense of personal style?
    c. Noticeable movements: Do they have tics or any physical mannerisms that seem excessive or draw your attention?
    d. Does the person have a distinctive smell? Are they malodorous? Do you detect the scent of alcohol or marijuana?
2. Level of alertness: Do they appear awake and well rested? Are they sleepy? Do they nod off at times? Do they appear intoxicated?
3. Level of cooperation: Is the person generally forthcoming with personal information? Does the person appear guarded, irritable, or suspicious? *"Why do you need to know that?"*
4. Are they an accurate historian? Does the story they tell you line up with what you know about them from other sources (old records, reports from family, information obtained from prescription monitoring systems, etc.)? Are there significant discrepancies?

5. Mood and affect:
   a. Mood: How does the person describe his or her current emotional state? "How are you feeling today?" If they describe themselves as feeling anxious, depressed, or some other emotion, see if you can get them to quantify the severity. Numeric scales can be useful here. "On a scale of 1 to 10, with 10 being the most severe, describe your current state of sadness, nervousness, anxiety, anger."
   b. Affect: How do you read/perceive the person's emotional state(s) based on facial expression, tone of voice, and body language? How do they appear to you? Does their expression change fluidly in response to the material being discussed?

   Does an incongruity exist between the person's stated mood and what you observe of his or her emotional state (discordant mood and affect)? An example would be when a woman tells you her depression is a 10 out of a possible 10, and yet she appears pleasant and smiles throughout the course of the evaluation.

6. Speech and Language: What do you notice about the person's speech?
   a. Is English their strongest language?
   b. If not, ascertain whether or not an interpreter is required.
   c. Is the volume of their speech normal, too loud, or do you have to strain to hear them?
   d. Do they speak so rapidly that you have to interrupt them to ask questions, as is often seen in people who are manic, hypomanic, or under the effects of cocaine, other stimulants, and some hallucinogens.
   e. Do they stutter or slur their words?
   f. Do they struggle to find words?
   g. Is there a normal range of inflection in their speech, or is there a flatness and dullness of tone, as is sometimes seen in psychotic disorders, such as schizophrenia?

7. Thought processes: An assessment of thought processes is typically based on the flow of the conversation and speech patterns, but can also include the person's self-report on how they experience their thoughts.
   a. Do the person's thoughts flow one to the next in logical sequence? Do conversations contain a natural back and forth, or do you struggle to understand what the person has just said? Does one thought seem disconnected from the next, as is sometimes seen in psychotic disorders, such as schizophrenia and various intoxication states?
   b. How does the person describe his/her own thinking? Do they experience their thoughts as going too slow or as racing? Do they get stuck on particular topics and can't let go (ruminative thinking)?
   c. Are they able to accurately interpret standard expressions, or do they struggle with metaphorical thought? This difficulty is frequently assessed with the use of common sayings, such as: "Tell me what it means when I say people in glass houses shouldn't throw stones?" A correct answer would be along the lines of "We all have our faults and shouldn't judge others." An indicator of more "concrete thinking" would be an answer such as "Your windows would break." This kind of thinking can be associated with certain disorders, such as schizophrenia, as well as with people who have limited cognitive abilities.

8. Thought content: What topics does the person seem most concerned with?
   a. Is the person largely concerned with realistic stresses in his/her life?

b. Do they repeat the same material over and over (perseverate)?

c. Do they focus on depressive themes, such as hopelessness, helplessness, and low self-esteem?

d. Grandiosity. Do they have an inflated sense of their self-worth or abilities?

e. Suspiciousness. Are they worried that people are out to harm them. This finding can be along a continuum of healthy wariness to outright paranoia.

9. Cognitive style and cognitive distortions: How do they view their world, others, and themselves? Do they use specific distortions, such as black-and-white thinking, catastrophizing, overgeneralization, labeling, and so on? (For a more thorough discussion of cognitive distortion, see the discussion of cognitive behavioral therapy, or CBT, on pages 105-111).

10. Delusions: Delusions are fixed false beliefs that, unlike cognitive distortions, leave the realm of reality. Some can seem plausible, but on further investigation turn out to be false, such as the unshakeable belief that a person's spouse is cheating, when they are not. Or they can be markedly odd and bizarre, such as the belief that someone is Napoleon Bonaparte or is taken by aliens every night to work in a factory making shampoo. Common delusional themes include the following:

a. Paranoid and persecutory delusions: The unrealistic belief that others (possibly named individuals but could be unnamed or agencies such as the IRS, the police, or CIA) are out to harm the person. Such delusions can include the belief that the person is under surveillance or has been harmed or interfered with (physically, sexually, or emotionally) by the feared entity or individual.

b. Grandiose delusions: Here the person has an unreal belief in his/her abilities, which can extend to thinking he/she is a famous person, such as a prophet, messiah, or ruler.

c. Thought insertion and mind reading: Here, the person believes others are putting thoughts into their head, or that they can accurately read other people's minds.

d. Thoughts of reference: This is where someone perceives special messages where they don't in fact exist. Examples include special messages in newspaper articles or on television, believing that the serial numbers on dollar bills contain significance to the individual.

e. Erotomanic delusions. The belief that another person, often a famous person the individual may have never met, is in love with them. These thoughts can progress to stalking behaviors.

f. Other delusional themes can include the belief that someone is pregnant when they are not (pseudocyesis), has been replaced by aliens, or the belief that a person's family has been replaced by imposters (Capgras delusion/syndrome).

11. Hallucinations:

a. Auditory hallucinations. Does the person hear voices?

b. Visual hallucinations. Do they see visions or things others don't?

c. Tactile hallucinations. Do they have the experience of bugs crawling on their skin (formication) or other unreal sensations involving the sense of touch?

d. Olfactory hallucinations. Do they smell things that aren't there? Do they believe they are omitting an odor that isn't reality based? When present, olfactory hallucinations often involve unpleasant and noxious odors.

12. Orientation to person, place. and time (Often noted as "orientation times 3"):
    a. Does the person give their correct name?
    b. The correct day, date, and year?
    c. Can they tell you where they are currently? Often assessed by asking the person to tell you the name of the facility or address of where the assessment is taking place.)

13. Level of literacy: This factor can be assessed by having the patient read a short paragraph and write out answers to related questions. Similarly, by using any of the handouts and homework sheets in the book, you will quickly ascertain whether the person has difficulty with reading, writing, and comprehension.
    a. Is the person able to read and write?
    b. Is English their first language?
    c. Can they read and write at a level consistent with their age, and expected level of development?
    d. Do they describe specific learning disabilities?

14. Focus and concentration: Are they able to perform basic tasks involving concentration?
    a. Serial sevens. Ask the person to subtract backward from 100 by sevens. Have them do this for at least five sequential calculations ($100 - 7 = 93 - 7 = 86 - 7 = 79 - 7 = 72 - 7 = 65$). Prior to selecting this task, make certain they have an educational background that should allow them to do this.
    b. An alternative task of concentration would be to have the person spell the word *WORLD* forward and then backward (DLROW).

15. Memory:
    a. Immediate recall: Can the person repeat back three words immediately after you say them (door, ball, string).
    b. Short-term memory: Does the person report difficulty remembering things that happened in the last couple minutes? Do they start to do something and completely forget what it was they were doing? A standard test for this capability would be to have them repeat three words (door, ball, string) and then ask the person to remember the words three to five minutes later.
    c. Long-term memory: How good is the person at remembering details of their personal history? Does what they tell you correspond with information you have from other sources. Is their story consistent, or does it change?
    d. Do they tell you about significant gaps (amnestic periods) in their history.
       • "I can't remember anything about my childhood."
       • "Everything around the time of my motorcycle accident is a big blur."
       • "I know I had electroconvulsive therapy, but don't ask me to remember a thing about it."

ASSESSMENT OF DANGEROUSNESS (SUICIDALITY AND/OR HOMICIDALITY)

According to the Centers for Disease Control, suicide is the tenth leading cause of death in the United States. And depending on the age group, homicide is the second to fifth leading cause of death in those under the age of 44. Thoughts of wanting to kill oneself or others are a critical part of the mental status evaluation. Where those thoughts can also represent a medical/behavioral health emergency, it is crucial to thoroughly and frankly assess a person's current and past thoughts of suicide and/or homicide.

At times people will experience both thoughts of wanting to kill themselves and others. The most dire outcome is a murder/suicide. High-risk scenarios for that include:

- A person with paranoid delusions who believes their spouse, or significant other, has been unfaithful.

- Marginalized teens, more common in boys than girls, who fantasize about committing acts of violence and then taking their own lives.

- Women with postpartum depression or psychosis, must be carefully assessed for not just suicidal thinking, but for thoughts of wanting to harm their children and infants.

- While not considered as a mental disorder, certain religious, or ideological, zealots can view murder, or mass murder, combined with their own suicide as being a sacrifice for a greater good.

If in the course of the evaluation you determine that this person is at imminent risk, every state has statutes around involuntary hospitalization (often starting with an emergency room evaluation) for people who are suicidal and/or homicidal. When in doubt, err on the side of safety, even if you're concerned that calling 911 will damage the therapeutic relationship. Remember, relationships can be repaired, but only if your patient is alive.

While there are no perfect approaches to assessing risk, there is good evidence that a careful assessment of risk factors and protective factors can help the clinician, both in the assessment of dangerousness, as well as in its treatment. One method is to identify specific risks and determine whether they are static (those things that cannot be changed) or dynamic (things that can change and might become the focus of treatment interventions).

Static Risk Factors (things that cannot be changed)

1. Past behavior is the best predictor of future behavior. If a person has made serious suicide attempts in the past or has a history of violence toward others, this information should be given significant weight. How lethal were any attempts in the past? A person who required medical hospitalization or admission to an intensive care unit (ICU) demonstrates the potential for future lethal attempts. Have they killed or seriously hurt someone before? Did they go to prison for this?
2. Does the person have a mental disorder, or more than one?
3. Is there a family history of completed suicide?
4. Gender: Even though women make more suicide attempts than men, men of all ages have higher rates of completed suicide and typically choose more lethal methods (79% of suicides are men). Men also have much higher rates of violence toward others (including homicide) than do women.
5. Age: The single-highest risk group for completed suicide is older white men, especially in the setting of a major loss or illness.

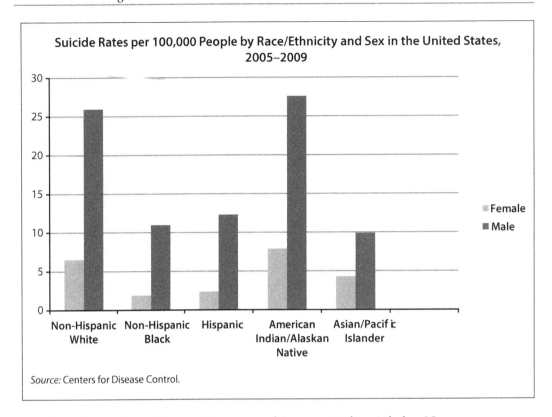

Suicide Rates per 100,000 People by Race/Ethnicity and Sex in the United States, 2005–2009

Source: Centers for Disease Control.

6. Race: Statistically, white non-Hispanics and American Indians/Alaskan Natives are at greater risk for suicide than non-white Hispanics and African Americans. African Americans, especially young men, are at the greatest risk for being victims of homicide.

Dynamic Risk Factors (things that can change and may become a focus of treatment)

1. Lethal means. Does the person own a firearm? Guns are the most frequent means of suicide, especially among men (56%). Having access to a firearm increases the risk of suicide threefold, and of being murdered, twofold. Have they been stockpiling medication, or accumulating street drugs for a fatal overdose? Poisoning/overdose is the most common form of suicide in women (37.4%).

2. Are they currently experiencing potentially treatable symptoms of mental illness?
   a. Are they currently depressed? Do they endorse symptoms of hopelessness (can't see a future)? Hopelessness is a significant finding that carries significant risk for completed suicide.
   b. Manic or hypomanic? Do they have mixed features (symptoms of both mania and depression at the same time)?
   c. Are they actively delusional? In particular, do they believe they are being threatened or are in danger (paranoia)? If they believe they're being persecuted is it by a particular person or entity?
   d. Are they hearing voices? Are the voices telling them to harm him/herself or anyone else? (command auditory hallucinations)?
   e. Is the person experiencing a worsening of PTSD? OCD? Or other mental disorder?

3. Have they recently been diagnosed with a major mental illness? The greatest risk of suicide for a person with schizophrenia is in the first year after diagnosis.
4. Are they currently using drugs and/or alcohol. Rates of both completed suicide and violence toward others rises dramatically when drugs and/or alcohol are involved.
5. Do they have medical problems, or a recent medical diagnosis?
6. Does the person have active legal problems? A high-risk period for suicide—especially among young men—is around the time of arrest.
7. Recent losses.
   a. Financial setbacks, such as the loss of a job, or foreclosure on a home?
   b. Death in the family or loss of a close friend?
   c. Death of a significant other?
8. Relationship stresses.
   a. Breakup of a relationship (including divorce)?
   b. Marital or relationship discord?
   c. Custody battles?
9. Planning and preparation. Have they recently purchased a firearm? Have they engaged in other practicing or preparatory behaviors (tying a noose, going on Internet suicide sites, stalking an intended victim)?

Protective Factors (things that help prevent a person from engaging in suicidal or homicidal behaviors)

Note: As with risk factors, some of these protective factors are static (unchangeable) and some are dynamic (can change).
1. Faith, religious beliefs, and spirituality.
   • "It's against my religion. I don't want to go to hell."
   • An ability to draw strength from one's faith.
2. Family ties and responsibilities.
   • "I couldn't do that to my children."
   • Family members who display active concern and a willingness to help their distressed family member.
3. Fear of the outcome of acting on their urges.
   • "Sure I'd love to see him drop dead, but I'd never actually go through with it. I'd never survive prison."
4. A belief that the person will get through their current difficulties.
   • "I know I'll get through this."

The Suicide Ladder

One approach to obtaining the suicide assessment is to start with open-ended questions that become increasingly specific. This is sometimes referred to as a suicide ladder.
1. Have you ever had thoughts of hurting yourself?
2. Have you ever tried to hurt yourself?
3. Tell me about the time(s) you tried to hurt yourself?
   a. What led up to it? (a breakup, loss of a job, felt too depressed and hopeless, etc.)

b. How did you hurt yourself?

c. Was the intent to die or something else? (Nonsuicidal self-injury, such as cutting, burning, head banging, is a common feature in personality disorders, such as borderline personality disorder.)

d. What happened afterward? Did you seek treatment? Did you require medical hospitalization? Psychiatric hospitalization?

e. Did you sustain any lasting physical damage from the suicide attempt?

4. Do you currently have any thoughts of hurting yourself?

5. What way(s) are you thinking of hurting yourself? (Do they have a present plan? Most people who contemplate suicide, have at least an idea of how they'd do it.)

a. Do you have access to carry out your plan? (firearms, a lethal overdose)

b. Have you made preparations or practiced carrying out the plan? (This can include identifying a beam or tree that could hold their weight if they tried to hang themselves, or purchasing a gun. Changes in behavior around firearms they already own, such as taking a gun from the safe and loading it.)

c. Have you made other preparations?
   • Updated a will?
   • Purchased an insurance policy?
   • Written a suicide note?
   • Given away possessions and/or returned things borrowed from others?

6. What's the likelihood that you'll carry out this plan?

7. What stops you from carrying through with your plan?

If the person is actively psychotic (hallucinating, delusional, and/or displaying grossly disorganized speech and/or behavior), the clinician will also want to assess for the presence and nature of any current delusions or hallucinations.

1. Are you currently hearing voices?

2. What are the voices saying?

3. Do these voices ever tell you to hurt yourself or anyone else?

4. Have you ever done what these voices tell you to do?

Assessment of Dangerousness to Others

1. Have you ever gotten into physical fights?

2. Have you ever injured anyone?
   a. If yes, what did you do?

3. Have you ever been arrested for any kind of assault? (If yes, explore the specifics.)
   a. How badly injured was the other person?
   b. Did they require medical treatment?
   c. What charges were brought?
   d. Was jail time served?

4. Have you ever killed anyone? (If yes, explore the specifics.)
   a. What were the circumstances (military, gang involvement, while committing another crime, etc.)?

b. Were charges brought?

c. Was jail time served?

5. Do you currently have any thoughts of hurting another person? (If yes, explore the specifics.)

a. Do you have a plan?

b. Do you have the means to carry out this plan?

c. What's the likelihood that you'll carry out your plan?

6. What stops you from carrying through with your plan?

If the person is actively psychotic (hallucinating, delusional, displaying grossly disorganized speech and/or behavior), the clinician will also want to assess for the presence and nature of any current delusions (especially persecutory ones) or hallucinations.

1. Is there someone or something that wishes you harm?

2. How certain of this are you?

3. How much time do you think about this?

4. Have you taken steps to protect yourself from this person(s) or thing(s)?

5. Are you currently hearing voices?

6. What are the voices saying?

7. Do these voices ever tell you to hurt yourself or anyone else?

8. Have you ever done what these voices tell you to do?

Assessment of Strengths

Through the course of an evaluation and ongoing in treatment, you will observe and assess your client's abilities in a number of situations. What things does the person do well? What strengths do you identify, and what strengths/positive attributes can they see in themselves? The ongoing assessment of strengths is useful for a number of reasons. It provides realistic points to help validate your client when they may be struggling with more negative thoughts about himself/herself, "You may be having a hard time now, but no one can take away the fact that you went eight years without a drink." A person's self-identified strengths let you know something about how they view themselves and about the person they'd like to be. Strengths a person possesses can also be called upon in the course of treatment to help move the person toward stated goals. "You mentioned that your faith is especially important to you. Have you considered taking on some volunteer work at your church, especially on the weekend where you're struggling to not drink?"

Areas to consider when assessing strengths include the following:

1. Relationships. Are they able to maintain close and loving relationships?

2. Do they have a strong social support network (family, friends, coworkers, faith community)?

3. Are they socially skillful?

4. Do they demonstrate an ability to get their needs met. How well do they navigate systems?

5. Assertiveness. Are they able to ask for what they want and effectively say no to unreasonable requests?

6. How well do they handle disappointment and frustration?

7. How motivated are they to work on their substance use and mental health problems?

a. Have they had significant prior successes in treatment?

8. Ability to complete tasks and goals. What things do they do well and take pride and ownership in?
   a. Do they have special skills and talents?
   b. Do they excel in school or the workplace?
   c. Are they athletic?
   d. An involved parent?
9. What strategies have they used in the past to achieve success? This might include past periods of sustained abstinence, or times where they've gone for extended periods without emotional/behavioral problems.
10. Do they have a strong work history and work ethic?

CHAPTER 3

The Comprehensive Assessment Part Two: Substance Use, Medical Histories, and Collateral Sources of Information

OVERVIEW

People with co-occurring disorders often receive wrong diagnoses; it's not surprising. Someone experiencing a withdrawal from alcohol or opioids, or crashing from a cocaine binge, can easily be confused with a person suffering with severe depression or an anxiety disorder, especially if they are not forthcoming with details of their substance use. People with bipolar disorder typically don't seek help when manic or hypomanic, but do when depressed. As a result, they are at risk for misdiagnosis, missed diagnoses, and the wrong treatments.

The potential for harm related to missed and wrong diagnoses is great. An unrecognized withdrawal from alcohol or Valium-type drugs (benzodiazepines) can lead to dangerous—even fatal—withdrawal syndromes. Just treating the depressed half of bipolar disorder can precipitate mania and worsen irritability and agitation, which in turn can worsen the accompanying substance use problem(s)—"I needed the booze to shut down my racing thoughts."

To make things more challenging, among the core symptoms of substance use disorders are minimization, and outright denial, of the problem.

- "I just drink socially."
- "Cocaine's not a problem."
- "The pills are prescribed. I have pain. I'm not an addict."
- "I don't take Xanax all the time, just when I need it."

So too, stigma, denial, and cultural and religious attitudes toward mental illness and drug use can make frank discussions about emotional and behavioral symptoms difficult.

In order to tease apart a person's substance use and mental health diagnoses, getting a careful history and looking for objective data are critical. We need to identify individual symptoms and put them together with the entirety of who the person is, where they came from, their genetics, epigenetics (those things that cause particular genes to be expressed or not), experience, culture, age, gender, beliefs, spirituality, goals, and aspirations.

THE SUBSTANCE USE HISTORY

The first step in understanding a person's use, and overuse, of a substance is the taking of a careful history. When did the use first occur? How has this use progressed over time? When did the person first identify that it was a problem? Or perhaps they don't view their use as problematic.

For those clinicians working in Joint Commission and Commission on Accreditation of Rehabilitation Facilities (CARF) accredited clinics and facilities, this patient history will be part of an intake assessment that maps out each substance used, duration, and quantity consumed. It typically includes questions about any legal, occupational, medical, and/or social consequences from the use, such as arrests for possession or driving under the influence (DUI/DWI), work-related problems, negative health consequences, or damage or loss to major relationships.

It is important to gather information about all aspects of substance use. Why does someone use cocaine versus marijuana or alcohol?

Understanding a person's drug(s) of use, gives clues to other domains of their life, and to the presence of co-occurring mental health problems. Is the primary goal in taking the substance to get high? To be social? Or is the goal to try and alleviate some kind of emotional or behavioral symptom?

- "Pot's the only thing that makes me calm."
- "I know it sounds strange, but cocaine lets me focus."
- "If I don't drink, I don't sleep."
- "I like the buzz."
- "I can't stand parties, but if I throw a few back I can have a good time."

An interesting gender difference is that on average more women who use substances do so to medicate away painful emotions, versus men who are more likely to use drugs and/or alcohol to get high.

It's useful to view the assessment process, which is ongoing, as similar to an investigative reporter trying to get the full and balanced story. This process uses the core questions behind any good mystery—who, what, when, where, why, and how.

The most widely used diagnostic manual in the United States, the DSM-5, provides a checklist of 10–12 common symptoms for each potential substance use disorder. Significant changes between this manual and its predecessor—the DSMIV-TR—are the elimination of the terms *abuse* and *dependence* and the inclusion of a severity rating for a person's substance use disorder as being mild, moderate, or severe. The severity is assigned based on the number of symptoms present, as well as clinical judgment. The "mild" diagnosis replaces the older DSM-IV-TR substance abuse diagnosis, and "moderate" and "severe" correspond to the substance dependence diagnosis. Other notable changes in the DSM-5 include elimination of recurrent legal problems as a criterion, inclusion of cravings and strong urges to use, and raising the number of criteria required to make the lower level (mild) diagnosis from one to two.

Although the DSM-5 criteria are specific for each substance, the general approach is as follows:

Over a 12-month period, a pattern of substance use leads to significant distress and/or impairment (this could be at work, home, in relationships, neglecting important obligations, etc.), accompanied by two or more of the following:

1. Increased consumption of the substance over time.
2. A desire to quit or cut down and/or unsuccessful attempts to do so.
3. Considerable time spent trying to obtain the substance and/or recover from its effects.
4. Cravings and urges to use the substance.
5. Continued use of the substance results in failure to meet obligations at home, work, or in other settings.
6. Continued use of the substance results in social or relationship problems.
7. Giving up important activities—social, work, family—as a result of the substance.
8. Using the substance in potentially dangerous situations, such as driving while intoxicated.
9. Continued use despite the realization that the substance is causing health and/or emotional problems.
10. Tolerance to the substance—needing to take larger amounts to get the same effect, or possibly no longer able to achieve the same effect.
11. Withdrawal symptoms—specific to the substance in question, ranging from potentially life-threatening withdrawals as can be seen with alcohol and Valium-type drugs (benzodiazepines), to more mild syndromes as are seen with caffeine. This criterion is also met if the person takes the substance in an effort to avoid withdrawal symptoms, such as someone who is opioid dependent who may need to dose themselves multiple times a day.

Exhibiting two to three of the preceding symptoms is considered mild, four to five moderate, and greater than six symptoms severe.

Once a likely problem with a substance has been identified, it is important to get the details. Handout 3, which can be completed with a client as a structured interview or given as a take-home or in-group/in-session assignment, helps flesh out the individual's relationship with their substance(s) of use. It can also be used to clarify the presence of a substance use disorder and its severity.

Assessment Tools and Questionnaires for Substance Use

Helpful for assessing the presence and severity of substance use disorders are screening and assessment questionnaires and tools, of which there are many.

The CAGE Questionnaire: Perhaps the simplest is the widely used four-item CAGE questionnaire for detecting alcohol use problems. (CAGE is an acronym, with each letter corresponding to one of the four questions.)

The CAGE Questionnaire

Instructions: Two or more yes answers indicate the possibility of alcoholism and should be investigated further.

1. Have you ever felt you needed to **Cut** down on your drinking?

2. Have people **Annoyed** you by criticizing your drinking?

3. Have you ever felt **Guilty** about drinking?

4. Have you ever felt you needed a drink first thing in the morning (**Eye-opener**) to steady your nerves or to get rid of a hangover?

Scoring the CAGE is simple: two or more positive answers correspond with a likely problem and the need for further evaluation.

Although the CAGE is specific to alcohol, the first three questions can easily be adapted to other substances. The fourth question—the eye opener—speaks to the presence of being physically addicted or dependent on a substance and needing to use it to avoid withdrawal symptoms. The fourth question can be modified for many other substances that cause physical dependence and withdrawal syndromes, such as opioids (heroin, methadone, buprenorphine/Suboxone, pain pills, etc.) and benzodiazepines (Valium, Xanax, Librium, Ativan, etc.).

A modified version of the CAGE, adapted to include drugs, the CAGE-AID, is available at the following link: www.ncdhhs.gov/mhddsas/providers/DWI/dualdiagnosis/CAGE-AID.pdf.

The Addictions Severity Index (ASI): The ASI, developed by Thomas McLellan, is a semi-structured interview that takes approximately one hour to complete. This is typically done at the start of an episode of treatment, such as upon admission to a rehabilitation facility. It focuses both on the historical use of substances over the person's life, as well as usage in the past 30 days. The final score is based on a scale of 0–10, with 0 being no problem and no need for treatment and 10 being an extreme problem with treatment absolutely necessary. The ASI has been used as both an assessment and outcome measure in numerous studies.

Alcohol Use Disorders Identification Test (AUDIT): Specific to alcohol, the AUDIT is a well-validated 10-item questionnaire designed for use in primary care settings, although it is easily incorporated into evaluations in other settings. Copyright for the AUDIT is through the World Health Organization. It may be downloaded and reproduced without cost. Several full text versions are available online.

Links to the AUDIT:

- pubs.niaaa.nih.gov/publications/Audit.pdf
- whqlibdoc.who.int/hq/2001/WHO_MSD_MSB_01.6a.pdf?ua=1 (This link includes both the screening tool and guidelines for its use and scoring.)
- pubs.niaaa.nih.gov/publications/arh28-2/78-79.htm

Family Substance Use History

It is clear that genetics and family history play important roles in the likelihood that someone will develop a substance use problem. Genetic factors alone (i.e., others in the family with substance use disorder) accounts for as much as 50 percent of the likelihood that someone will go on to develop a problem.

So, too, social and family factors help shape a person's understanding of their substance use. If drinking wine at a meal is the norm, it is important to know this, as it may create issues for a person in recovery from an alcohol use disorder. If the person's mother has/had problems with substance use, was she actively using when she was pregnant with the identified client?

In addition to obtaining the history of the person's family and which members have had substance use problems, it is important to clarify who in their life currently uses. Are others in the home drinking or drugging? Is a significant other currently using?

HANDOUT 3
CORE QUESTIONS ON SUBSTANCE USE AND ABUSE

Instructions: Please answer the following questions completely. If you need additional room, write on the back or add additional pages.

1. What is your favorite drug of use?

2. How much do you use?

Substance used	Age of first use	Amount used/day	Last used	Number of days/ week used	Cost/ day of use	Method of use— smoked, injected, snorted, drank

3. What do you experience from each substance?

Substance	Effects

4. Write a brief description of how your use of substances has developed over your lifetime. (Write on the back if necessary.)

5. Has the amount you used changed over time? (Describe how your usage has changed over time.)

6. How do you obtain your alcohol or other drugs?

7. How much time do you spend obtaining drugs?

8. When do you use (times of day)?

9. Who is present when you use?

10. Where do you use?

11. Why do you use this substance?

12. What are the consequences of your use?

   a. Financial

   b. Occupational

   c. Emotional

   d. Health

   e. Social

f. Legal

g. Recreational

h. Other

13. How do you feel about your use?

14. What is the longest period of time you've gone without using substances?

15. What symptoms of withdrawal—if any—have you experienced when going without substances?

16. What is/are your current level(s) of craving for any drug of use or abuse (using a 10-point scale, with 10 being the highest possible craving)?

17. What makes your level of craving increase or decrease?

18. Has anyone in your family (currently or in the past) had problems with drugs and/or alcohol?

19. Does anyone in your current household use drugs and/or alcohol?

20. If you have a significant other (husband, wife, partner), does he/she currently use drugs or alcohol?

    a. Has that use been an issue for him/her in the past?

21. If you have problems with your mood or behavior, including prior psychiatric diagnoses, did your emotional problems come before or after your drug use?

22. Do you ever use substances to medicate away unpleasant feelings or emotions? If yes, please describe.

Seeing Beyond Denial and Lies: A Behavioral Approach

Honesty may be the best policy, but anyone familiar with the nature of substance use disorders knows that deception, denial, minimization, and outright lies, both to oneself and to others, are symptomatic of these disorders and not an indictment of the person. From sneaking cigarettes, to hiding empty bottles, to avoiding arrest when committing illegal activities around obtaining the next fix of heroin, pain pills, or methamphetamine, lying and minimization can become an unquestioned part of the addicted person's life.

To complicate matters, an interesting two-sided equation around dishonesty and trust presents itself. People have both a natural tendency to believe one another, and to get upset when they realize they've been lied to. Lies can destroy relationships, both in families and in clinical settings. The loss of trust is a source of pain for both the person with the substance use problem and for those who care about that person. Clinicians face the potential pitfall of labeling the person as a sociopath, incorrigible, or a lost cause.

- "He swore to me he'd stopped, and now I find he's hiding bottles in the woods."
- "I can smell it on her clothes."
- "His PlayStation is missing; last time this happened he pawned it for drugs."
- "He's just here because it's court mandated. He's not really interested in getting clean."

In order to address both halves of this equation it is useful to start with a nonjudgmental attitude that views the words out of a person's mouth as just one source of information. A person's behaviors—especially when looking at substance use disorders—are more important than the person's words. And third, heavy substance use and physiologic dependence are often accompanied by physical signs and symptoms that can help get you through the densest layers of denial and deception.

It is useful to assume the stance of a behaviorist and ask: What are the functions of the denial and the lies? What are the connected emotions?

On the surface these questions might appear obvious; knowing why someone engages in a problematic behavior, such as lying to conceal or minimize drug use, gives us insight into a person's view of the world, of self, and of others. The purpose of the lie or minimization may also give clues as to the person's level of motivation (see Chapter 4) to do something about their substance use. In essence, by denying or minimizing the problem, it's likely that the individual is still in a precontemplative stage of change. Helping them achieve a more accurate appraisal of their substance use will support forward movement into contemplation and action stages of change.

The following table gives some common lies and minimization statements:

The Minimization and/or Lie	Related Emotion(s)	Function(s)
My drinking is not a problem.	Shame: "I don't want anyone to know." Fear: "I can't stop." Anger (irritation): "It's no one's business!"	To maintain the habit. To assure oneself and others that things aren't so bad.
Minimization of the amount of a substance used. • "It was just two beers." • "I'm a social drinker."	Annoyance Shame	To maintain the habit. To conceal the extent of the substance used. To reassure others that this is not a problem.
Hiding signs of drug or alcohol use.	Fear Shame Guilt	To maintain the habit. To avoid negative consequences of the behavior, such as arrest, loss of relationships, loss of job, loss of custodial rights.
Misrepresenting (exaggerating or outright lying about) the amount of a substance used or severity of psychiatric symptoms to gain access to treatment.	Cool detachment Desperation	To receive controlled substances (opioid replacement medication, benzodiazepines, stimulants) for personal use or for possible diversion (sale, or use not intended by the prescriber).

MEDICAL HISTORY

A person's medical history often contains clues to current difficulties with substance use and psychiatric disorders. So too, negative health consequences can, and do, result from substance use disorders, as well as from the effects of many psychiatric medications.

- Did a football injury lead to an addiction to narcotics?
- Did recurrent illnesses and surgeries as a child lead to posttraumatic stress disorder and recurrent depression?
- Did someone develop diabetes after being on medication for bipolar disorder or schizophrenia?
- Did someone contract hepatitis or HIV from using intravenous drugs?

At a minimum, the following information should be gathered, either as part of a structured interview or by having the patient/client complete a health screening form. This form is similar to what is completed in most medical and dental offices, and can be completed by a client prior to the first visit.

HANDOUT 4
HEALTH SCREENING FORM

Name:_____   Date:_____

Date of Birth:_____

Please answer the following questions.

	Yes	No
Do you have a primary care physician or nurse practitioner?		
Name of your primary care physician or nurse practitioner		
Have you seen your primary care physician or nurse practitioner in the last year?		
Do you have an obstetrician/gynecologist?		
Name of your obstetrician/gynecologist		
Have you seen your obstetrician/gynecologist in the last year?		
Do you have a dentist?		
Name of your dentist		
Have you seen your dentist in the last year?		

Please provide the names of any other health providers you are currently seeing.

Name of provider	Reason for seeing them

Please answer the following questions. For yes answers, please specify the nature of the problem.

	Yes	No
Do you have eye or vision problems?		
Have you had a vision exam within the past year?		
Do you have dental problems?		
Do you have nasal (nose) problems or any problems with breathing?		
Do you have problems with your hearing?		
Do you have any skin problems?		
Do you have high blood pressure?		
Do you have high cholesterol?		

(Continued)

(Continued)

	Yes	No
Do you have diabetes?		
Is there a family history of diabetes? (If yes, specify who.)		
Do you have heart disease?		
Is there a family history of heart disease? (If yes, specify who.)		
Do you have lung disease such as asthma, emphysema, bronchitis, or COPD?		
Is there a family history of lung disease? (If yes, specify who.)		
Do you have stomach problems, such as constipation or diarrhea?		
Do you have problems with urination?		
Do you have neck or back problems?		
Have you ever had a seizure?		
Have you ever had a head injury?		
Have you ever had a head injury where you lost consciousness?		
Do you have thyroid problems?		
Do you have any gynecological problems?		
Are your periods regular?		
Are you currently pregnant?		
Have you ever had kidney disease?		
Do you have liver disease (cirrhosis)?		
Have you ever had Hepatitis A, B, and/or C? (If yes, specify which.)		
Do you have HIV or AIDS?		
Do you have a history of sexually transmitted diseases?		
Have you ever had tuberculosis?		
Have you been tested for tuberculosis in the past year?		
Other (Please fill in any additional information about your medical history you feel is important.):		

Please answer the following questions.

	Yes	No
Has your weight changed in the past six months? (If yes, complete the following questions>)		
Was the weight change intentional?		
How much did you weigh six months ago?		
How much did you weigh one month ago?		

Medical/Surgical hospitalizations: Please list all surgical procedures and inpatient medical hospitalizations you have had. If further space is required, write on the back.

Reason for surgery or inpatient hospitalization	Age at the time
1.	
2.	
3.	
4.	
5.	

Allergies (List all known allergies to medications and/or other substances.): _____
_____

Current Medications: Please provide a complete list of all your prescribed and over-the-counter medications, including nutritional supplements and herbs you are taking.

Medication	Dose	Times per day	Reason taken	Prescriber
1.				
2.				
3.				
4.				
5.				
6.				
7.				

PAIN ASSESSMENT

If your client is experiencing physical pain, it needs to be assessed and addressed. An assessment of pain should include:

- Location: Where does it hurt?

- Quality of the pain: Is it stabbing, crushing, pins and needles?

- Duration: Does it come and go, or is it constant?

- Circumstances related to the pain: Do certain things or activities make the pain better or worse?

- Severity of the pain. Using a 10-point scale, with 0 being no pain and 10 being the worst pain imaginable, rate your level of pain.

PHYSICAL EXAMINATION, REVIEW OF SYSTEMS, AND LABORATORY STUDIES

When working to clarify substance use diagnoses, it is important to identify physical or laboratory findings that can support the diagnoses. These results will be reviewed in detail for each of the major drugs of abuse later in this book. Similarly, some laboratory and physical findings can provide additional information about the person's history, including the presence of mental illness.

Objective physical and laboratory findings serve a number of purposes. They range from helping increase the individual's level of motivation to curb or stop their substance use, to uncovering active medical issues that need to be addressed (may or may not be a direct consequence of substance use), to discovering that someone is pregnant.

Finally, a medical workup (history, physical, and lab work) is often a prerequisite to using medication. This step helps to decrease the likelihood that the person will experience particular side effects and adverse reactions to medications, and also to obtain baseline information.

A standard medical component of the assessment will include a physical examination.

Physical Examination with Review of Systems

- Vital signs (temperature, blood pressure, pulse, height, weight)
  - An elevated blood pressure or pulse could be a sign of withdrawal from alcohol or benzodiazepines.
  - Malnourishment can be associated with several drugs of abuse, including advanced alcohol disease and heavy methamphetamine use.
  - Central obesity is a common finding in people who have been on a number of psychiatric medications.
- Skin
  - Are there signs of intravenous drug use (track marks, scars left by abscesses)?
  - Psoriasis can be associated with long-term alcohol use, as well as being a side effect of lithium.
  - Sores and picking lesions are common in people with stimulant (amphetamines, methamphetamine) use disorders and in individuals in withdrawal from opioids.

- Old scars may indicate deliberate nonsuicidal self-injury (cutting) or past suicide attempts.
- Heavy smokers may have nicotine stains on the fingers and on facial hair in men.

- Head, eyes, ears, nose, throat
  - Size of the pupils (pinpoint when people are using opioids, wide when they are in withdrawal)
  - Condition of the teeth

    Often poor in people who have been neglecting their overall health secondary to substance use or social deprivation.

    Erosion of tooth enamel, especially on the front teeth, can be associated with frequent vomiting, as is seen in some people with eating disorders (bulimia and anorexia).
  - Nasal problems can be associated with use of inhaled/snorted drugs.

- Digestive system
  - Diarrhea can be a symptom of opioid withdrawal. Constipation is a frequent side-effect of opioid use. It can become severe and lead to total bowel obstruction, perforation, and death.
  - Frequent nausea and vomiting are common in advanced alcohol disease and may be a sign of pancreatitis.
  - A distended abdomen, with evidence of fluid in the abdominal cavity (ascites) can be a sign of serious liver disease and is often seen in late-stage alcohol disease.

- Urinary system
  - Difficulty urinating can be a sign of intoxication with opioids and some frequently abused over-the-counter cold preparations, such as dextromethorphan.

- Cardiovascular system (heart and blood vessels)
  - Heart murmurs can be a residual symptom from intravenous drug users who have had bacterial endocarditis.
  - Swollen ankles can be a sign of serious heart problems or may be a side effect of medications or illicit drugs.

- Respiratory system (lung)
  - Abnormal breath sounds (wheezing) and restricted lung expansion are common in smokers of tobacco, cannabis, or cocaine (crack).

- Musculoskeletal
  - Cramping and flu-like symptoms can be signs of opioid withdrawal .
  - Complaints of pain need to be carefully explored; they may provide information about the cause of a physical dependence on a substance.

- Nervous system
  - Tremors and increased deep tendon reflexes can be signs of withdrawal from alcohol or benzodiazepines.

Laboratory

- Drug screens. Drug screening is to the treatment of substance use disorders what checking a blood sugar is to the treatment of diabetes.
  - o Ideally, drug tests should be supervised, because it is common for people with substance use disorders to attempt to alter the results.
  - o Urine is by far the most common means, and depending on the setting where you work, samples can be "dipped" or sent to a lab.
  - o In legal or forensic settings, where test results can be entered as evidence, you will need to follow written policies to ensure chain-of-custody handling of the specimen.
  - o Drug tests need to be specific for the individual and the substances of abuse. For instance, a person who is opioid dependent and on replacement therapy, such as methadone or buprenorphine (Suboxone/Subutex/Zubsolv), needs to have screens that can detect both potential opioids of abuse (oxycodone, heroin) as well as confirm that the person is in fact taking the prescribed medication. Where these replacement medications have significant street value, this extra step is an important safeguard against diversion.
- Blood work will be specific to the individual and their drugs of use, medications, and other medical problems. Typical lab studies might include:
  - o Complete blood count (CBC)

    Can detect an anemia (abnormally low blood count) that is often found in long-term drinkers

    Can indicate the presence of infections

    Can reveal serious medication adverse reactions, such as dangerously low white blood cells in people taking certain medications, such as Clozapine/Clozaril and Carbamazepine/Tegretol
  - o Liver enzymes

    Particular enzymes (SGOT, SGPT) may be elevated in long-term drinkers.

    These are often elevated in intravenous drug users with hepatitis (liver inflammation).

    Certain psychiatric medications carry a risk for liver disease.
  - o Lipids (cholesterol, triglycerides, high-density and low-density lipoproteins) are often elevated in people with metabolic syndrome.
  - o Amylase and lipase are enzymes typically elevated in people with alcoholic pancreatitis.

FAMILY AND OTHER SOURCES OF INFORMATION (COLLATERALS)

In addition to getting a careful history from the person in treatment, outside sources, such as family, spouse, other health care providers, probation officers, and case workers, can be helpful. This information gathering needs to be done with the signed permission of the person in treatment.

It is best to establish the importance of having outside sources at the start of treatment. It is optimal to have the person in treatment sign releases of information (forms that give specific permission for you to talk with others about the patient) at the first meeting.

The yield of information from family and others can make all the difference in clarifying not only the substance use history, but it also provides clues to the presence of co-occurring mental health problems, family histories of mental illness and substance use disorders, and potential barriers to successful treatment, such as a partner or family member who is actively using drugs and/or alcohol.

Outside sources of information are important; and in certain situations, not communicating with them can lead to serious problems later in treatment:

- Children and adolescents. Each state will have specific statutes as to what parents need to be informed of in the treatment of their children.
- Young adults living with a parent(s).
- People involved with the criminal justice system who have been mandated for treatment.
- Other situations where treatment is being dictated to the patient, such as employee assistance programs (EAP), where the person's ability to keep her job is dependent on successfully completing a substance use program.

A practical approach to obtaining outside sources of information is to indicate to the client, at the start of treatment, that this communication is the norm. Although it is within the person's right to refuse access to family, spouse, and others, it may not be in their best interest and should raise concern as to the reasons why access to collateral sources is being withheld.

Prior Records

No evaluation is complete without a review of past treatment. Although often challenging to obtain, getting copies of prior records is desirable. As the assessment progresses, keep track of facilities and/or prior and current providers. Obtain releases of information so that you can talk to current providers and request records be sent.

Some individuals may have copies of their records, they should be encouraged to bring these documents.

State-Operated Prescription Monitoring Programs (PMPs)

Almost all states now maintain prescription monitoring sites (see Appendix A). At a minimum, these sites will provide information on what controlled substances (opioids, benzodiazepines, certain sleeping medications, stimulant medication for ADHD, medical marijuana, certain hormones) the patient has been prescribed. Each state has specific rules about who is able to access this information—typically prescribers, doctors (MDs and DOs), nurse practitioners (APRNs), and physician assistants (PAs) with prescriptive authority, and pharmacists.

Both at the beginning and periodically throughout treatment, it's important to check this site. By doing so, you may discover that a person's use of opioids and/or benzodiazepines is much greater than claimed. These sites also provide information as to whether the person has been getting prescriptions from multiple prescribers (doctor shopping) and if they're using multiple pharmacies in an attempt to conceal their overall use of controlled substances.

In some instances this information, when combined with drug testing, may increase your suspicion that some—or all—of these medications are being diverted. For instance, a person who is getting monthly prescriptions for diazepam (Valium) but has a negative drug screen for benzodiazepines should raise serious concerns.

CHAPTER 4

The Comprehensive Assessment
Part Three: Stage of Change and
Level of Motivation for Change

> **Overview**
> **Stage of Change Theory**
> **Assessment of Motivation for Change**

OVERVIEW

From the early stages of treatment (engagement and persuasion), through the final phase (termination), it is important to understand the patient's current readiness to address his or her substance use and other behaviors or situations that person finds problematic. As a clinician you need to monitor this level of readiness like the temperature on a thermometer:

- What is the person's current level of motivation?
- How does this level of motivation correspond to the person's current stage of change?

Readiness and motivation are moving targets and seldom progress in a linear fashion. When someone wakes up hungover, that person might swear to never again drink. Come five o'clock and happy hour, the hangover is forgotten, urges to drink and craving take over, and thoughts of abstinence are just a memory. Or individuals might go from not thinking their drinking was a problem, to suddenly deciding they absolutely must quit after being told they have alcoholic hepatitis, cirrhosis, or serious alcohol-related heart disease (alcoholic cardiomyopathy).

STAGE OF CHANGE THEORY

Developed by Prochaska and DiClemente, stage of change theory provides a useful model for assessing a person's readiness for change. Although initially used in the setting of substance use and addictive disorders, a stage of change approach can be applied to any behavior or circumstance a person is looking to change, such as leaving a problematic relationship, starting an exercise regimen, or taking a new medication.

The stages can be conceptualized as follows:

1. Precontemplation. The person is unaware a problem exists.

2. Contemplation. The person is aware a problem is present, but is not yet ready to make a change.

3. Preparation/Planning. The person plans to do something about the problem.

4. Action. Decisive action is taken to address the problem.

5. Maintenance. The problem has been fixed, and now efforts are in place to keep the change.

6. Relapse/Recycle. A lapse and recurrence of the problem behavior or substance use requires a return to earlier stages to get things back on track. The severity of the lapse can be minor to extreme.

7. Termination. The problem no longer requires effort to maintain the change.

Stage of Change	Thoughts	Behaviors
Precontemplation The person is unaware a problem exists.	• My drinking is not a problem. • I have no interest in giving up cigarettes. • I just use cocaine socially. • The pills are prescribed. I don't have a problem with them and I'm certainly not addicted to them. • I don't have an eating disorder. • Nothing wrong with my thoughts. So what that I hear voices? • It's just the way he is. It doesn't bother me when he gets in one of his moods.	Problem behavior continues without change.
Contemplation The person believes a problem is present, but is not yet at a point of readiness/willingness to take definitive action.	• I sometimes drink too much. • Cigarettes are expensive and they are not good for me. • I wish I could stop using cocaine, but the cravings are too strong. • I might be getting into trouble with the pills the doctor prescribed. Whenever I go without them, I feel sick. • It's not normal for me to make myself throw up every day. • The voices are real to me, but they're interfering with my ability to get stuff done. • When he yells and screams it makes me frightened. I know I shouldn't have to put up with this, but I can't leave him.	Problem behavior continues; some early attempts to change the behavior may be evident.

Stage of Change	Thoughts	Behaviors
Planning/Preparation The person makes plans to do something about the problem.	• I'm going to call the clinic to make an appointment. • I'm circling my quit date on the calendar. • I've got a friend in NA. I'll ask her to take me to a meeting. • I'm going to need a detox program to get off these pills. • I have to find someone who knows how to treat eating disorders. • I'm going to make an appointment to see a psychiatrist. • I've started to put together an escape plan. I'm worried he might actually hurt me if he knows about it.	Problem behavior continues; some early attempts to change the behavior may be evident.
Action The person views the substance use, or other behavior, as problematic and is at the point of taking concrete steps to address it.	• Today, I'm not going to drink. • Today, I'm putting on a patch and will not smoke. • I've deleted the number of my drug dealer and have blocked her calls. I will not use. • I've started to taper off the pain meds. If it doesn't work, I'll go onto opioid maintenance treatment. • I've started cognitive-behavioral therapy for my bulimia, and I might take medication, as well. • I've started medication for the voices, and have found an Internet peer group of people who hear voices. • I moved out when he was at work and am staying at a safe house.	Plans are implemented. The problem behavior decreases or stops.
Maintenance The substance use, or other behavior, has been changed (typically stopped) and the person engages in strategies to strengthen and reinforce the positive changes.	• I'm going to attend AA for the foreseeable future to support my sobriety. • I've gotten rid of all the ashtrays and am using the money I would have spent on cigarettes to take a vacation. • I no longer associate with my old drug friends. • I know that I need to stay away from pain pills. If my doctor offers, I'll ask for alternatives. • I'm still seeing my therapist, but not as often, and keep focused on healthy eating. • I take my medication daily, and when I feel like stopping it, I remind myself of how much more I'm able to get done without the voices. • The relationship is over. I don't take his calls and have blocked him from my Facebook page.	Strategies to maintain the new behavior are continued, although possibly at a diminished level.

(Continued)

(Continued)

Stage of Change	Thoughts	Behaviors
Relapse/Recycle The person experiences a lapse and recurrence of the problem behavior or substance use and must renew efforts to get things back on track.	• Not good. I got myself in a situation where I drank (smoked, did cocaine, took a pain pill). I thought I could handle it, and now the drinking is escalating back to where it was. I need to put a stop to this. • I can't believe I just made myself puke. I thought I had this under control. Apparently not. • I was out of meds and didn't fill them in time. I think on some level I wanted to see what would happen if I just didn't take them, because I've been doing so well. • He caught me in a moment of weakness, and now he thinks we're going to pick up right where we left off. I can't let that happen.	The person needs to reinvest in recovery and put plans into motion (action phase) that will get him/her back on track. Also, a careful examination of what led up to the lapse, possibly using a behavioral chain analysis (see Chapter 8) may yield areas for further work.
Termination Changes to the substance abuse, or other behavior, are firmly embedded and the person no longer experiences any cravings or significant thoughts related to the past use, or behavior.	• I'm someone who just can't drink. • I'm an ex-smoker. • I know I have to stay away from cocaine. • I'll only let them give me opiates if there's no other choice. • I had bulimia, and now I don't. • Taking my medication is just a part of my daily routine. • I was once in an abusive relationship. That won't happen again.	No further actions are required. Changes made have been incorporated into the person's daily life.

ASSESSMENT OF MOTIVATION FOR CHANGE

Along with understanding where a person is in the change process, it is important to understand the various factors that fuel his or her motivation. Is someone seeking substance use and/or mental health treatment on his/her own initiative (intrinsic motivators), or are outside forces at play (extrinsic motivators)?

Although nothing is wrong with having extrinsic motivators, their presence is important to note, because treatment issues and willingness for change may be compromised in some circumstances.

- "The minute I'm off probation, I'm out of here."
- "I'm just doing what I have to do to keep my job."
- "They wouldn't let me out of the hospital if I wasn't taking the medication. Now that I'm out I don't want it or need it."
- "My parents gave me an ultimatum, either get off drugs or get out of the house."

Frequently, a combination of motivating factors is what leads a person into treatment. It is important to identify the item(s) that tipped the scale in favor of someone seeking help.

Intrinsic Factors	Extrinsic Factors
"Sick and tired of feeling sick and tired."	Court-ordered (drug court, jail diversion, mandated treatment following a DUI).
Health concerns. "My doctor told me I've damaged my liver from the drinking."	Family pressure/tough love. "My mom told me either I get clean or I find somewhere else to live."
"I don't want this lifestyle anymore."	Mandated by work—Get into treatment or risk losing the job.
"I want to be a better role model for my children."	Involuntary psychiatric commitment. In most states, this action centers around imminent risk of harm to self or others, and possibly grave disability, as well.
"I don't want to end up like my father."	Treatment mandated as part of divorce or custody proceedings.
"I don't want to be depressed anymore."	Treatment stipulated by a child-protective agency.
"I know I need help."	Treatment/assessment stipulated by another agency, such as the department of motor vehicles.
"My substance use and the way I'm behaving go against my moral beliefs. I have to stop."	I'm starting a new job and they drug test. I've got to ditch the pot.

A person's level of motivation and where they are in the change process are closely linked. When motivation is high, a person is more likely to change, and vice versa. This connection between motivation and change provides the underpinning for the therapeutic strategy of motivational interviewing (MI), which is discussed in Chapter 8.

CHAPTER 5

Creating a Problem/Need List and Setting Goals and Objectives

---

Overview

How to Generate a Problem/Need List

    Problem/Need List Exercise One

    The Findings

    Constructing the List

Establishing Goals and Objectives

    Goals and Objectives Are Specific to the Individual

    Goals and Objectives Are Realistic

    Goals and Objectives Are Measurable

    Goals and Objectives Are Behaviorally Based

    Goals and Objectives Are Desirable

OVERVIEW

The prior three chapters focused on the collection of large amounts of information (data) about your patient. They incorporated most items found in standard assessment or intake tools in facilities and organizations that are accredited through the Joint Commission and the Commission on Accreditation of Rehabilitation Facilities (CARF).

However, data that are collected and not interpreted and utilized serves no purpose. This chapter focuses on the process of looking at all the information collected and organizing it into a workable problem/need list, and from there establishing the goals and objectives for treatment.

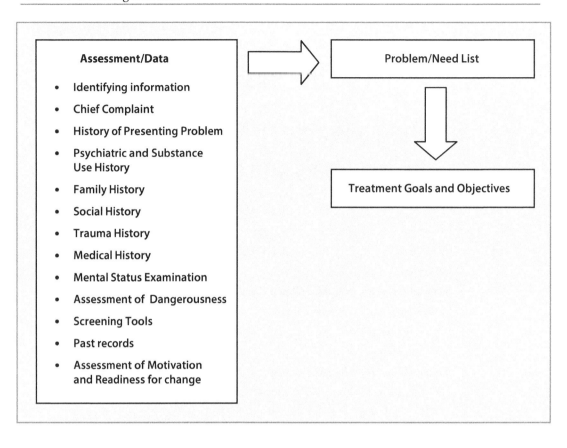

THE PROBLEM/NEED LIST

Problem/need lists serve a number of useful purposes:

- They help both the client and the clinician focus on the issues of greatest urgency and concern.
- They incorporate and reflect the client's aspirations.
- They serve as the backbone of treatment plans and will guide the creation of specific goals and objectives.
- They will be used when providing services reimbursed by third-party payers (insurance companies, Medicare, Medicaid).
- They can help clarify diagnoses.

HOW TO GENERATE A PROBLEM/NEED LIST

The simplest method to construct a problem/need list is to go through all of the data collected and identify anything that might be considered significant. This will include anything abnormal, out of range, a potential focus of treatment, barriers to treatment, client strengths, and so on. Then it is a matter of taking those bits of data, either lumping them together by themes or natural connections, or separating them apart to have them stand as their own problem or need. The two strategies could be summed up as lump the data or list the data.

The problem/need list typically contains the criteria used to generate diagnoses, but it is not a reiteration of the diagnoses. Rather the problems/needs are an articulation, based on the data, of what needs to be worked on, accompanied by some indication of the severity of the situation and the evidence to support the existence of the stated problem/need.

Problem/Need List Exercise One

Instructions: Make a copy of the following case study (a referral to an outpatient clinic) and highlight or circle every piece of information (data) that can be considered abnormal, out of range, or significant. Complete this review prior to turning the page.

CASE STUDY
JAMES TRENT

Identifying Information: James Trent is a 34-year-old divorced Caucasian father of two, who works for a state agency, and comes referred for substance abuse treatment by his employer's employee assistance program (EAP).

Chief Complaint: "If I don't get into treatment and stop using cocaine, I'll lose my job."

History of Presenting Problem: Mr. Trent reports he recently tested positive for cocaine during a random drug test. It is the second time in the past five years he tested positive. He works as a supervisor for the Department of Children and Families and is on leave, pending his successful completion of a drug program. He states that since he gave the positive urine two weeks ago, he has been acutely anxious with diminished sleep and appetite. He reports lying awake at night worrying about bills, such as making his mortgage payment and not falling behind in child support for his 6- and 8-year-old sons. "I don't have a cushion. If I don't go back to work, I'll lose everything."

He has never sought treatment for what he views as recreational cocaine use, but adds, "I'm totally ready to give it up."

Past Psychiatric History: Mr. Trent states he was in counseling as an adolescent around the time of his parent's divorce: "just a few sessions when I was 14." He remembers feeling depressed through much of high school, and took an overdose of Tylenol after a breakup with a girlfriend when he was 17. He never told anyone and did not seek treatment. He has never been hospitalized. He has never been on psychiatric medications, although his primary care doctor has recommended a trial of antidepressants in the past.

Family Psychiatric and Substance Use History: His mother has been treated for depression and anxiety; she is in recovery and has been sober for more than 10 years. His oldest brother has problems with drugs and alcohol, for which he has been in and out of multiple treatment centers.

Substance Use History: He first tried marijuana when he was 13. Because he knows that he will be drug tested, he gave up cannabis, but has tried synthetic cannabis, which he didn't like. He denies having more than three drinks/week, but adds when he does use cocaine, he will drink more than usual (up to a pint of hard liquor, and several beers).

He first tried cocaine in college, and states that this and stimulants, such as Ritalin and amphetamines, are his drugs of choice. "They make me feel invincible." He has also tried "legal" stimulant alternatives such as bath salts. Initially he'd snort cocaine, but in recent years has preferred to smoke crack for the more-intense rush. He has never used needles. He reports long periods (as much as a year) where he has gone without using cocaine. He currently uses on the weekends, typically on Friday night, but that lately his usage has increased. He currently spends $200–$400/week on cocaine.

He smokes a half pack of cigarettes/day and has done so since he was 16.

Medical History: He had asthma as a child. He had an appendectomy. He has no allergies and is on no medications. He was told he has hypertension, but has not followed up with treatment recommendations.

Social History: Mr. Trent is the second of four children. His parents separated when he was a teenager. "My father was cheating on my mother." He reports being a B student, being athletic, and having friends. He graduated high school, attended a four-year community college and has worked for the state since graduation. He was married to a woman he met in college, they have two sons, and he has limited custody (one evening/ week). He admits that the breakup of the marriage "was all my fault. It was the cocaine, and she caught me with somebody."

He currently lives in a condominium, pays child support, and is not in a significant relationship. "I go to work, I come home. It's gotten to where the only thing I look forward to is getting blasted on the weekends."

Mental Status Examination: Mr. Trent appears of normal weight and is appropriately dressed and groomed. He makes good eye contact and is cooperative throughout the evaluation. He describes his mood as highly anxious (9 out of a possible 10) and moderately depressed (5 out of 10). He appears anxious, and his speech is at times pressured, although he is easily redirected. His concerns focus on being able to return to work, and he expresses a high level of motivation to not use cocaine.

When specifically asked about suicidal thoughts, he denies having any. However, he adds that if he were to lose his job, he doesn't know how he would cope. He has no thoughts of wanting to harm anyone else. He has no psychotic symptoms.

He is fully oriented, and his memory is intact.

The Findings

CASE STUDY
JAMES TRENT

Identifying Information: James Trent is a 34-year-old divorced Caucasian father of two, who works for a state agency, and comes referred for substance abuse treatment by his employer's employee assistance program (EAP).

Chief Complaint: "If I don't get into treatment and stop using cocaine, I'll lose my job."

History of Presenting Problem: Mr. Trent reports he recently tested positive for cocaine, during a random drug test. It is the second time in the past five years he tested positive. He works as a supervisor for the Department of Children and Families and is on leave, pending his successful completion of a drug program. He states that since he gave the positive urine two weeks ago, he has been acutely anxious with diminished sleep and appetite. He reports lying awake at night worrying about bills, such as making his mortgage payment and not falling behind in child support for his 6- and 8-year-old sons. "I don't have a cushion. If I don't go back to work, I'll lose everything."

He has never sought treatment for what he views as recreational cocaine use, but adds, "I'm totally ready to give it up."

Past Psychiatric History: Mr. Trent states he was in counseling as an adolescent around the time of his parent's divorce: "just a few sessions when I was 14." He remembers feeling depressed through much of high school, and took an overdose of Tylenol after a breakup with a girlfriend when he was 17. He never told anyone and did not seek treatment. He has never been hospitalized. He has never been on psychiatric medications, although his primary care doctor has recommended a trial of antidepressants in the past.

Family Psychiatric and Substance Use History: His mother has been treated for depression and anxiety; she is in recovery and has been sober for more than 10 years. His oldest brother has problems with drugs and alcohol, for which he has been in and out of multiple treatment centers.

Substance Use History: He first tried marijuana when he was 13. Because he knows that he will be drug tested, he gave up cannabis, but has tried synthetic cannabis, which he didn't like. He denies having more than three drinks/week, but adds when he does use cocaine, he will drink more than usual (up to a pint of hard liquor, and several beers).

He first tried cocaine in college, and states that it and stimulants, such as Ritalin and amphetamines, are his drugs of choice. "I like the way they make me feel invincible." He has also tried "legal" stimulant alternatives such as bath salts. Initially he'd snort cocaine, but in recent years has preferred to smoke crack for the more-intense rush. He has never used needles. He reports long periods (as much as a year) where he has gone without using cocaine. He currently admits to using on the weekends, typically on Friday night, but that lately his usage has increased. He currently spends $200–$400/week on cocaine. He smokes a half pack of cigarettes/day and has done so since he was 16.

Medical History: He had asthma as a child. He had an appendectomy. He has no allergies and is on no medications. He was told he has hypertension, but has not followed up with treatment recommendations.

Social History: Mr. Trent is the second of four children. His parents separated when he was a teenager. "My father was cheating on my mother." He reports being a B student, being athletic, and having friends. He graduated high school, attended a four-year community college, and has worked for the state since graduation. He was married to a woman he met in college, they have two sons, and he has limited custody (one evening/week). He admits that the breakup of the marriage "was all my fault. It was the cocaine, and she caught me with somebody."

He currently lives in a condominium, pays child support, and is not in a significant relationship. "I go to work, I come home. It's gotten to where the only thing I look forward to is getting blasted on the weekends."

Mental Status Examination: Mr. Trent appears of normal weight and is appropriately dressed and groomed. He makes good eye contact and is cooperative throughout the evaluation. He describes his mood as highly anxious (9 out of a possible 10) and moderately depressed (5 out of 10). He appears anxious, and his speech is at times pressured, although he is easily redirected. His concerns focus on being able to return to work, and he expresses a high level of motivation to not use cocaine.

When specifically asked about suicidal thoughts, he denies having any. However, he adds that if he were to lose his job, he doesn't know how he would cope. He has no thoughts of wanting to harm anyone else. He has no psychotic symptoms.

He is fully oriented, and his memory is intact.

Constructing the List

In the example of James Trent, one can identify more than 40 individual bits of information that could be considered significant. When examined, the majority of this information can be divided into two large categories: those related to his substance use, and those related to his current and past difficulties with his mood.

Substance Use–Related Data	Mental Health–Related Data
Referred by EAP for positive urine	Acutely anxious (rates it 9 out of 10)
Second cocaine positive urine	Can't sleep
Fears he'll lose his job	Financial worries
Spends $200–$400/week on cocaine	History of mood disturbance as a teenager
Began to use cocaine in college	Primary care doctor has suggested antidepressants in the past
Switched from snorting to smoking to increase the euphoric effects of cocaine	Can't see a future for himself if he were to lose his job
Divorced in part because of drug use	Mother with history of depression and anxiety
Serious financial concerns because of drug use and threatened loss of job	Past suicide attempt in the setting of a relationship breakup
High level of motivation to quit using cocaine	Depressed mood (rates it 5 out of 10)
Past history of cocaine use, as well as other drugs, going back to age 13	
Increased use of alcohol when using cocaine	
Smokes cigarettes	
Has never been in drug treatment	
Mother and brother with problems with drugs and alcohol; mother with long period of recovery	
Has gone long periods in the past without cocaine	
Identifies cocaine use as the high point of his week	

While most of the information is easily divided into one of these two large topics, some could fit into both. It is not clear how much, if any, of his depression and anxiety are related to the direct effects of cocaine, such as is seen following a binge (cocaine crash). And other pieces of information, such as his childhood asthma and untreated hypertension might not fit into either, but could be addressed with the creation of a third heading.

Medical Issues
Asthma as a child
Untreated hypertension

Moving forward into treatment, all of this information must be captured, and the problem/need list is one way to start. That said, it is not necessary, or desirable, to relist information you've already captured. Rather the goal is to distill the material into succinct statements around which you and your client will construct treatment.

Problem/need statements should be complete and readily understandable by the clinician, the patient, and quite possibly the insurance reviewer, who will need to know that the stated problem(s) is/are something for which reimbursement can be authorized.

Finally, the order in which the problems/needs are listed will be based on what you and your client view as the most pressing concern. The first problem is also typically the issue for which services are being billed.

Continuing with the example of Mr. Trent, a first problem/need list might look as follows:

Problem/Need List

1. **Active and severe substance use**, as evidenced by (AEB), increased use of cocaine, threat of job loss, loss of a major relationship secondary to drug use, increased consumption of alcohol, use of "legal" intoxicants, significant financial burden of continued drug use, cigarette smoker.
2. **Moderate to severe depressive and anxious symptoms**, with disturbances in sleep and appetite and anxious ruminations. Past history of a suicide attempt and inability to see a future should he lose his job.
3. **Active and past medical problems**: Untreated hypertension (active) and childhood asthma (resolved).

ESTABLISHING TREATMENT GOALS AND OBJECTIVES

The goals and objectives you set with your client serve as the rudder for treatment. Whether or not you are moving in the right direction—accomplishing the goals—will help you evaluate the interventions and strategies you have selected.

Organizations and agencies such as the Centers for Medicare and Medicaid Services (CMS) and the Joint Commission define goals and objectives differently, but for the sake of this book they will be used as follows:

- *Goals* could be considered the end product or finish line of a course of treatment, such as a lasting sobriety or complete resolution of depressive symptoms.
- *Objectives* (short-term goals) are the stepping stones on the way toward achieving the bigger goal, such as making it through an alcohol detoxification or starting therapy and possibly taking medication for depression.

When setting treatment goals and objectives, keep the following five key points in mind:

1. They are specific to the individual.
2. They are realistic.
3. They are measurable.
4. They are behaviorally based (something is being done).
5. They are desirable.

Goals and Objectives Are Specific to the Individual

All treatment starts and ends with your client. What is it that this person hopes to achieve over the course of treatment? Outside of your office, what things matter to them and how have these been affected by their current and past difficulties?

Your client's treatment plan needs to reflect who they are and their aspirations. Programs with prescriptive "cookie cutter" treatment plans will fall short of these goals, and be out of compliance with treatment standards and policies as set forth by the Joint Commission and the Centers for Medicare and Medicaid Services (CMS).

When setting goals with your patient, it is important to hear what it is they want from treatment and from life. The simplest approach is to ask, "What is it you'd like to get out of treatment?" or, "Where would you like things to be six months from now? A year from now?"

When eliciting a person's aspirations, it's important to remember that their goals for themselves, and the goals you as a clinician might want them to have, might be different. For instance, someone who presents with depression and problematic alcohol consumption might not be ready to have abstinence from alcohol as a goal. Or someone in an abusive relationship that clearly impacts their level of anxiety and depression, might not view leaving their significant other as desirable and/or financially realistic at the present time. In these examples, it is important to understand the client's perspective and to consider a harm-reduction strategy of meeting that person where they are. This doesn't mean this goal won't change in the future, but that at this point in time, this is where the client is.

To demonstrate that all goals are in fact the client's, some organizations, including the Joint Commission, want to see goals in the client's own words, or at least that their ideas are clearly represented. This creates a level of complexity when combined with the other necessary components of goals (Measurable, Realistic, Behaviorally based, and Desirable). In order to achieve this, clinicians will sometimes need to construct goal statements that incorporate the clients' own words and ideas with terms that fulfill the requirements of an acceptable goal statement.

Example: "I want to stop using drugs and alcohol." In this instance the client's statement fulfills all requirements. The measurement is 100 percent (abstinence).

Example: "I want to be less depressed and anxious." Client will experience a 30 percent or greater decrease in depression and anxiety as measured on 10-point scales. In this case measurable outcomes need to be added to the client's expressed goals.

Another approach, which is used throughout this manual, is to capture the client's goals in their own words, and then develop them with language that is measurable, behavioral, and so forth in the body of the treatment/recovery plan.

Goals and Objectives Are Realistic

When constructing treatment it's important to keep track of what can reasonably be accomplished over the course of treatment and with the specific individual. This varies greatly depending on the setting, the client, and their particular needs.

A realistic goal for a brief inpatient hospitalization might be elimination of the suicidal thinking and behavior that were the grounds for the current admission. Whereas realistic goals for a six-week outpatient co-occurring program, such as an intensive outpatient program, might be a 50 percent decrease in depressive symptoms and 42 days without using illegal drugs or alcohol. In ongoing individual outpatient therapy for co-occurring anxiety and cocaine use, realistic goals might include sustained abstinence and remission of all psychiatric symptoms.

As you work with clients to create their goals and objectives, it is useful to think about what they might be able to do easily, and then to push a bit further. For an adolescent who dropped out of school as a result of emotional, behavioral, and drug problems, what would it take for that teen to re-enroll or to get their equivalency diploma? Is this goal realistic? For someone with recurrent relapses with drugs and alcohol, what are some obtainable changes that person can make to decrease the likelihood of a next relapse? If they are someone who never went to 12-step groups, maybe that's a change that could be made. To push further, could you get them to commit to seven meetings in seven days, or better still, thirty in thirty?

Goals and Objectives Are Measurable

Both the Centers for Medicare and Medicaid Services (CMS) and the Joint Commission have specific policies and/or standards that require all treatment goals and objectives be measurable. Beyond this requirement, being able to quantify progress is helpful to both the client and the clinician, allowing you to look back and see what progress has been made and what remains to be done.

The use of scales and measurements (metrics) can provide a useful language between the clinician and their client as they progress through treatment. "So, how's the anxiety today?" "It's good, no more than 2 out of 10."

However, putting numbers and measurements to concepts as complex as depression, mood swings, and anxiety can be challenging, and it is among the most-frequently cited deficiencies by the Joint Commission.

The following list contains practical strategies to ensure that your treatment goals and objectives are measurable.

1. Absolutes—Words such as *all, none, yes,* and *no.* Or the person *will* or *will not* do something. Here the measurement is either 0 or 100.

   Example: Caleb *will* obtain affordable housing by the end of the month.

   Example: "I *will* be abstinent from alcohol."

   Example: The client will take *all* medication as prescribed.

   Example: "I want to stop cutting." Margaret will engage in no self-injurious behaviors.

2. Use of numerical scales.
   a. Likert scales. Five-point scales, where 1 is typically never or none, and 5 is all the time or extreme.

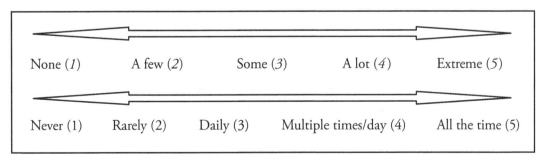

None (*1*)   A few (*2*)   Some (*3*)   A lot (*4*)   Extreme (*5*)

Never (1)   Rarely (2)   Daily (3)   Multiple times/day (4)   All the time (5)

Example: "I want to be less anxious." Using a 5-point scale, the patient will report anxiety as being no greater than a 2.

Example: The client will report a decrease in the frequency of panic attacks from a 4 (multiple times/day) to a 2 (rarely/less than one per week).

b. Subjective units of distress (SUDs). A 100-point scale that is defined by the client. Zero is usually no distress, and 100 is the most distress possible. SUDs are frequently used when doing cognitive-behavioral and other related therapies.

Example: "I want to be less depressed." Using a 100-point scale (100 being the worst), the patient will report depression no greater than a 30.

c. Other scales, such as a 10-point scale, as is often used when rating the severity of pain, 0 is no pain, and 10 would be the worst imaginable.

Example: Using a 10-point scale (10 being the worst), Sheila will report her anxiety never going above a 4.

Example: "I want my drug cravings to go away." Using a 10-point scale, the client's craving for heroin will never go above a 2.

3. Standardized screening tools and assessment scales.

   a. Tools to measure signs and symptoms of drug and alcohol withdrawal, such as the Clinical Institute Withdrawal Assessment (CIWA) and the Subjective Opioid Withdrawal Scale (SOWS).

Example: The patient's symptoms of alcohol withdrawal will be managed so that she scores no greater than a 2 on the CIWA.

   b. Tools to measure mood and anxiety symptoms, such as the Beck Depression Inventory, Patient Health Questionnaire-9 (PHQ-9), PTSD Checklist, Yale-Brown Obsessive-Compulsive Scale (Y-BOC), World Health Organization's Disability Assessment Schedule (WHODAS 2.0).

Example: "I don't want to be depressed." The patient's depression will be no higher than a 7 on the PHQ-9.

Example: Lorna will exhibit a 30 percent, or greater, decrease in her obsessive-compulsive symptoms as measured with the Y-BOC.

4. Parameters and specific amounts. The use of "less" or "more" *accompanied by specific amounts.*

Example: Frank will attend three or more AA meetings per week.

Example: Carla will utilize three or more dialectical behavior therapy (DBT) coping skills and record them on her weekly diary card.

Example: "I've got to stop washing my hands a hundred times a day." Jean will decrease her hand washing behavior to less than five times/day.

Goals and Objectives Are Behaviorally Based

Goals and objectives imply something is being achieved by the patient, and as such all require an action word (verb). Useful examples include *achieve, apply, demonstrate, experience, identify, maintain, master, obtain, show, understand, utilize.*

Example: Carl will <u>achieve</u> abstinence from cocaine.

Example: "I want to be less anxious." The client will <u>experience</u> a 30 percent decrease in anxious symptoms as measured using a 10-point scale.

Example: Carl will <u>attend</u> an AA meeting daily for the next four weeks.

Goals and Objectives Are Desirable

Having desirable goals may seem obvious, but sometimes getting you and your client to agree on what is desirable will be a challenge. Most frequently this occurs where the clinician, or sometimes a program, has a goal that is different from the patient's. At times this becomes an issue when someone has been mandated for treatment, especially if they do not believe there is a problem.

- "I'm not ready to stop drinking. I want to be able to keep drinking socially."
- "I plan to use synthetic cannabis, because I know my probation officer doesn't test for it."
- "I'm just here for court. The second that's done, I'm out of here."
- "I've always been depressed. I always will be depressed. I'm not interested in doing anything about that."

In these instances the challenge is to come up with mutually acceptable goals and objectives. This might involve the use of a harm-reduction approach where you start where the client is, and begin the process of motivating and persuading them to change.

- "I'm not ready to stop using." The client will attend three or more substance use groups per week, and will complete a pros and cons list around her current usage.
- The client will attend weekly substance use education and weekly motivational interviewing sessions, with a focus on cannabis.
- "I don't want to go to jail because of pot." The client will attend program, with the goal of being substance free, at least until his legal issues have resolved.
- The client's level of depression will be assessed and at least two treatment options that she has not previously tried, will be made available to her.

CHAPTER 6

Treatment and Recovery Plans

Overview
Principles of Treatment and Recovery Planning
Interventions
Structure of Treatment and Recovery Plans
Sample Treatment and Recovery Plan
Dynamic and Changing Aspects of Assessment and Treatment

OVERVIEW

Clinicians who treat substance use and mental health disorders are often faced with a difficult dichotomy when it comes to documentation and treatment planning. On the one hand, it is critically important to identify your client's strengths, dreams, and aspirations and to build on those elements. But the realities of insurance reimbursement are such that what needs to be recorded focuses on deficits, or what is wrong, diagnosable, and disordered. If you cannot document the medical necessity for your services, you will not get paid.

In recent years this split between what must be recorded so that services can be reimbursed and the benefits of strength-based assessments and treatment planning have led some organizations and providers to create two sets of treatment plans. One that demonstrates medical necessity and the other as a more client-friendly document, sometimes referred to as a recovery or wellness plan.

While there are merits to having both the medical-model treatment or care plan and the client-friendly recovery or wellness plan, there are also potential pitfalls, such as overvaluing one and undervaluing the other. There's an increased paperwork burden and the risk that the focus becomes less about treatment and more about the thorough completion of forms.

For the sake of this text, both halves of this equation—the need for strength-based treatment and documentation of medical necessity—will be included in a single treatment/recovery plan. Beyond the specifics of forms, the more important point is that treatment planning is a process with real clinical value. It's the blueprint for treatment.

Treatment/recovery plans flow naturally from the ongoing distillation of information you get from your patient, the problem/need list, and the goals and objectives you've established.

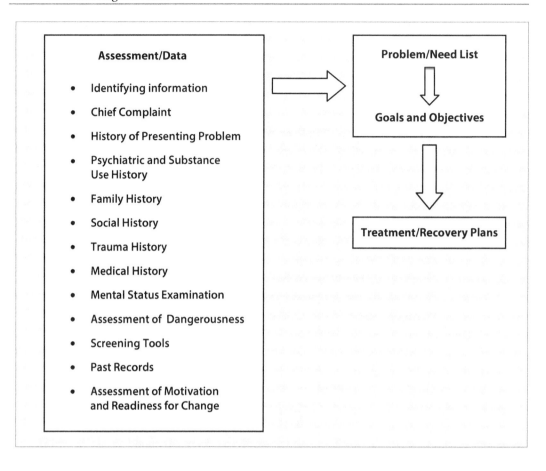

Principles of Treatment and Recovery Planning

Treatment/recovery plans will include the following aspects:

1. Plans are developed collaboratively between the client and the clinician.
2. Plans are developed and centered around the client's particular needs, aspirations, challenges, and problems. One approach is for clinicians to view themselves as a consultant to their client. The focus is always on the client's specific goals and what needs to be done to achieve them.
3. Treatment/recovery plans represent a process. They are not set in stone, but are constantly reassessed and revised based on the client's changing circumstances.
4. All potential resources for positive change can be incorporated into plans (not just interventions considered clinical). Taking the dog for a daily walk, going to the gym on a regular basis, having lunch with a sober friend, getting involved in a religious organization, or taking a course at the local college are real-world activities that can help move a person toward their stated goals.

Interventions

Interventions are the specific strategies, treatments, skills acquisition, utilization of peer support systems, faith-based communities, family, friends, and other resources that will be used in helping the person move toward specific goals and objectives. Interventions, then, are the tools in your client's and your respective toolkits. And like hammers and screwdrivers it's all about having the right tool for the right job. Just as you wouldn't try to hammer a screw into a piece of drywall, mismatched or one-size-fits-all treatment strategies won't get the job done. Do they have the necessary tools already, or is part of the work of treatment about helping them expand the range of what's in their toolkit?

The range of potential interventions is massive, so for the sake of the treatment and recovery planning process, interventions should all include the following domains:

1. Interventions are specific to the client's goals and objectives.
2. Interventions are specific to the problem/need list.
3. There is ownership of the interventions. Someone is responsible for seeing that they get done (this might be more than one person, especially where the clinician or other member of the multidisciplinary team and the client have a role in getting the intervention accomplished.)
4. Interventions have specific parameters. Just as all the goals and objectives need to be measurable, so too the interventions should have specific parameters. How many sessions, of what length, over what period of time, and so forth. If there is an anticipation that an intervention will continue indefinitely, such as taking particular medications for persistent conditions, that should be noted.
5. Interventions are realistic. They are in the realm of what can be accomplished by the client and the clinician.

STRUCTURE OF TREATMENT AND RECOVERY PLANS

At a minimum treatment/recovery plans would contain the following:

1. The active problems/needs that are the focus of treatment
2. The specific goals and objectives tied to the problems and needs
3. Interventions (treatments, strategies, family, peer and community resources, etc.) that will be employed in moving the person closer to their goals

The Treatment and Recovery Plan: The following form, which can be used as is or adapted to your organization, incorporates Joint Commission standards for treatment planning as well as those required for most insurers, including Medicare and Medicaid (CMS). In addition, specifics related to peer activities and a strength-based recovery philosophy have been incorporated into the form.

TREATMENT/RECOVERY PLAN

Patient's Name: Date of Birth: Medical Record #:	

Level of Care

ICD-10 Codes	DSM-5 Diagnoses

The individual's stated goal(s):

1. Problem/Need Statement:
Long-Term Goal:
Short-Term Goals/Objectives: Target date: 1. 2.

2. Problem/Need Statement:
Long-Term Goal:
Short-Term Goals/Objectives: Target date: 1. 2.

3. Problem/Need Statement:
Long-Term Goal:
Short-Term Goals/Objectives: Target date: 1. 2.

Interventions					
Treatment Modality	Specific Type	Frequency	Duration	Problem Number	Responsible Person(s)

Identification of strengths:

Peer/family/community supports to assist:

Barriers to treatment:

Staff/client-identified education/teaching needs:

Assessment of discharge needs/discharge planning:

Completion of this treatment/recovery plan was a collaborative effort between the client and the treatment team members:

SIGNATURES		Date/Time
Client:		
Physician:		
Treatment Plan Completed By:		
Primary Clinician:		
Other Team Members:		

SAMPLE TREATMENT/RECOVERY PLAN

Using the case study, the related problem/need list, and goals and objectives of James Trent in the previous chapter, the following treatment/ recovery plan can be assembled.

TREATMENT/RECOVERY PLAN

Patient's Name: James Trent	
Date of Birth: 2/12/1980	
Medical Record #: XXX-XX-XXXX	

Level of Care: Intensive Outpatient (IOP)

ICD-10 Codes	DSM-5 Diagnoses
F14.20	**Cocaine use disorder, moderate**
F32.9	**Unspecified depressive disorder with mixed and anxious features**
F12.20	**Cannabis use disorder, moderate**
F17.200	**Nicotine use disorder, moderate**

The individual's stated goal(s): "I want to get clean and be a better father to my children. I don't want to lose my job, and I'd like to have a girlfriend."

1. Problem/Need Statement: Active and severe substance use, as evidenced by (AEB), increased use of cocaine, threat of job loss, loss of a major relationship secondary to drug use, increased consumption of alcohol, use of "legal" intoxicants, significant financial burden of continued drug use, cigarette smoker.
Long-Term Goal(s):
1. To be completely abstinent from illicit drugs and alcohol, as well as "legal" intoxicants, AEB-negative urine toxicology screens, and self-report.
2. To maintain employment.
3. To become a nonsmoker.
Short-Term Goals/Objectives (with target date):
1. To stop using cocaine, cannabis, and "legal intoxicants." (immediately)
2. To maintain employment. (4/15/2014)
3. To develop a plan to stop smoking cigarettes. (4/15/2014)

2. Problem/Need Statement: Moderate to severe depressive and anxious symptoms, with disturbances in sleep and appetite and anxious ruminations. Past history of a suicide attempt and inability to see a future should he lose his job.

Long-Term Goal(s):

To be free from symptoms of anxiety and depression, AEB depression and anxiety no greater than a 2 on a 10-point scale (10 being the worst).

Short-Term Goals/Objectives (with target date):

1) To clarify the psychiatric diagnoses. (4/15/2014)

2) To achieve a 50 percent reduction in anxious and depressive symptoms using a 10-point scale. (4/15/2014)

3. Problem/Need Statement: Active and past medical problems: Untreated hypertension (active) and childhood asthma (resolved).

Long-Term Goal(s):

To have all medical issues adequately addressed and treated.

Short-Term Goals/Objectives (with target date):

To obtain a primary care physician or nurse practitioner, and have a first appointment. (5/15/2014).

Interventions					
Treatment Modality	**Specific Type**	**Frequency**	**Duration**	**Problem Number**	**Responsible Person(s)**
Group Therapy	CBT with co-occurring focus	3X/week	50 minutes/ group for one month	1,2	Mr. Trent, primary clinician, or designee
	Chemical dependence education and relapse prevention	3X/week	50 minutes/ group for one month	1	Mr. Trent, primary clinician, or designee
	Multiple family meeting	1X/week	One hour	1,2	Mr. Trent, identified family member(s) or S.O.
Individual Therapy	CBT individual therapy with co-occurring focus	2X/week	Fifty minutes/ for one month	1,2	Mr. Trent, primary clinician

Nursing Assessment	Nursing assessment	One time, and as needed	One hour	1,2,3	RN
Initial Psychiatric Assessment	MD/Nurse practitioner	Once	One hour	1,2,3	MD/APRN
Psychopharmacology	Medication evaluation	Weekly	15–20 minutes	1,2,3	MD/APRN
Labs	Blood work/ other studies as indicated	Upon admission, and as needed	N/A	1,2,3	MD/APRN
Specimen Collection	Breath analysis/ urine drug screen	As ordered	One month	1,2	Clinician, or designee
Peer Support	12-step	2–3 meetings/ week	One month	1	Mr. Trent
Other	Obtain medical referral	Once	Brief	3	Mr. Trent, program MD/ APRN

Identification of strengths: Strong work ethic, highly motivated to achieve abstinence and to not lose his job. Takes his role of being a father seriously and wishes to be more involved in his children's lives. Views himself as a moral person.

Peer/family/community supports to assist: Mr. Trent views his mother as a significant support. She has been in recovery for more than 10 years and has offered to go with him to NA meetings. She has also expressed willingness to attend multiple family meetings at the IOP. Mr. Trent says he will obtain a sponsor through NA. He also identifies supports through his work, but is cautious about what he divulges to coworkers.

Barriers to treatment: Mr. Trent identifies the financial burden of being on leave from work. He hopes to return to work as soon as possible, but realizes it may create scheduling difficulties with treatment.

Staff/client-identified education/teaching needs: To better understand the nature of his substance use, and to identify specific triggers and vulnerabilities. To identify and understand possible connections between his depressive and anxious symptoms and his substance use.

Assessment of discharge needs/discharge planning: Mr. Trent will be free from illicit drug use, and follow-up treatment will address both relapse prevention and ongoing assessment and treatment of any residual mood or anxiety symptoms.

Completion of this treatment/recovery plan was a collaborative effort between the client and the following treatment team members:

SIGNATURES		Date/Time
Client:	James Trent	3/15/2014 2pm
Physician:	Charles Atkins, MD	3/15/2014 3:15pm
Primary Clinician:	Gloria Anderson, LCSW	3/15/2014 2pm
Other Team Members	Peter Green, CaDaC	3/15/2014 4pm
	Lois White, RN	3/15/2014 4pm

Dynamic and Changing Aspects of Assessment and Treatment

A final point to make when discussing assessment and treatment is that these are fluid and dynamic processes. When working with people who have co-occurring disorders, it is crucial to be open to changing needs and clinical presentations. Both substance use and mental disorders change over time, they can have relapsing and remitting courses, and the symptoms of one can obscure and confuse the symptoms of the other.

Someone who presents in opioid withdrawal complaining of severe depression and anxiety may be depression free once they are out of withdrawal and on opioid maintenance treatment. However, you may now notice that they fidget throughout sessions and groups and are easily distracted. Both they, and their mothers, tell you these problems have been present since they were young. Suddenly the initial problems/needs list, which included depression and anxiety, needs to be revised to address the emerging presentation of ADHD, which is common (see Chapter 9) in people with substance use disorders.

Or even someone you have had in treatment for years, with a diagnosis of a depressive disorder, may suddenly present as manic or hypomanic. The earlier diagnosis of unipolar depression, along with aspects of the treatment, need to be changed to account for what is likely a bipolar disorder.

And with treatment, people do improve, and this needs to be reflected in the changing problem/need list, treatment/recovery plans, and the treatment itself. If a problem has resolved, this should be indicated, and plans get updated and reworked based on changing levels of care, changes in the clinical focus, clarification of diagnoses, and so on. For those who bill Medicare and Medicaid and/or are Joint Commission or CARF accredited, additional standards will mandate how frequently, and under what circumstances, plans need to be revised/updated or rewritten.

CHAPTER 7

Levels of Care

LEVELS OF CARE

One of the slogans of co-occurring treatment is "there is no wrong door." The intent of this statement is correct. When someone reaches out for help, that person needs to be met with open arms…and a correct level of care. For instance, it would be dangerous to attempt treating a manic individual in serious alcohol or benzodiazepine withdrawal in an outpatient clinic. However, should such a person walk through your door, you wouldn't turn them away. What you would do is attempt to keep them calm while making the necessary arrangements, which might include calling 911 to get an ambulance to transport them to an emergency room. Similarly, someone with mild depression and anxiety, who is smoking cannabis daily, is unlikely to require an inpatient stay, let alone have their insurance company be willing to reimburse for that level of service.

In addition to safety concerns, other factors need to be considered when matching a particular person to a correct level of care, treatment setting, and specific interventions. It won't just be a question of what is the best fit—although that issue is of great importance—but will need to take into account the real-world circumstances of community resources, the person's insurance or lack thereof, family resources, peer supports, active medical problems, level of motivation, personal preference, and so forth.

The concept of level of care can be thought of as a continuum that extends from inpatient settings, such as detoxification, medical and psychiatric units in hospitals, and freestanding substance use facilities, through residential programs, to a broad array of outpatient treatment options, both those run by professionals, as well as peer and mutual self-help options.

In some instances, level of care will need to take into account legal difficulties individuals might have. If they are incarcerated and require acute psychiatric or substance use treatment, then transfer to a hospital or specialty behavioral health unit will need to occur. Increasingly, through various mandates, the correctional system is required to address the behavioral health and substance use needs of inmates, and so even when people are incarcerated these principles of best fit can be applied.

Another concept to keep in mind is that both substance use and mental disorders respond well to treatment, but are also subject to relapses and clinical setbacks. Inpatient settings are reserved for individuals in high-risk situations who require acute and intense, possibly life-saving, treatment. When the acute need has passed, it is appropriate for that person to step down to a less-intense level of care, such as a residential rehabilitation program, partial hospital program (PHP), intensive outpatient program (IOP), or other form(s) of less-restrictive outpatient treatment.

WHEN TO USE AN INPATIENT SETTING

When deciding on what is the most appropriate level of care, the first question to be answered is: Does this person require, or desire, an inpatient option, such as a medical detoxification unit or psychiatric unit? The key issues here include the following:

1. Safety and medical concerns (It's important to familiarize yourself with your state's statutes and procedures concerning involuntary hospitalization and psychiatric/substance use commitment. These guidelines generally focus on the person being at imminent risk of harming himself or someone else, and often include language that extends to extremely disordered and dangerous behaviors.)
   a. Active suicidal or homicidal behavior
   b. Serious and active medical issues, such as alcohol or benzodiazepine withdrawal
   c. A person who requires detoxification who has co-occurring serious medical issues and/or a history of severe withdrawal syndromes in the past, such as alcohol or benzodiazepine withdrawal seizures and/or delirium tremens (DTs—see Chapter 16).
   d. Substance use patterns, which require detoxification that cannot be safely monitored on an outpatient setting (An example would be someone who is simultaneously dependent on opioids and another central nervous system depressant, such as benzodiazepines.)
   e. Grossly disorganized and dangerous behaviors (This will include substance-induced manic and psychotic states, such as can be seen with PCP, synthetic cannabis, hallucinogens, amphetamines, bath salts etc.)
   f. Grave disability that directly results from the substance use and/or mental disorder (This can involve the person's behavior deteriorating to the point where they no longer can manage basic self-care such as adequate nutrition, shelter, and clothing.)

2. Need for a higher level of care than what the person is currently receiving (It is often the case that someone initiates treatment as an outpatient, but circumstances require a move to a higher level of care, such as a medically monitored drug detoxification, residential program, or psychiatric inpatient unit, for a period of time. Reasons for this include:
   a. The emergence or reemergence of serious safety issues, as spelled out previously
   b. An inability to achieve specific treatment goals as an outpatient
   c. Recurrent serious relapses with drugs and/or alcohol where the individual is unable to achieve any significant periods of abstinence

3. Personal preference. It might be that someone has the resources and the willingness to begin treatment on an inpatient basis. For them this might be the most efficient way to start a course of treatment.
   - "I know myself, if there's even a chance I can get near booze I'm going to drink. I need to break the cycle by getting into a rehab program for a few weeks."

4. Mandated reasons for inpatient.
   - Circumstances where the individual has no choice but to be admitted to an inpatient unit, such as court-mandated for evaluation and treatment.

Inpatient Options

The selection of one inpatient setting over another will be driven by the individual's particular needs, preferences, and to some extent, personal resources (insurance, entitlements, transportation, available facilities, access to family and other supports, etc.). The two most-important questions to answer when selecting an inpatient option are:

1. What are the goal(s) for this admission? For the person with co-occurring disorder, this takes on particular significance as many inpatient facilities specialize in psychiatric disorders or substance use disorders, but not both. Which leads to the next question:

2. Can this facility meet the specific need(s)/goal(s) that are driving this admission?

The following sections describe the broad categories of inpatient facilities.

Medical Hospital/Acute Medical Unit

The current standard of care for severe alcohol and benzodiazepine withdrawal involves management on medical units. This is on account of the potentially life-threatening nature of these conditions and the need to access a broad-range of medical interventions, from intravenous medications to, in severe situations, the use of life-support equipment, such as can be found in intensive care units.

Access to behavioral health services, both to assist in the assessment and management of delirium and other psychiatric co-occurring conditions, is through consultation with either the hospital's psychiatric service (psychiatrist, APRN, social worker) or the person's treating psychiatrist, if they have privileges (are approved to see patients) at the hospital.

Medical units are typically unlocked and if there is a need for suicide precautions, or the individual is confused and at risk for self-harm, sitters or other interventions will be required to safely monitor the person.

Length of stay is driven by the need for ongoing acute medical hospitalization. At the point the active medical concern has been safely addressed, the person will be discharged, or transferred to the next appropriate level of care.

Community Hospital–Based Behavioral Health (Psychiatric) Units

These units are typically locked (with some exceptions) and are part of a larger medical hospital. Increasingly, psychiatric units have protocols to handle mild to moderate cases of alcohol and benzodiazepine withdrawal, while addressing severe psychiatric symptoms (mania, psychosis, suicidality). A potential advantage to hospital-based units is the access to medical care and ancillary hospital services, such as radiology and laboratory.

On average inpatient admissions are brief (4–10 days), and at the point the person no longer meets criteria for an inpatient admission (suicidal, homicidal, gravely disabled, and/or in withdrawal), the patient is discharged and referred to a less-restrictive level of care.

Free-Standing Private Psychiatric Hospitals

These facilities are separate from medical hospitals, although they typically have formal agreements (memorandums of understanding) with area hospitals, should a patient require transfer to an acute medical setting. Many freestanding hospitals have areas of expertise, which might make one of them a best-fit for a particular individual, such as specialized treatments for eating disorders, personality disorders, psychotic disorders, and so on.

Each facility's ability and willingness to work with co-occurring substance use disorders vary and should be assessed prior to admission. Any specific concerns about the potential for a dangerous withdrawal need to be clarified at the onset. "Do you treat alcohol withdrawal? If the person goes into serious withdrawal (has a seizure, Delirium Tremens, hallucinosis) how do you handle those situations?" "Do you work with people who are opioid dependent? Do you provide opioid replacement therapy?"

Veteran's Affairs (VA) Hospitals

There are Veterans Affairs Hospitals and Clinics throughout the United States, the Philippines, Guam, and the Virgin Islands. Services are available to active service members, their families, and some veterans with service-connected benefits. There are available substance use disorder services as well as mental health services, and these vary by state and location. Admission to a VA inpatient detoxification unit, general psychiatric unit, or specialty unit (such as a PTSD or co-occurring unit) will be based on the same symptom acuity that would necessitate admission to a community, state, or freestanding unit or facility. A central point of contact and information can be obtained through the Bureau of Veteran's Affairs at www.va.gov or by calling the VA crisis line at 1-800-273-TALK/8255.

State-Run Psychiatric and Substance Treatment Facilities

While nationwide the availability of state psychiatric hospitals has diminished greatly, most states still maintain facilities for individuals who meet their "target population criteria." These are typically people with histories of severe and persistent mental illness, often accompanied by substance use disorders.

Each state will have specific admission criteria, which will include the presence of acute and severe psychiatric symptoms. In the case of substance use disorders, state-operated detoxification facilities will use admission criteria based on historical information (history of seizures, DTs, etc.) as well as current presentation (acutely intoxicated or actively in withdrawal). Many states rely on the ASAM Patient Placement Criteria, described at the end of this chapter, when making level-of-care decisions, especially as they pertain to accessing state beds.

The length of stay in state hospitals is variable, but there is typically greater leeway for longer lengths of stay. In some cases, this can be on the order of months.

Detoxification Units

Detoxification units specialize in safely managing withdrawal, mostly from alcohol and benzodiazepines. Detoxification admissions from alcohol range from a few days to a week or more depending on the severity of symptoms. A complete and safe detoxification from heavy benzodiazepine use can take on the order of weeks, although the latter stages can be managed in a rehab setting with adequate medical oversight. Some detoxification units also offer treatment for opioid-dependent individuals. This might include a medically managed taper off opioids or the use of opioid-replacement therapy with methadone or buprenorphine (Suboxone, Subutex, and available generics).

Specialized detoxification units can be found in various settings, from general medical hospitals, state psychiatric hospitals, VA hospitals, and freestanding psychiatric hospitals, to residential substance use programs and centers with integrated detoxification and rehabilitation programs. Things to consider when selecting an inpatient option might include the following:

- If the person requires a medically supervised detoxification from alcohol or benzodiazepines, does this facility have a record for successfully providing this treatment? (medical unit, detoxification unit)

- If the person is manic, psychotic, or suicidally depressed and abusing opioids, will this facility be able to handle both the psychiatric component and the substance use component, which may require opioid replacement, such as buprenorphine or methadone? (inpatient psychiatric unit with co-occurring capacity)

- In addition to acute psychiatric and/or substance use symptoms, does this person also have serious and active medical issues that need to be addressed? (hospital-based psychiatric unit)

- If the person is suicidal, is this facility adequately prepared to safely monitor and treat them? (inpatient psychiatric unit, freestanding psychiatric hospital, medical unit with 24/7 sitters)

RESIDENTIAL TREATMENT

The option to use a residential program, frequently after a medically monitored detoxification, can be a useful strategy when trying to break the pattern of addictive substance use. In residential programs the structure and therapy allow the individual to lay the groundwork for healthier habits, while providing a physical separation from triggers and cues that exist at home and in community settings.

Residential options include standard four-week (28-day) rehabilitation programs to lengthier residential settings, some of which include options for the individual to obtain work either within the facility's campus or in the outside community.

Once the mainstay of both substance use and mental health treatment, like acute inpatient stays, residential treatment options are now reserved for individuals who cannot get their needs adequately met in a less restrictive setting.

For people with co-occurring disorders it is important to evaluate, prior to admission, whether a particular residential program is able to meet both their substance use and mental health needs. It was once the norm that residential programs would not admit people with significant mental disorders. While this has changed somewhat, residential programs can be lumped into three broad categories:

1. Addictions only programs. These programs only address the substance use issues. They will likely exclude individuals who have active mental health problems. Psychiatric services and mental health services are not provided.

2. Co-occurring (dual diagnosis) capable. These programs have some mental health services available, but are still mostly focused on the substance use issues. Available mental health services will include access to a psychiatrist or psychiatric APRN, and some attention to the interplay between mental health and substance use.

3. Co-occurring (dual diagnosis) enhanced. These facilities assess and treat both the substance use and mental health disorders. They are more able to manage the needs of people with significant active emotional, behavioral, and cognitive symptomatology. Some will specialize in particular diagnoses, such as schizophrenia-spectrum disorders, severe personality disorders, affective disorders, PTSD, etc.

Partial Hospital Programs (PHP)

Partial hospital programs (PHPs) were developed both as a step down from inpatient hospitalization, as well as a strategy to try and prevent inpatient hospitalization. The basic idea of a PHP is that a person can access an almost inpatient level of multidisciplinary services, but be able to go home at night. PHPs typically run five to seven days per week, for four or more hours per day, and include a multidisciplinary approach, which includes a psychiatrist/psychiatric APRN, nursing, some medical services, such as laboratory services, and a range of group, individual and family therapies. To meet the Medicare requirement for PHP there must be at least 20 hours/week of programming.

PHP programs are often specialized—geriatric, adolescent, personality disorder, general adult, eating disorders, co-occurring, substance use, etc. PHP treatment is largely group based, but may include individual therapy as well, based on the person's goals and preferences. Medication management and psychiatric oversight (psychiatrist and/or APRN) are integral parts of partial hospital programs.

Admission criteria for PHPs center on the likelihood that without this level of care the person would require an inpatient hospitalization, and most insurers, including Medicare, require the admitting physician to sign an attestation statement to this effect. For insurance purposes, PHP is most often billed through an individual's inpatient benefit. Length of stay in PHP is typically on the order of one to a few weeks.

Some substance use and co-occurring PHPs include ambulatory detoxification services, which might be appropriate for a person with mild alcohol withdrawal. Others offer services for opioid-dependent individuals, including the use of opioid replacement therapy.

INTENSIVE OUTPATIENT PROGRAMS (IOP)

Similar to PHP, intensive outpatient programs (IOPs) involve treatment on multiple days per week (3–5) for at least three hours per day. IOP programs are often specialized (co-occurring, substance use, child, adolescent, geriatric, personality disorder, eating disorder, etc.). IOPs utilize a multidisciplinary treatment team (psychiatrist/APRN, social work, other clinicians, nursing, possibly occupational and other rehabilitative therapists, psychologists, etc.).

Admission criteria to IOP programs include symptom acuity below the level of inpatient or PHP severity. This might include moderate to severe depression, some suicidal thinking without plan or intent, some self-injurious behavior, psychosis, hypomania where the person is not engaged in dangerous behaviors, moderate to severe anxiety symptoms, and active substance use disorders.

Lengths of stay in IOP programs range from a few weeks to a couple months.

ASSERTIVE COMMUNITY TREATMENT TEAMS (ACTT)

Assertive community treatment teams (ACTT) are community-based services, largely reserved for people with severe and persistent mental illness, including those with co-occurring substance use disorders. Historically, ACTT services and community mental health centers (CMHCs) developed as large state hospitals were downsizing and closing. The intent was to create wrap-around community-based services for those with the greatest need.

ACT teams, which are typically housed in CMHCs or other state-run or -funded mental health clinics, provide an intensive level of multidisciplinary support. ACTT services are community based, with an emphasis on working with people in their own home and in the community. Treatment is guided by the individual's needs and can include daily, sometimes multiple times a day, visits from a case manager and/or peer specialist.

Core Components of an ACT Team

- Case managers with small caseloads 10:1 ratio.
- Nurses and physicians/APRNs are formally a part of the team and have relatively small caseloads in order to address the needs of the clients served.
- The ACT team works collaboratively. All clients belong to the team, and vice versa. There are frequent team meetings to review treatment, and progress toward goals.
- ACT services are typically not time limited. Once enrolled, clients may continue with ACT for as long as the services are required.

- Continuity of staffing is encouraged, so that clients are familiar with the ACT team members and able to develop relationships.
- The team includes peer specialists.
- Clients are a part of the team.
- The team includes a substance abuse specialist.
- The team includes a vocational specialist.
- The team includes a housing specialist.
- Crisis service is available 24/7.
- Any inpatient admissions and discharges are coordinated with the ACT team.
- The emphasis is on providing services and supports in the community, versus in clinics or offices.
- Outreach and engagement strategies are emphasized.
- A dual diagnosis approach is used with clients who have co-occurring disorders, which includes motivational strategies, mutual aid groups, and an emphasis on matching the level of service/treatment to the individual's level of motivation. The overall goal is abstinence from problem substance use, but there is a willingness to work with clients at all stages of change.

Case Management and Targeted Case Management are similar to ACTT in that they are community based and work with the person in their home and in the community. They typically are less intense, with visits from a case manager occurring a couple times per week, or less.

ACTT and CM/TCM are often funded through a state's department of social services or mental health agency. In some states these are run by the state agency and in others by a variety of non-profit providers, including some in-home nursing agencies. (For a listing of state agencies with contact numbers and websites see Appendix A.)

OUTPATIENT THERAPY DELIVERED BY PROFESSIONALS

There is a vast array of effective outpatient treatments. This runs from individual therapy with a licensed psychologist, social worker, psychiatrist, or other professional licensed by the state, to groups held in mental health clinics, private practices, and many other settings. For people with co-occurring disorders the selection of particular therapists, modes of therapy, and settings for therapy will be driven by the person's goals, clinical needs, preferences, and resources. In the diagnosis-specific chapters of this handbook, recommendations for particular forms of therapy will be made.

Some general points to consider when constructing an outpatient treatment/recovery plan include the following:

1. If psychiatric medications are involved, can they be safely managed by the person's primary care physician or medical nurse practitioner? If not, ensure that the person has regular follow-up with a psychiatrist or psychiatric nurse practitioner. If this person is not also providing

the therapy component, make sure that there is communication between the prescriber and the therapist.

2. Therapy should be specific to the person's goals, needs, and preferences. This customization might include specialized/diagnosis-driven therapies, such as are available for trauma, borderline personality disorder, obsessive-compulsive disorder, depression, anxiety disorders, psychotic disorders, and so forth.

3. A key component is the fit between the person and the therapist. In general, having a positive relationship with a therapist corresponds to overall better treatment outcomes. It is important that, whatever form of therapy the person selects, they trust and feel comfortable with their therapist. Although reductionist, a critical question to be answered is, do you like your therapist?

4. Are all the person's therapeutic needs and goals being met by the particular form(s) of therapy? For people with co-occurring disorders, answering this question will mean that the mental health components and the substance use disorder(s) are both being addressed.

MATCHING TREATMENT AND SETTING TO THE PERSON AND DIAGNOSES

Does the level of care provide all, or most, of the services this person requires? For a person with co-occurring this will ideally mean that both their substance use and mental health needs can be attended to in the same location (fully integrated treatment). If fully integrated treatment is not possible, and it frequently isn't, then it becomes a matter of putting together a treatment and recovery plan that fills in the missing pieces. Examples include the following:

1. A person who has both opioid dependence and schizophrenia. She might need to get her mental health services at an outpatient clinic or private practice, while getting opioid replacement treatment through either a methadone clinic or physician who prescribes buprenorphine (Suboxone, Subutex, generics) for opioid maintenance.

2. Someone who has severe problems with emotion regulation, as is seen in borderline personality disorder, and also has a severe alcohol use disorder. An ideal program might be one where he can participate in dialectic behavior therapy (DBT) with a dual diagnosis focus (see Chapter 15).

3. A woman with both a severe eating disorder, such as anorexia, and moderate amphetamine use disorder will need treatment that addresses both, including medical monitoring, with contingencies in place should her weight drop below a critical point or other medical complications develop.

4. A man with moderate to severe obsessive-compulsive disorder and alcohol use disorder will do best with a program or provider(s) that offers cognitive-behavioral therapy and specific medication(s) for his OCD, as well as treatment for his alcohol problem.

RESOURCE ISSUES AND BARRIERS TO TREATMENT

A person's resources, in the broadest sense, need to be taken into account when formulating realistic treatment/recovery plans and accessing services. In the process of evaluating resources, barriers to treatment will emerge and need to be addressed. Factors to consider include the following:

- Personal preference. Is the recommended course of treatment something the person agrees with?

- Motivation. Is the person's level of motivation at a level where they are likely to participate in the recommended treatment?

- Transportation. Can they make it to treatment?

- Ability to pay for the recommended services, insurance limitations; ability to afford prescribed medication.

- Employment constraints. Will this person need to take time off from work? How will they manage this? Can treatment be provided in such a way, or at such times, where there is minimal disruption to their work life?

- Housing. If someone is homeless, or in jeopardy of being homeless, this creates a front-burner issue that must be addressed as soon as possible.

- Sober supports. Is the person living in an environment where others are actively using drugs and alcohol? Having others in the house who are using greatly decreases the likelihood that someone will be successful in stopping their drug and/or alcohol use. Conversely, having friends and family who are involved in recovery can provide everything from an understanding ear, to a ride to a 12-step group, with coffee and a piece of pie afterward.

- Friends and family. Who in this person's life do they want to be involved in their treatment? In what ways can these others help support the person in their recovery?

- Availability of specialty services.

- Medical barriers to treatment. Is the person physically well enough to participate in therapy? Will they require special accommodations to make that possible?

AMERICAN SOCIETY OF ADDICTION MEDICINE (ASAM) PATIENT PLACEMENT CRITERIA

Developed initially in the 1980s to help providers determine a best level of care for individuals with substance use disorders, the ASAM Patient Placement Criteria have gone through revisions, with an increased attention to people with co-occurring disorders. The criteria, along with clinical judgment, help clinicians and organizations, such as state agencies and insurance companies, look at a particular person and assess what would be the best fit for that person at this point in treatment. This evaluation is done with the use of a multidimensional (six dimensions) assessment:

1. Acute intoxication/withdrawal potential. Is this person at risk for a serious withdrawal, either based on current presentation or history?

2. Biomedical condition and complications. What factors need to be considered with this person's current and/or historical medical history and conditions?

3. Emotional, behavioral, or cognitive conditions and complications. What are this person's emotional, cognitive, and mental health needs and issues?

4. Readiness to change. What is the person's current level of motivation to change?

5. Relapse, continued use, or continued problem potential. What is this person's history of relapse? Does this person continue to use despite negative consequences of that use?

6. Recovery/living environment. What is the status of the person's living situation? Does the person have sober supports, or is their current living situation one that presents challenges and barriers to recovery?

The ASAM criteria look at levels of care along a numerical continuum from 0 = no treatment required to 4 = medically managed intensive inpatient treatment. It utilizes five levels of care that are further articulated based on program focus, intensity, and capacity for managing co-occurring mental, social, and medical needs. The five levels are:

- 0.5: Early intervention
- 1: Outpatient treatment
- 2: Intensive outpatient/partial hospitalization
- 3: Residential/inpatient treatment
- 4: Medically managed intensive inpatient treatment

The ASAM criteria are an industry standard, and 30 states utilize them when making determinations about placement in state-funded treatment facilities and programs. An updated version of this manual was published in October 2013.

CHAPTER 8

Key Psychotherapies, Mutual Self-Help, and Natural and Peer Supports

Overview

Motivational Interviewing

Cognitive Behavioral Therapy

Styles of Cognitive (Thought) Distortion

Behavioral Chain Analysis

Mindfulness Training

Psycho Education

Family Interventions

Relapse Prevention

Skills Training

Wellness

Mutual Self-Help

Alcoholics Anonymous

Narcotics Anonymous

Al-anon and Nar-anon

Adult Children of Alcoholics

Double Trouble in Recovery and Dual Diagnosis 12-step

OVERVIEW

Throughout this book, specific social, therapeutic, and medication strategies will be discussed in each of the major diagnostic categories. As will become apparent, certain therapies and approaches, such as mutual self-help groups (Alcoholics Anonymous, Narcotics Anonymous, etc.), cognitive behavioral therapy, motivational interviewing, and mindfulness training have benefits that cut across diagnostic boundaries, and in a sense become building blocks for treating co-occurring disorders.

Motivational Interviewing (MI)

Developed by William Miller, Ph.D., and Stephen Rollnick, Ph.D., motivational interviewing (MI) is a therapeutic approach that helps the individual make positive movement around problem behaviors. While initially studied in substance use, motivational technique can be applied to a broad range of behaviors, from cigarette smoking, to lifestyle changes (exercise, nutrition), to adherence with medication regimens.

Motivational interviewing is change-based and empowers clients to make their own decisions. It steps back from a traditional advice-and-consent model ("I'm the doctor and this is what you must do") to one where the person must weigh the pros and cons of their own action ("I've got to stop doing this; it's really hurting me"). The theory behind motivational interviewing is that you let the person explore and resolve his or her ambivalence (both sides of the argument) around the problem behavior, the pros and the cons. In the process, the therapist helps the person heighten the internal discomfort (dissonance) around the behavior, to where they are more likely to change it.

In motivational therapy it is the therapist's task to engage the client, to help them focus and articulate the area for change, as well as why the change might be important. Finally, the therapist helps the person plan and implement the steps needed to realize the desired change. Techniques used in motivational interviewing include the following:

- Empathy and reflective listening. The clinician listens closely to what the individual is saying, and then reflects back the material presented, to see if they have in fact gotten it right. This should not turn into in an exercise in parroting the person's words, but rather in assuring the client that they have been completely understood.

  Client: "I really don't feel like stopping the booze. It's the only thing that calms me down at night. But if I don't my girlfriend says she's going to end things."

  Therapist: "So you don't want to stop drinking, because you like the way it calms you down, but it sounds like you're worried that if you don't, your girlfriend will leave. Is that correct?"

- A nonjudgmental stance on the part of the clinician. This includes maintaining a neutral stance in both verbal and nonverbal expression. It's important that the clinician not step in and take over either side of the person's struggle with the behavior, as this may push them in the direction you're trying to move away from.

- Nonconfrontational and noncoercive. The therapist does not challenge the person's behaviors, attitudes, or beliefs, but rather helps the person look at their own concerns regarding their behaviors. It's the difference between saying, "Can't you see your drinking is killing you and destroying your relationship" to "You seem conflicted about the effect your drinking is having on your relationship with your girlfriend and on those elevated liver enzymes; am I getting that right?"

- Roll with resistance. It's natural, when looking at long-held behaviors to not want to give them up. There are reasons why people continue to engage in problem behavior, and these must not be ignored or discounted. For therapists doing motivational interviewing, it can be a challenge to not step in on the side of the behavior you are trying to support.

Incorrect (judgmental and blaming):

Client: "I'm just not ready to give up the drinking."

Therapist: "But if you don't, your wife is going to leave you. Is that what you want? Do you want your drinking to be the reason your marriage falls apart?"

Correct (reflective listening with neutral stance):

Client: "I'm just not ready to give up the drinking."

Therapist: "I can see you're struggling with giving up the drinking. Tell me about that."

- Heighten the internal dissonance (discomfort): This is where the therapist serves as a sort of repository of the pros and cons the client has presented about their behavior, and strategically feeds them back. The challenge is to do this in such a way that you support the person's forward movement with change.

  Therapist: "I think I see your dilemma. On the one hand you really like the way alcohol makes it possible for you to feel comfortable in social situations. Yet on the other hand, you say things have gotten to the point where you can no longer control the amount you drink, and it's resulted in some really bad consequences. How do you think you're going to resolve this?" Other strategies employed in a motivational approach might include the following:

- Use of pros and cons (decisional balance). Have the individual write down all the things they like and dislike about a targeted behavior, such as substance use.

- Use of scales to assess readiness for change. "On a 10-point scale, 10 being ready to do it today, how primed are you to stop using alcohol?"

- Directive questioning around preparation for change. "Do you have a quit date for your smoking?"

- Validate and acknowledge all positive change. "Three 12-step groups last week? That's tremendous, well done!"

COGNITIVE BEHAVIORAL THERAPY (CBT)

Cognitive behavioral therapy (CBT) is a present-focused therapy that has its roots in behaviorism and cognitive therapy (Aaron Beck, Albert Ellis). The connections between what we think, feel, and do provide the overall focus of CBT.

CBT has been studied extensively as a research model and has a large body of evidence to support its usefulness in the treatment of anxiety disorders, depression, and a broad range of mental disorders, from ADHD to schizophrenia. It is one of the building blocks of numerous important therapies, including evidence-based manualized treatments for trauma, therapies for working with people with bipolar-spectrum and schizophrenia-spectrum disorders, as well as being one of the foundations of dialectic behavior therapy (DBT) for borderline personality disorder (see Chapter 15).

CBT requires that as a client learns techniques in therapy, they then practice them in the real world. To help generalize material learned in session, homework assignments are a typical component of CBT-based therapies.

In the CBT model, a thought, whether accurate or distorted, leads to an emotional response, which prompts the doing of a related behavior.

Thought 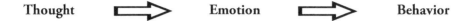 **Emotion** **Behavior**

In some cases, it may actually be the emotion that precedes the thought, such as the surge of panic when an eighteen-wheeler cuts you off on the highway, which leads you to immediately swerve out of the way, with the corresponding rush of adrenalin and catastrophic thought, "I could have been killed." Regardless of the order, CBT provide the linkages between what we think, feel, and do.

As therapy, CBT helps the client identify and then challenge distorted thinking, which leads to painful emotions and maladaptive/problem behaviors. The approach of the therapist in working with the client is to help them see how these present-day distortions are likely based on some deeper-held beliefs, which may or may not be accurate or fully accurate. As therapy progresses, these beliefs can be challenged and reframed with more accurate appraisals.

Identifying distorted thinking, which the person is often unaware of, requires tremendous attention to the specifics of the situation. A truism of CBT is that all emotional changes are preceded by some kind of triggering or automatic thought, "What were you thinking right before you slammed down the phone on your mother?"

In doing CBT, it is important to be familiar with common forms of cognitive distortion and ways to challenge them. The style of therapy is conversational, directive, and frequently didactic as skills and techniques are taught by the therapist. When homework is assigned, it is crucial that it be reviewed at the next session to ensure that the material was understood and practiced. Homework review also provides an opportunity to fine-tune skills and to help coach the client to use them more effectively.

Styles of Cognitive (Thought) Distortion, as well as challenges/cognitive restructuring/reframing, include but are not limited to the following:

- Black-and-white thinking. This is where people or situations are perceived as being all one way or another. Someone is their friend or their enemy. There is no gray.

  Example: "I can't do anything right."

  Challenge: "Well, as I look at things objectively, I do some things quite well, and others are a challenge. And when I struggle or do something incorrectly it brings up these feelings of frustration and failure."

- Catastrophic thinking. With this type of thinking, a small setback is magnified into something larger.

  Example: "I just know this headache is the sign of some horrible medical problem. It's probably a tumor."

  Challenge: See a doctor, get objective data. Maybe it's a brain tumor, but it's probably not.

- Emotional reasoning. Taking an emotional state to be a factual truth.

  Example: "I feel unlovable. Therefore I am unlovable."

Challenge: "Everyone is lovable. But when I'm feeling blue, I sometimes think it makes me less of a person."

- Generalization. A portion of something is taken to represent the whole.

  Example: A nurse with a difficult patient, saying, "the entire unit is out of control."

  Challenge: "No, it's really just this one person who's taking most of my time and energy. It's making me anxious because it's impacting my ability to care for my other patients."

- Labeling (judging). A pattern of reducing people and situations to a single attribute or descriptor.

  Example: "My mother is a control freak."

  Challenge: "At times my mother's insistence that things be done her way really gets to me. But there's much more to her than that."

- Mind reading. The belief that you know what others are thinking. Typically this involves inaccurate interpretation of facial cues, body language, tone of voice, and so on. The distortion typically centers on the belief that the other person is thinking negatively about you. This particular distortion is common in people with social anxiety disorder.

  Example: "You can just tell he hates me."

  Challenge: Strike up a conversation and try to get a more accurate read on what the other person is thinking. "You seem upset. Is everything okay?"

- Blaming. Other people are responsible for the person's actions.

  Example: "You made me mad."

  Challenge: Other people don't have the power to change our emotions. It is something we do with our own thoughts.

- Shoulds. An unrealistic expectation of always being able to do everything perfectly.

  Example: "I should be able to make the 10 types of Christmas cookies my mother did, while taking care of the kids and working a full-time job. Why can't I? What's wrong with me?"

  Challenge: "That's being unrealistic, my mom stayed at home and didn't have to pay the kinds of bills I do. That said, I wish I had time to do more of that holiday stuff. I really miss it."

- Fallacy of fairness. A misplaced belief in some universal sense of fairness.

  Example: "After all I did for her, the least she could do is show me some respect."

  Challenge: There is no universal code of fairness. What one person thinks is fair, another might not agree with.

- Fallacy of change. A belief that wanting another person to change, or trying to make them change, will in fact get them to change. An elegant challenge to this distortion is found in the Al-Anon literature, and is referred to as the 3 C's—I didn't cause this, I can't control it, and I can't cure it.

  Example: "If he really loved me he'd stop drinking."

  Challenge: It is impossible to make someone else change. It's something they have to do themselves.

Behavioral Chain Analysis

CBT, which has been adapted and incorporated into many therapeutic models, can be extremely helpful when trying to understand and piece together the events surrounding problem behaviors, from a suicide attempt to a relapse with cocaine. This is commonly done with a technique called a behavioral chain analysis, which requires going into exquisite detail over what happened, what led up to it, what the person was thinking and feeling, and what other factors might have contributed to the undesired outcome. The therapist and client are able to identify causal factors, which become the focus of problem solving, cognitive challenges, and other techniques to try and lessen the likelihood that the behavior and related negative emotions will reoccur.

How to Construct a Behavioral Chain Analysis One way to construct a behavioral chain analysis is to begin with the problem behavior or emotion. From there, clarify everything that was going on prior to the event. Help the client focus on what they were thinking and feeling. Ask them what other factors might have led up to the event (vulnerabilities), such as being too tired, hungry, already upset over something, bored, or other factor.

It is common, when first working with someone on a behavioral chain analysis, for them to struggle with reconstructing the various thoughts, feelings, and events that led up to the problem. "It just happened, I don't know what I was thinking." Be diligent, it may take a number of prompts and some encouragement to flesh out the particulars. In some ways, a behavioral chain analysis is like being a detective or a reporter, you want to know the who, what, when, where, and why. It is time well spent, as what will emerge will help you and your client understand the behaviors and emotional states that person is trying to get a handle on. Beyond that, identifying where things got off track provides the information needed to strategically teach skills that will help them through similar situations.

The following is an example of a completed behavioral chain analysis, with a blank copy on the subsequent page that can be reproduced.

Example: A chain analysis for a woman following a serious relapse with alcohol.

Therapist: "Let's work backward from your slip with alcohol, and go through everything you were thinking, feeling, and doing beforehand."

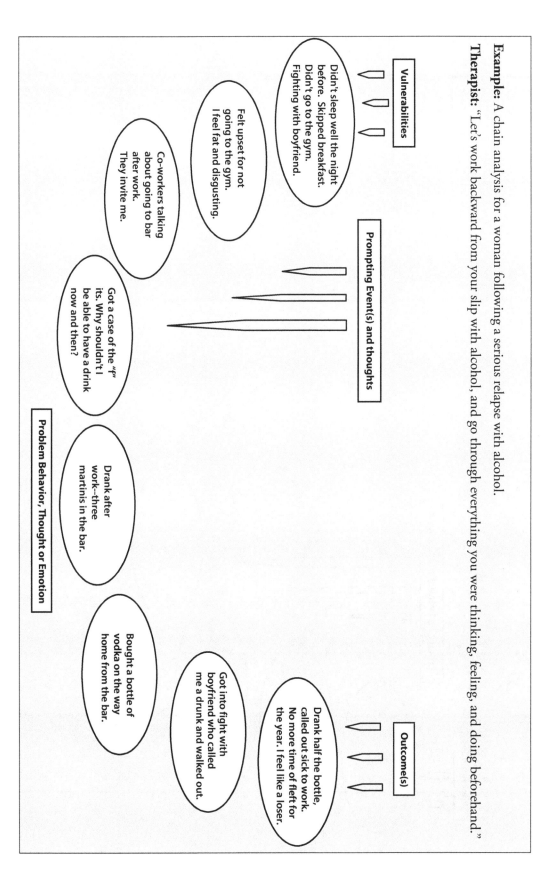

Vulnerabilities

Didn't sleep well the night before. Skipped breakfast. Didn't go to the gym. Fighting with boyfriend.

Felt upset for not going to the gym. I feel fat and disgusting.

Co-workers talking about going to bar after work. They invite me.

Prompting Event(s) and thoughts

Got a case of the "f" its. Why shouldn't I be able to have a drink now and then?

Problem Behavior, Thought or Emotion

Drank after work--three martinis in the bar.

Bought a bottle of vodka on the way home from the bar.

Got into fight with boyfriend who called me a drunk and walked out.

Outcome(s)

Drank half the bottle, called out sick to work. No more time of fleft for the year. I feel like a loser.

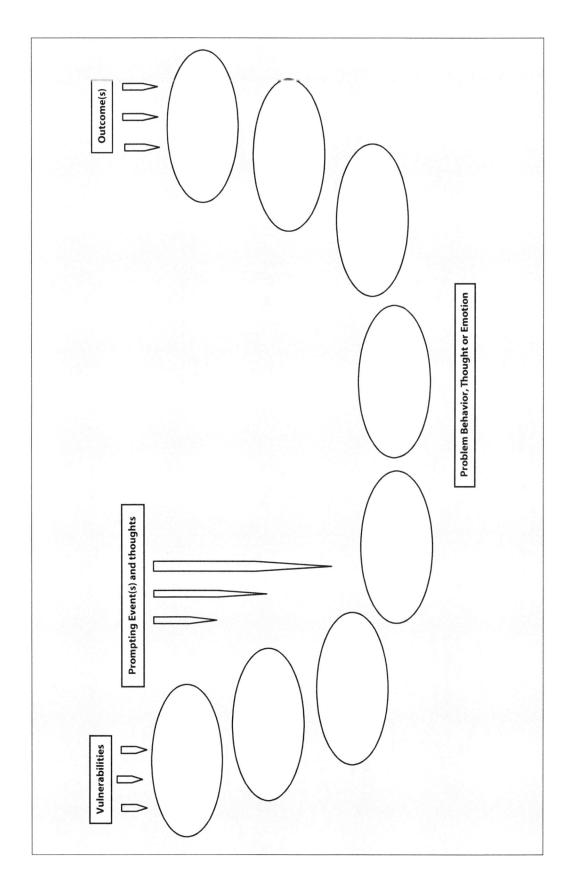

Discussion: In the completed behavioral chain analysis, the therapist and client will be able to identify a number of areas to work on, these include:

Cognitive distortions

- Emotional reasoning: "I feel fat and disgusting."

- Naming/labeling/judging: "I'm nothing but a drunk."

- Catastrophizing: "I don't think I'm ever going to get better."

- Black-and-white thinking: "It's like the last four months without a drink are just gone, and I'm back to step one."

Skills deficits

- Drug/drink refusal

- Emotional vulnerability and need for self-care:
  o Need to focus, and problem solve, on getting adequate sleep, exercise, and nutrition

Applications of Cognitive Behavioral Therapy (CBT) CBT connects the dots between thoughts, emotions, and behaviors, and as a result has nearly limitless applications. When working with CBT, the therapist and client identify targets, which could be dysfunctional emotions, distorted thinking, and/or problematic behavior. Strategies, such as the behavioral chain analysis, help clarify the connections and point out areas for specific interventions, such as cognitive reframing, and other skills training.

CBT, as a stand-alone therapy, is considered an evidence-based practice for the treatment of:

- Obsessive compulsive disorder
- Panic disorder
- Generalized anxiety disorder
- Specific phobias
- Depressive disorders

When combined with other modalities, such as psychopharmacology, traditional substance use treatment, motivational interviewing, and mindfulness, as will be seen throughout this book, CBT provides an important component of many new and emerging best practices including the treatment of:

- Substance use disorders
- Personality disorders
- Posttraumatic stress disorder
- Bipolar spectrum disorder
- Attentional disorders
- Schizophrenia spectrum disorders

MINDFULNESS TRAINING

Founded in Zen and other ancient Eastern traditions, mindfulness-based techniques, used alone and combined with other therapies, have demonstrated robust benefits in a broad-range of conditions from pain, depression, and anxiety to problem substance use. Studies that have included brain imaging before and after mindfulness training reveal interesting and exciting changes, including enhanced connectivity between areas of the brain associated with arousal and attention.

While based in contemplative religious practices, mindfulness can be taught and practiced free from any religious connotation or affiliation. Where its origins are in Eastern traditions, mindfulness practice is fully compatible with Judeo-Christian and other religious and secular practices.

Mindfulness involves bringing one's attention to the present moment. Fundamentals of mindfulness include:

- Complete attention to the moment.
- A nonjudgmental awareness of thoughts, sensations, and feelings.

- Fluid awareness. One does not hold onto thoughts and feelings but lets them pass through consciousness.

Most approaches to teaching mindfulness begin with a focus on the breath, which then expands to include an awareness of thoughts, feelings, and sensations as they pass through the mind and the body.

There are many ways to develop a mindfulness practice, and in order for it to become something of benefit, it's best done on a daily basis. Common mindfulness exercises include the following:

- Seated meditation. With the legs comfortably crossed, focus on the breath as it enters and leaves the body. Observe the feeling of the breath as it passes in and out of the nostrils. Observe your thoughts without becoming fixed or attached to them. Let them come and go like clouds passing across the sky.
- Walking mindfulness. Take a walk focusing on each footstep as it connects to the ground. Observe what you see, feel, and think.
- Counting the breath. While seated, lying down, or walking, count your breaths. A cycle of inhalation and exhalation will be 1, and count up to 10. If you get lost or lose your place, return to the number 1 and begin again. Alternatively, you can count the lengths of your inhalations and exhalations.
- Mindfulness with daily activities. Identify things you do every day and commit to doing them with total awareness. This could include mindful eating, brushing the teeth, shaving, gardening, etc.
- Mind-body practices such as yoga, qigong, tai chi, and others.

PSYCHO EDUCATION

Through every stage of treatment, from engagement through relapse prevention, teaching clients about their disorders, their treatment choices, how therapy works, what medications do and don't do, principles of wellness, and so forth is key to helping them gain mastery over their own recovery. It's the truisms that, "knowledge is power" (Francis Bacon), and "The beginning of wisdom is the definition of terms" (Socrates). In its broadest sense, psychoeducation is about client empowerment and sharing the answers in the teacher's manual.

Methods for providing psychoeducation are both formal, such as specific groups and courses, and informal, as can occur in many professional and even nonprofessional interactions like those found within the peer self-help communities. With the ready availability of information through the Internet, psychoeducation is often self-directed and clinicians need to be aware, and comfortable with, perspectives and information that may be in conflict with their treatment beliefs and approaches or with which they are unfamiliar.

As a building block of treatment, psychoeducation is frequently woven into therapeutic themes. This includes learning about the brain's reward system and how this may create challenges, especially during early recovery, to understanding the potential benefits and risks of specific therapies, including medications, and how they are thought to work.

Psychoeducation plays an important role in understanding wellness and illness management. Topics for any given individual will be tailored to their specific needs, diagnoses, cognitive abilities, as well as interest level. One cautionary note is that especially early into recovery, it is common to inadvertently trigger craving through the use of materials that contain graphic depictions of drug use, such as are found in popular movies and TV shows.

For prescribers, psychoeducation around medication may include the following:

- Verbal and written material on any medications prescribed. This includes the potential risks and benefits of any medication, as well as what to do should they have questions or problems.

- Time to ask questions about medications, as well as to ask about options, including the option to not take a specific medication. For clinicians, it can be as simple as asking, "Do you have any questions? And, if you don't have any now and some occur to you, write them down and we'll talk about them next time."

- The prescriber asking the client questions about his/her medications, to ascertain whether or not they fully understood what they're taking, why they're taking it, and how they're supposed to take it.

FAMILY INTERVENTIONS

Including family, significant others, and key friends and supports in therapy has been shown in numerous studies to be of benefit and to improve outcomes. The type of interventions that make sense will be specific to the person in treatment and the constellation of that person's friends and family. Common approaches to family work include the following:

- Individual family therapy. Here the goals are often centered around enhanced communication and decreased conflict.

- Family psychoeducation. Often conducted in a multifamily format. Here information around mental and substance use disorders is provided and discussed. This can be with, or without, the person in treatment being present.

- Diagnosis-specific family work. There are specific treatments, such as the family-focused therapy for bipolar disorder (Chapter 11), which provide psychoeducation and skills training to help improve outcomes and prevent relapse.

- Mutual self-aid for family/friends where the person in treatment may not be present. Among these self-help groups are those that specifically address substance use problems, such as Al-anon and Adult Children of Alcoholics, and those that focus more on the mental disorders, such as support groups through the National Alliance on Mental Illness (NAMI).

NAMI (www.nami.org) is the largest grassroots advocacy and education organization for people with mental illness and their families. It offers a variety of support groups, both for family members and for people with mental illness. NAMI also funds research and broad-reaching campaigns to raise awareness and understanding about mental illness. In addition to support groups, which are free, NAMI offers low-cost, up-to-date trainings, such as family-to-family trainings (12 weeks) and a peer-to-peer training (10 weeks).

RELAPSE PREVENTION

Relapse prevention typically involves consolidating gains people have made in the process of becoming abstinent from problem substance use. It can be provided in both group and individual sessions. Twelve-step programs, such as AA, NA, and others, are often included when thinking about how to construct strong relapse prevention programs.

In a broader sense, relapse prevention can also be applied to mental disorders that have the potential for relapse. Here the emphasis is on maintaining and practicing skills and overall attention to wellness, so that relapses can be prevented or caught before they become severe.

Specific approaches to relapse prevention include:

- Avoidance of high-risk situations. In 12-step lingo this becomes, "people, places, and things" associated with past substance use behaviors.
- Strengthening of sober supports. This can include friends and family as well as involvement with mutual self-help groups, such as AA and NA.
- Maintaining physical and emotional health. Attention to getting adequate sleep, exercise, and good nutrition, and attending to physical and emotional problems.
- Education around the risks of relapse and the nature of addictive disorders.
- Fill the time. Boredom and too much unstructured time can increase craving. Part of a recovery plan can be the development of new sober activities, which might include hobbies, social activities, or learning new skills.
- Avoid triggering materials that show graphic depictions of substance use.

SKILLS TRAINING

Where cognitive behavioral therapy (CBT) helps the client understand the connections between dysfunctional emotions, thoughts, and behaviors, skills training provides the tools to develop healthier ways to manage emotions, relationships, and life in general. Skills training can include broad-based strategies, such as developing a daily mindfulness practice and achieving competence at recognizing and reframing distorted thinking, to specific tasks such as effectively turning down alcohol or drugs in a social setting or using repeated exposure techniques to lessen the anxiety associated with a specific phobia.

Skills training, which can be done in group and individual settings, shares much in common with an educational model. Manualized therapies use skills training as a core component, where a typical session includes discussion of the day's topic, with some degree of psychoeducation, followed by the teaching of one or more particular skills and the assignment of practice or homework. Effective skills training typically involves:

- The transmission/teaching of the information in a way that helps the client to fully understand the task at hand, through readings, focused discussion, and handouts.

- Practice of the skill within the session.

- Assignment of at-home practice to help generalize the skill to the real world.

- Checking in to see if the skill is being practiced and performed correctly and effectively. If the client is struggling with the skill, this is an opportunity to coach them into using it correctly.

A prime example of an evidenced-based therapy that utilizes skills training is dialectic behavior therapy (see Chapter 15), which breaks down an array of skills into four major modules: mindfulness, distress tolerance, emotion regulation, and interpersonal effectiveness.

WELLNESS

Just as there are clear correlations between protracted stress and physical and emotional problems, there is an equally robust literature—and growing daily—that demonstrates the benefits of establishing and maintaining healthful activities, habits, and attitudes. Lumped under the heading of "wellness" are major lifestyle components that are key to the development and maintenance of full, healthy, and meaningful lives. Among the most important are the following:

- Adequate restorative sleep

- A healthy diet

- Maintenance of important positive relationships

- Productive and meaningful activity: Work, hobbies, volunteerism

- Connection(s) to the greater community, including faith communities

- Adequate and regular exercise

- Attention to emotional and physical problems

MUTUAL SELF-HELP

On the substance abuse side of the co-occurring equation is a long and well-established track record for the usefulness of self-help groups such as AA, NA, and others. There are many variants on the 12-step paradigm, and matching the person to groups where he or she will feel comfortable and supported is important.

For people with co-occurring substance use and serious and persistent mental disorders, mutual aid groups, such as Double Trouble in Recovery and Dual Diagnosis 12-step, provide greater freedom to talk about medications as well as psychiatric symptoms and syndromes.

The benefits to mutual-aid groups include:

- Sober support

- Sober setting

- No cost (sometimes a donation is requested for coffee and snacks)

- Connection with others who have similar concerns and struggles
- Access to mentors and possibly sponsors with more experience and time in recovery
- Freedom from the power structure of traditional treatment settings
- Validation for efforts in recovery
- Availability

Available mutual-aid programs include:

Alcoholics Anonymous (AA)

Mutual self-help 12-step groups, such as Alcoholics Anonymous (AA) and Narcotics Anonymous (NA), are the oldest and largest peer support networks in the world for people with substance use disorders. They have meetings, and now online meetings, across the United States, Canada, and most other countries. For many, 12-step meetings provide the tools necessary to achieve and to maintain sobriety.

Alcoholics Anonymous (www.aa.org), founded in 1935, with an estimated membership of well over 1 million in the United States alone, is the original 12-step program. Membership is based solely on a shared desire to stop drinking. Groups are apolitical, peer/nonprofessional run, and free. (Donations may be accepted to keep the meetings self-sufficient and to pay for snacks.)

While the primary focus of AA is abstinence from alcohol, people with other substance use problems are welcome. AA is open to all, and people with co-occurring mental disorders can benefit greatly from the meetings. The 12-steps, which utilize introspection and changing of problem behaviors and patterns of thought, are compatible with other psychotherapies, such as cognitive behavioral therapy.

Major criticisms of AA involve the use of God and giving over control to a "Higher Power." Even the Serenity Prayer, by American theologian Reinhold Neibuhr, which has been adopted by AA, NA, and other 12-step groups involves the use of a deity. "God grant me the serenity to accept the things I cannot change, courage to change the things I can, and the wisdom to know the difference."

Another concern with 12-step groups that are focused on alcohol and/or drugs is that individuals with co-occurring mental disorders may find pushback from other group members about their need for psychiatric medications or maintenance medications such as methadone or buprenorphine. Both AA and NA have literature that specifically addresses the need for appropriate medication.

A recommendation for all clinicians, in order to be familiar with 12-step programs and their format, is to attend a number of open meetings.

Narcotics Anonymous

NA (www.na.org) grew out of AA in the 1940s. The program is similar to AA, and the goal is for people who have used substances to come together with a common goal of getting and staying abstinent.

Al-anon and Nar-anon

Twelve-step programs have also been established to support family and friends of people with substance use disorders. In certain locations, simultaneous meetings of AA and Al-anon (NA and Nar-anon) meetings are held.

Adult Children of Alcoholics

This 12-step program is geared to help individuals raised in alcoholic and otherwise dysfunctional households overcome problems rooted in their childhoods. It emphasizes the shedding of passivity and victimhood in pursuit of happy and healthy adult relationships.

Double Trouble in Recovery and Dual Diagnosis Recovery Groups

These 12-step format groups are geared for individuals who have both substance use and significant mental disorders. They are peer run, and while they do not have a national organization, they are frequently hosted/located in mental health clinics or are affiliated with outpatient hospital clinics.

SECTION II

Mental Disorders, Their Presentation(s), and Treatment Approaches with Co-Occurring Substance Use Disorders

CHAPTER 9

Co-Occurring Attention Deficit Hyperactivity Disorder and Related Disorders

OVERVIEW

Attention deficit hyperactivity disorder (ADHD), a persistent problem with attention and focus often accompanied by hyperactivity and impulsive behavior, is associated with significant impairment in a child's development and achievement in school, social settings, and at home. Once thought to be rare in adults, studies have shown that it persists from childhood in as many as 75 percent of adolescents and 50 percent of adults, making it a lifelong condition.

It is estimated that between 5 percent and 9 percent of children and 2.5 percent to 5 percent of adults meet criteria for ADHD (4.4% in the National Comorbidity Survey). The figure for adults will likely rise with the change in the DSM-5 criteria going from six criteria for each of the categories related to inattention and hyperactivity/impulsivity, down to five for adults. (It is still six for children and adolescents younger than 17.)

The relationship between attention deficit hyperactivity disorder (ADHD) and all forms of substance use disorders (SUDs) is well established. Studies that have looked at the overlap between ADHD and SUDs have found that between 10 percent to 24 percent of adults with ADHD will also have at least one non-tobacco SUD.

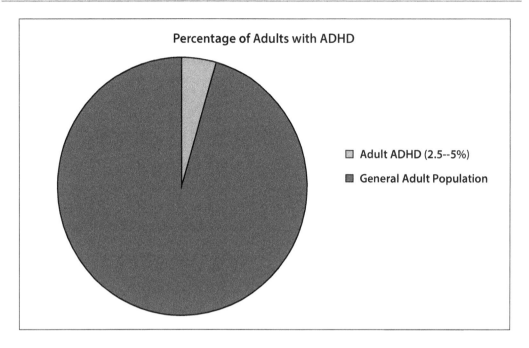

In addition to the close relationship between ADHD and SUD are the findings that oppositional defiant disorder (ODD) and conduct disorder (CD), the latter, which involves disregard for rules and the rights and feelings of others, and is considered the child and adolescent precursor to adult antisocial personality disorder, are closely linked as well.

Conduct disorder (CD) in particular carries a high lifetime co-occurrence with all substance use disorders. Studies that looked at individuals with CD, ADHD, and SUD found the link/overlap between CD and SUD to be greater than the link between ADHD and SUD. Some researchers have proposed a model whereby ADHD leads to conduct disorder, which in turn greatly increases the risk of developing substance use disorders.

ADHD, where it is most-frequently first diagnosed in childhood, is somewhat unique among co-occurring disorders. In many instances, it is clear that the mental disorder preceded the substance use disorder. As such, a diagnosis of ADHD in a child or adolescent can be considered a significant risk factor for the development of one or more substance use disorders. In individuals who also meet criteria for conduct disorder (CD), this risk increases as much as threefold.

For parents and those who work with children and adolescents, diagnoses of ADHD, oppositional defiant disorder, and conduct disorder should be warning flags to assess for the presence of substance use problems and to begin early interventions to prevent their development.

Overall, children with ADHD are at an increased risk for problems with drugs and alcohol. They begin substance use at a younger age, and progress more rapidly to regular use and dependence. Substance use findings among children, adolescents, and adults with ADHD include:

- As many as 50% of adolescents with substance use disorders have ADHD.
- Childhood ADHD is linked to alcohol and drug use disorders in adults.
- Earlier onset and greater severity of substance use disorders are seen in adults with ADHD.
- Adults with ADHD are less likely to stop smoking.

- ADHD is associated with early onset of cigarette smoking (under age 15), which in turn is associated with other substance use disorders.

Because of the strong relationship between ADHD and substance use disorders, and the persistence of symptoms into adulthood, it is important to assess for ADHD in people seeking treatment for substance problems. This assessment is especially true for women, who more frequently exhibit the inattentive symptoms as children and adolescents, and are less frequently given the diagnosis.

Studies that assessed the presence of ADHD in adults with substance use disorders find consistently high rates between 15 percent and 35 percent. This finding contrasts sharply with the number of people in those same studies (less than 5%) who had been previously diagnosed with ADHD as children. This disparity underscores the importance of assessing for ADHD symptoms in adults with substance use disorders.

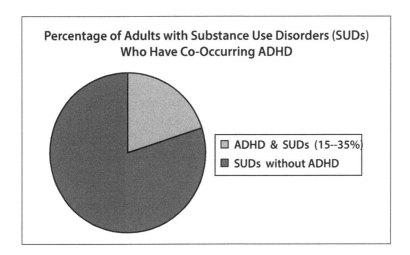

Among individuals with co-occurring substance use disorders and ADHD, preferred substances include cannabis, cocaine, stimulants, alcohol, and tobacco.

ADHD, SUDs, AND MULTIPLE CO-OCCURRING MENTAL DISORDERS

While the overlap between ADHD, substance use disorders, and other "externalizing" disorders such as oppositional defiant disorder (ODD) and conduct disorder (CD) is robust. It's important to note that other psychiatric disorders, such as depression, bipolar disorder, PTSD, personality disorders (antisocial and borderline, in particular), and anxiety disorders commonly co-occur with people who have both ADHD and substance use disorders.

The implications for treatment and prognosis with people who have multiple psychiatric disorders are significant. They are prone to greater disability and severity of substance use problems. The complexity of their symptoms can complicate and confuse diagnosis:

- Is the hyperactivity and inability to sit still from their ADHD?
- Are they in a hypomanic or manic state?
- Is the individual's current state a symptom of opioid withdrawal? Stimulant intoxication?

As with all co-occurring disorders, the presence of multiple psychiatric disorders needs to be addressed, and diagnostic confusion can be clarified over the course of treatment.

Assessment of ADHD

Children and Adolescents

The assessment and diagnosis of ADHD in children and adolescents typically involve multiple sources of information: parents, teachers, and possibly other clinicians, such as a school psychologist, social worker, or nurse. Where there is a strong genetic component to ADHD, the presence of ADHD in other close family members (parents and siblings in particular) should be explored.

In the current diagnostic manual, the DSM-5, symptoms must have been present for at least six months and be accompanied by six or more inattentive and/or hyperactive/impulsive symptoms. Several of these symptoms must have been present before the age of 12 (in the DSMIV-TR this was age 7), the symptoms occur and cause impairment or disrupt multiple aspects of the individual's life (school, home, sports, recreation, friendships). And finally, the symptoms are not the result of some other medical condition, mental disorder, medications, drugs, or alcohol.

Standardized questionnaires and screening tools completed by parents, teachers, and possibly clinicians and the child, combined with direct observation and clinical assessment are the mainstays of making the diagnosis of ADHD in children and adolescents.

Commonly used screening tools and questionnaires for children and adolescents include:

- Attention Deficit Disorders Evaluation Scale (ADDES-3)
- ADHD rating Scale-IV
- SNAP-IV Rating Scale (The SNAP-IV is available in its entirety on the American Psychiatric Association's website: www.psychiatry.org/practice/dsm/dsm5/online-assessment-measures#Level2.)
- Conners' Rating Scale

Adults

Assessing ADHD in adults with co-occurring substance use disorders, and possibly other mental disorders as well, presents challenges. It is important to differentiate signs and symptoms that might be associated with active drug use and/or withdrawal and intoxication syndromes from the inattention, impulsivity, and fidgeting seen with ADHD. Similarly, symptoms such as hyperactivity, easy distractibility, and inattention are found in other mental disorders, such as bipolar-spectrum disorders. Certain medical conditions, such as hyperthyroidism, can also mimic ADHD.

Keys for accurately assessing ADHD in adults include the following:

- Does the person have a prior childhood diagnosis of ADHD?
- If there's not a prior diagnosis, is there evidence that symptoms of ADHD were present before age twelve? (DSM-5 criteria)

- Is there a family history of ADHD?

- Does the person display the requisite number (at least five for adults) of hyperactive/impulsive and/or inattentive symptoms, as specified in the DSM-5? And have these persisted since childhood?

- Multiple sources of information. Just as with assessing children and adolescents, having multiple informants can be helpful to not just assess and make the diagnosis of ADHD, but to rule out other conditions that might cloud the picture. Having a parent, significant other, and clinician(s) who have worked with the individual provide their observations can aid in diagnosis.

- Rule out potential medical causes for the observed symptoms.

- Screening tools. As with children and adolescents, the use of screening tools in adults—while not diagnostic—adds important information. When used as part of an intake process, they can also help flag previously undiagnosed cases of ADHD. Screening tools for adults include:

  a. Conners' Adult ADHD Rating Scales-LV (CAARS) (A 66-item self-report and observer scale that uses Likert 0–4 ratings. A score greater than 65 is suggestive of ADHD.)

  b. Brown Attention Deficit Disorder Scale (BADDS) (Developed by Dr. Thomas Brown, a variety of age-specific scales are available. A 40-item scale for adults and adolescents uses Likert 0-4 ratings. A score greater than 50 is suggestive of ADHD.)

  c. Wender Utah Rating Scale for ADHD (This 61-item Likert-based scale assesses ADHD symptoms in adults based on the individual's ability to recollect what symptoms were present during childhood.)

  d. Adult ADHD Self-Report Scale (ASRS-v1.1) (An 18-item questionnaire completed by the patient. It is copyrighted by the World Health Organization (WHO) and is reprinted here in its entirety. The entire instrument takes approximately five minutes to complete.)

     1) Adult ADHD Self Report Scale (ASRS-v1.1) Screener includes the first six items (Part A) in the ASRS-v1.1 and can be used as a brief screening tool. It is not meant to be diagnostic, but can bring to attention the potential for ADHD. Four of the six items marked off in the shaded boxes of the form are suggestive of ADHD.

     2) No scores are assigned to part B, but items checked off in the shaded boxes should prompt further investigation for the presence of ADHD.

ADULT ADHD SELF-REPORT SCALE (ASRS-v1.1)
SYMPTOM CHECKLIST

Patient name		Today's date				
Please answer the questions below, rating yourself on each of the criteria shown using the scale on the right side of the page. As you answer each question place an X in the box that best describes how you have felt and conducted yourself over the past 6 months. Please give this completed checklist to your healthcare professional to discuss during today's appointment.		Never	Rarely	Sometimes	Often	Very Often
1. How often do you have trouble wrapping up the final details of a project once the challenging parts have been done?						
2. How often do you have difficulty getting things in order when you have to do a task that requires organization?						
3. How often do you have problems remembering appointments or obligations?						
4. When you have a task that requires a lot of thought, how often do you avoid or delay getting started?						
5. How often do you fidget or squirm with your hands or feet when you have to sit down for a long time?						
6. How often do you feel overly active and compelled to do things, like you were driven by a motor?						
						Part A
7. How often do you make careless mistakes when you have to work on a boring or difficult project?						
8. How often do you have difficulty keeping your attention when you are doing boring or repetitive work?						

Question					
9. How often do you have difficulty concentrating on what people say to you even when they are speaking to you directly?					
10. How often do you misplace or have difficulty finding things at home or at work?					
11. How often are you distracted by activity or noise around you?					
12. How often do you leave your seat in meetings or other situations in which you are expected to remain seated?					
13. How often do you feel restless or fidgety?					
14. How often do you have difficulty unwinding and relaxing when you have time to yourself?					
15. How often do you find yourself talking too much when you are in social situations?					
16. When you're in a conversation, how often do you find yourself finishing the sentences of the people you are talking to, before they can finish themselves?					
17. How often do you have difficulty waiting your turn in situations when turn taking is required?					
18. How often do you interrupt others when they are busy?					

Part B

Reference: Kessler, R. C., Adler, L., Ames, M., Demler, O., Faraone, S., Hiripi, E., Howes, M. J., Jin, R., Secnik, K., Spencer, T., Ustun, T. B., Walters, E. E. (2005). The World Health Organization Adult ADHD Self-Report Scale (ASRS). *Psychological Medicine*, 35(2), 245–256.

Treatment of Co-Occurring SUDs and ADHD

Developing effective treatment/recovery plans for people with co-occurring substance use disorders and ADHD is best achieved through both sequential and integrated treatment. While there are limited studies looking at co-occurring treatment for substance use disorders and ADHD, research, and clinical experience offer the following guidelines.

1. Acute and active substance use and/or withdrawal states will need to be addressed first. This makes sense both from a diagnostic and treatment perspective, because when a person is actively using or in a state of withdrawal, it is unclear what symptoms are being caused by intoxication, withdrawal, or the ADHD.
2. Psychosocial treatments such as cognitive behavioral therapy have been shown to be of benefit for both ADHD and substance use disorders. Results have been more uniformly positive in adults than in children.
3. Psychopharmacology might include medications that address the ADHD, as well as medications to treat cravings associated with specific substance use disorders, as well as opioid replacement, if appropriate.

Psychosocial Treatment of ADHD

Where well-controlled studies looking at particular therapies in adolescents and adults with co-occurring substance use disorders and ADHD are not available, clinicians need to look at what has been found to be effective for ADHD, and then incorporate it into the person's overall treatment. The evidence supports the use of behavioral and cognitive-behavioral therapy (CBT) in children, adolescents, and adults with ADHD. As with all CBT, success hinges on the client's willingness to participate both in session and through homework completion and practice, which is how they will develop the skills taught and generalize them into their daily lives. Particular areas of focus will include:

- Skills training to address:
  o Time management
  o Organization
  o Prioritization
  o Breaking down tasks into smaller manageable components
  o Identification of problems with task initiation and low motivation
  o Interpersonal skills training and communication skills
- Cognitive training to address distorted patterns of thinking, especially as they pertain to negative self-talk and perceptions the individual has about their capabilities to stay on task and to be successful. There is also an emphasis on helping people identify and work with impulses and behaviors, and to develop long-range goals, versus short-term gratification, as is found in the misuse of drugs and alcohol.

Medications for ADHD

FDA-approved medications for the treatment of ADHD include the following:

1. Psychostimulants. These are the first-line treatment for ADHD. They are effective in managing symptoms in children, adolescents, and adults. However, these medications include risks for abuse, misuse, diversion, and dependence, and recently a black box warning was added to all stimulants regarding the risk of sudden cardiac death. All stimulants can increase blood pressure and heart rate. Prior to starting one of these medications a medical history and physical examination, likely including an electrocardiogram (ECG) should be conducted, especially if there is a history, or family history, of heart disease.

   Common side effects and adverse effects of stimulants include decreased appetite and weight loss, increased energy, insomnia, behavioral and emotional changes, which can include anxiety, mania, depression, paranoia, and other psychotic symptoms.

Available stimulants:
   a. Methylphenidate hydrochloride

   - Ritalin and Ritalin SR (sustained release tablets)
   - Concerta (extended/osmotic-release tablets)
   - Metadate CD (extended release capsules)
   - Daytrana (a patch)
   - Methylin (liquid solution and chewable tablets)

   b. Mixed amphetamine salts

   - Adderall, Adderall extended release

   c. Lisdexamfetamine-dimesylate (Vyvanse)
   d. Methamphetamine hydrochloride

   - Desoxyn

   e. Dexmethylphenidate

   - Focalin, Focalin extended release

   f. Dextroamphetamine sulfate

   - Dexedrine

2. Nonstimulant medications for ADHD
   a. Atomoxetine (Strattera). Similar in structure to some of the older antidepressants, which act on the neurotransmitters serotonin and norepinephrine, atomoxetine is an FDA-approved medication for the treatment of children, adolescents, and adults. It is often tried as an alternative to stimulant medication and might be considered with someone who has a history of stimulant misuse.
   b. Bupropion (Wellbutrin). This antidepressant medication is used off label to treat ADHD, but is contraindicated in individuals with a history of seizure disorder and those with significant eating disorders.
   c. Guanfacine. Initially a medication for blood pressure (alpha-blocker), it is FDA-approved for the treatment of ADHD in children ages 6–17.

   - Tenex
   - Intuniv (extended release form)

d. Tricyclic antidepressants: Even though they do not carry the FDA indication for ADHD, there is good literature to support the off-label use of some of the older tricyclic antidepressants, which inhibit the reuptake of both serotonin and norepinephrine, in adults. In particular the medications desipramine and nortriptyline. Where these medications do not carry abuse potential, they may be an option with individuals who have a history of misusing stimulant medication. However, these medications are associated with significant cardiac side effects and can be fatal in overdose. An electrocardiogram should be obtained prior to starting one of these medications and again when the stable dose is achieved.

Abuse, Misuse, and Diversion of Stimulant Medications

Stimulant medications, such as amphetamines (Adderall, Dexedrine) and methylphenidate (Ritalin), are frequently abused for their euphoric effects and are a favorite among high school and college students when pulling "all-nighters." They can be misused by people looking to lose weight as well as those with eating disorders who take them for their appetite suppressant and weight loss side effects. Others, such as long-distance truck drivers have been known to use psychostimulants to ward off fatigue. Because of their energizing properties, these medications have significant "street value" and can be sold or traded.

Concerns about misuse and diversion of stimulant medication, both in minors and adults, need to be addressed when these medications are used, especially with people who have co-occurring substance use disorders. The risk of abuse and diversion increases further if there is a history of oppositional defiant disorder, conduct disorder, and/or antisocial personality disorder.

Strategies to decrease misuse/abuse and diversion include:

1. Use of long-acting versus immediate-release stimulants, these carry less of a euphoric effect, and are less readily snorted or injected. The transdermal preparation of methylphenidate (Daytrana) also carries a lower likelihood for misuse.
2. Urine toxicology screens help to ensure that the person is in fact taking the medication. Supervised urines have a greater degree of accuracy than unsupervised.
3. When prescribing stimulants to children and/or adolescents be aware of other family members who might be at risk for diverting the child's medication. Children and adolescents should have a responsible parent or guardian oversee their medication, and keep it secure.
4. For children and adolescents who take medication during school, it should be overseen by the school nurse (which is the law in most states).
5. Random pill counts can be used to see if any pills are missing.

Case Study: Caleb James

Caleb is a 22-year-old never married man, father of one, who currently lives with his parents. He presents for treatment to a chemical dependence and co-occurring clinic as a stipulation of the court. He is currently in a jail diversion program following his arrest for possession of narcotics (marijuana, cocaine, and opioids) with intent to sell. He has had several positive urines (opioids) and has been told if this continues he will serve jail time.

He has limited ability to leave his parents' home. He is wearing an ankle monitor. He arrives at the first appointment with his mother. He has difficulty sitting still and taps his feet and fidgets with his hands and cell phone through much of the appointment.

Caleb says that while treatment has been mandated, he would like to be off drugs. Aside from the threat of jail time, he wants to be an active part of his three-year-old daughter's life. She is currently in the custody of his girlfriend's parents. He is allowed a one-hour supervised visit weekly.

He identifies particular problems with opioids, which he has been using since he was 14, and cocaine. He smokes marijuana daily, but since his arrest two months ago switched to synthetic cannabis in an attempt to avoid positive drug screens. He has injected drugs in the past—heroin and cocaine. He reports he currently uses opioids daily, "whatever I can get my hands on." He has never been in a drug-treatment program, but thinks he needs to be on either methadone or buprenorphine as he's been unable to stop using opioids. Given a choice, he states he'd much rather be on buprenorphine as it does not require daily clinic attendance.

He says as a child he was diagnosed with ADHD, which his mother confirms. "He could never sit still and was always getting into trouble in school." She states he was placed on Ritalin by his pediatrician when he was 10. "They worked when he took them," she said. "Problem was he'd forget or didn't want to a lot of the time, and then he started hanging out with the wrong kind of kids, and it just went downhill from there." She adds that Caleb's father also has ADHD and takes stimulant medication. She believes other members on Caleb's father's side also have ADHD, and several have problems with drugs and/or alcohol. She knows of no other family psychiatric or substance abuse history.

Caleb was expelled his sophomore year of high school when he was found selling his stimulant medication and medications he'd taken from his father. He subsequently completed his GED and two semesters of trade school (plumbing). He has had multiple drug-related arrests, but has never served more than three days in jail. To date, he has no felonies and he has no history of violence.

His medical history includes multiple broken bones from skateboarding and dirt bike accidents. He describes being in diffuse physical pain (about 4–5 out of 10), but admits it is difficult to know what is from his old injuries and what is from going in and out of opioid withdrawal.

His physical examination and medical screening reveals evidence of mild opioid withdrawal—large pupils (meiosis), goose flesh (piloerection), complaints of diarrhea, and muscle and stomach cramps. He has fresh track marks on the back of his right hand and inside of his right arm (antecubital fossa). They are not infected, or warm to the touch. He has not been tested for HIV or hepatitis since his last arrest. He is uncertain if he has been exposed to hepatitis in the past.

His mental status exam is significant for mild anxiety (2–3/10), which he relates to the threat of jail and fear that he will not be able to see his daughter. He does not consider himself depressed. He has no evidence of psychosis and denies any thoughts of wanting to harm himself or anyone else.

Step One: Level of Care Determination

In thinking through this individual's current symptom severity, he would meet criteria for a number of levels of care. Where he's had minimal prior treatment, it would be reasonable to begin in a PHP or IOP setting with a co-occurring focus and ability to provide opioid replacement therapy (buprenorphine or methadone).

If such a combined program were not available, an alternative would be to get his opioid replacement and substance use treatment through an opioid treatment program, and receive psychiatric treatment (parallel) through a mental health clinic. Although, some opioid-treatment programs will be adequately structured to assess and address both his mental health and substance use needs.

Step Two: Constructing the Problem/Need List

The significant information (data) from the case study can be divided into three broad categories: substance use, ADHD/mental health, and medical. Some information will apply to multiple categories.

Substance Use	ADHD and Mental Health	Medical
Court-mandated to treatment	History of ADHD as a child	In mild opioid withdrawal
Arrested for possession, multiple prior arrests	Difficulty sitting still, fidgets	History of multiple broken bones
In a jail-diversion program	Multiple sources of information verifying ADHD history (mother and the patient, direct clinical observation, prior diagnosis by the patient's pediatrician)	Pain, unclear if from cramping and achiness of withdrawal, versus past injuries
Motivated by threat of doing jail time	Treated with stimulants as a child: "They worked when he took them."	Fresh track marks
Positive urines	Family history of ADHD (father and other relatives)	Unclear hepatitis and HIV status
Smokes cannabis daily	Mild anxiety	
Uses synthetic cannabis to try and avoid detection	No suicidality or homicidality	
History of intravenous drug use	Thrill-seeking, impulsive, and high-risk behaviors in the past (dirt bike riding, skateboarding)	
Uses opioids daily	Conduct problems and antisocial behaviors—stole and sold medication and drugs Expelled his sophomore year	
History of cocaine use		

Has never been in drug treatment		
Motivated to get on opioid replacement therapy with either methadone or buprenorphine		
Currently has limited involvement with his daughter; motivated to be more involved in her life		

Using these three categories, an initial problem/need list can be constructed.

1. Severe and active substance use problems, as evidenced by (AEB) opioid dependence and current withdrawal symptoms, daily cannabis use (currently synthetic), legal and social problems related to drug use. Currently using intravenous drugs (heroin and cocaine).
2. Active symptoms of ADHD with a well-documented history of a prior diagnosis and strong family history.
3. Active medical issues, including opioid withdrawal and possible exposure, through high-risk activity, to blood-borne pathogens.

Step Three: Establishing the Initial Goals/Objectives for Treatment

Using the three-item problem list, the patient and clinician will develop measurable, realistic, behavioral, and desirable goals for treatment.

1. Active and Severe Substance Use:
   - Short-term goal(s):
     1) Caleb will achieve abstinence from illicit drugs, AEB self-report and negative urine drugs screens.
     2) Caleb will start on opioid replacement therapy (buprenorphine).
     3) Caleb will be free from all symptoms of opioid withdrawal.
   - Long-term goal(s): Caleb will maintain abstinence from illicit drugs AEB self-report and negative urine toxicologies.
2. ADHD:
   - Short-term goal(s):
     1) Caleb will be assessed for the current severity of his ADHD symptoms when he is free from symptoms of acute opioid withdrawal.
     2) If ADHD symptoms are present and clinically significant (using the ASRS-v1.1), specific treatment options, including the use of medication and psychosocial interventions for ADHD, will be reviewed with Caleb.
   - Long-term goal(s): To control symptoms of ADHD to where they are no more than a 2 on a 5-point scale.

3. Medical:

- Short-term goal(s):

    1) Caleb will be free from symptoms of opioid withdrawal.

    2) He will be definitively assessed for HIV and hepatitis. The results will be reviewed with him, and he will receive counseling regarding high-risk behaviors and how to reduce them.

- Long-term goal(s): Caleb will obtain a regular medical provider and keep all scheduled appointments.

Step Four: Constructing the Treatment/Recovery Plan

Once the problem/need list and goals and objectives have been fleshed out, they are moved forward into the treatment/recovery plan where the specific interventions are identified, including frequency, duration, and who will be responsible for seeing that they happen.

TREATMENT/RECOVERY PLAN

Patient's Name: Caleb James

Date of Birth: 6/16/1992

Medical Record #: XXX-XX-XXXX

Level of Care: Co-Occurring Intensive Outpatient (IOP)

ICD-10 Codes	DSM-5 Diagnoses
F11.23	Opioid Withdrawal with Opioid Use Disorder, Severe
F90.2	Attention-Deficit/Hyperactivity Disorder Combined Presentation
F12.20	Cannabis Use Disorder, Severe (including synthetic Cannabis)
F14.20	Cocaine Use Disorder, Moderate
Z65.3	Problems Related to Other Legal Circumstances

The individual's stated goal(s): "I don't want to go to jail. I want to be on buprenorphine so I don't have to use dope. I want to get clean and sober. I want to go back to school and get my plumber's license. I want to be a better father to Jilly. I think I might need to go back on ADHD meds."

1. Problem/Need Statement: Severe and active substance use problems, as evidenced by (AEB), opioid dependence and current withdrawal symptoms, daily cannabis use (currently synthetic), legal and social problems related to drug use. Currently using intravenous drugs (heroin and cocaine).

Long-Term Goal(s):
Caleb will maintain abstinence from illicit drugs AEB self-report and negative urine toxicologies.

Short Term Goals/Objectives with target date:
1. Caleb will achieve abstinence from illicit drugs, AEB self-report and negative urine drug screens. (3/30/2014)
2. Caleb will start on opioid replacement therapy (buprenorphine). (3/20/2014)
3. Caleb will be free from all symptoms of opioid withdrawal. (3/21/2014)

2. Problem/Need Statement: Active symptoms of ADHD with a well-documented history of a prior diagnosis and strong family history.

Long-Term Goal: To control symptoms of ADHD to where they are no greater than a 2 on a 5-point scale.

Short-Term Goals/Objectives with target date:
1. Caleb will be assessed for the current severity of his ADHD symptoms when he is free from symptoms of opioid withdrawal. (3/30/2014)
2. If ADHD symptoms are present and clinically significant (using the ASRS-v1.1), specific treatment options, including the use of medication and therapy will be reviewed with Caleb. (3/30/2014)

3. Problem/Need Statement: Active medical issues including opioid withdrawal and possible exposure to blood-borne pathogens through intravenous drug use.

Long-Term Goal: Caleb will obtain a regular medical provider and keep scheduled appointments.

Short-Term Goals/Objectives with target date:
1. Caleb will be free from symptoms of opioid withdrawal. (3/21/2014).
2. He will be definitively assessed for HIV and hepatitis, and the results will be reviewed with him. He will receive counseling regarding high-risk behaviors and how to decrease them. (3/21/2014).

Interventions					
Treatment Modality	Specific Type	Frequency	Duration	Problem Number	Responsible Person(s)
Medical Assessment	History and physical	Upon admission, and follow-up as needed.	20–45 minutes	1,3	Physician/ APRN
Nursing Assessment	Nursing assessment	One time, and as needed.	One hour	1,2,3	RN
Psychiatric Assessment	Psychiatric diagnostic assessment and follow-up	Upon admission, and then as needed	One hour during the admission process, follow-up medication management as needed.	1,2,3	MD

Individual Therapy	CBT individual therapy with co-occurring (ADHD) focus	2X/week	50 minutes for one month	1,2	Mr. James and primary clinician
Group Therapy	Substance abuse education	3X/week	50 minutes for one month	1,2,3	Mr. James and group leader
	Co-occurring CBT	2X/week	50 minutes for one month	1,2	Mr. James and group leader
	Relapse prevention	3X/week	50 minutes for one month	1	Mr. James and group leader
	Family support and education group	1X/week	90 minutes	1,2	Mr. James, his parents, and group leader
Labs	Blood work/ electrocardiogram, other studies as indicated	Upon admission, and as needed	N/A	1,2,3	MD/APRN
Specimen Collection	Breath analysis/ urine drug screen	As ordered	One month	1,2	Clinician, or designee
Peer Support	12-step	2–3 meetings/ week	One month	1	Mr. James

Identification of strengths: Expresses a high-degree of motivation to not use drugs. Has clear career goals, and his parents have agreed to help him finance a return to trade school. Wants to be more involved with his daughter's upbringing.

Peer/family/community supports to assist: Views his parents as supports. Has a case manager through the jail diversion program whom he identifies as being a positive influence.

Barriers to treatment: High risk for relapse. Risk of incarceration.

Staff/client-identified education/teaching needs: To learn specific triggers for use and/ or relapse. To understand connections between ADHD and substance use. To identify effective strategies for managing symptoms of ADHD.

Assessment of discharge needs/discharge planning: To be free from symptoms of opioid withdrawal and to be in early abstinence. Appropriate linkages to next level of care will be in place.

Completion of this treatment/recovery plan was a collaborative effort between the client and the following treatment team members:

SIGNATURES		Date/Time
Client:	Caleb James	3/18/2014 2pm
Physician:	Peter Greene, MD	3/18/2014 3:15pm
Primary Clinician:	Melody Greenblatt, LCSW	3/18/2014 2pm
Other Team Members	Ogden Osgood, CADC	3/18/2014 4pm
	Bill Hodges, RN	3/18/2014 4pm

CHAPTER 10

Depressive Disorders and Co-Occurring Substance Use Disorders

---

Overview

Symptoms of Depression

Key Issues in the Assessment of Co-Occurring Depressive and Substance Use Disorders

Assessment and Screening Tools

The Patient Health Questionnaire 9 (PHQ9)

Psychosocial Treatment

Pharmacology

Antidepressants

Electroconvulsive Therapy, Transcranial Magnetic Stimulation, and Vagus Nerve Stimulation

Case Study

OVERVIEW

In any given year, nearly 7 percent of Americans will meet criteria for major depression, with women carrying a two- to threefold greater risk than men. A first episode of depression can occur at any age, with the greatest incidence in a person's late teens and twenties.

The lifetime prevalence of depression in the United States, based on two large surveys, ranges from 13 to 16 percent. Broken down, the lifetime prevalence of major depressive disorder alone is 7.41 percent, and the lifetime rate of major depression with a co-occurring substance use disorder is 5.82 percent. Rates of all substance use disorders are significantly higher among people with major depression than the general population.

Co-occurring depressive disorders occur in more than 40 percent of people with alcohol use disorders and in more than 17 percent of people with all non-tobacco substance use disorders. Depression with co-occurring substance use disorders is associated with more severe depression, multiple co-occurring mental disorders, and more suicide attempts.

The course of a depressive disorder is highly variable and often chronic. An untreated depressive episode can last from months to more than a year. The more episodes of depression a person has had increases the likelihood of future episodes. In many treatment guidelines, depression is viewed as a chronic medical condition, where recurrence is to be anticipated.

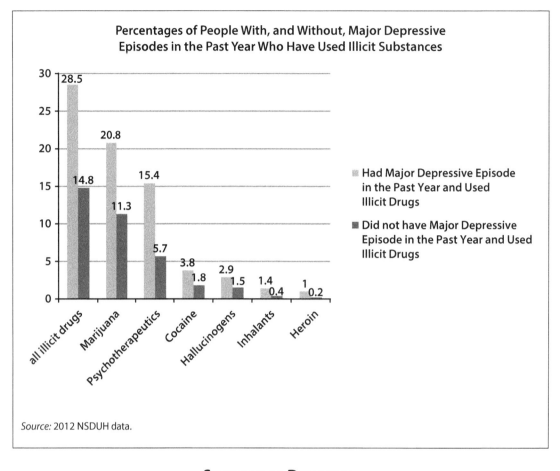

Percentages of People With, and Without, Major Depressive Episodes in the Past Year Who Have Used Illicit Substances

Legend:
- Had Major Depressive Episode in the Past Year and Used Illicit Drugs
- Did not have Major Depressive Episode in the Past Year and Used Illicit Drugs

Source: 2012 NSDUH data.

SYMPTOMS OF DEPRESSION

Key to the diagnosis of a major depressive episode is that it is a sustained mood state, in the current DSM, of at least two week's duration. Although people will typically report symptoms on the order of months, or even years.

A diagnosis of a depressive episode is based on a constellation of symptoms, one of which must be a depressed/sad/unhappy mood and the other is the loss of interest or pleasure (anhedonia). Other symptoms include:

- Changes in sleep. Either too much or too little.

- Changes in appetite. Either increased or decreased, and may be accompanied by weight loss or gain.

- Changes in energy. Typically loss of energy and chronic feelings of fatigue, but may also be agitated, irritable, and anxious.

- Poor concentration. The person finds it difficult to focus and to attend to activities that require sustained attention.

- Excessive and often inappropriate guilt.

- Feeling of worthlessness and low self-esteem.

- Hopelessness. The person feels they will never get better.

- Thoughts of death.
- Thoughts of suicide, including plans and/or attempts.

KEY ISSUES IN THE ASSESSMENT OF CO-OCCURRING DEPRESSIVE AND SUBSTANCE USE DISORDERS

Differentiating a primary depressive disorder from other mental disorders, such as bipolar disorder, PTSD, and borderline personality disorder, is not always straightforward. And many substances and medications can cause depressive syndromes. For instance, alcohol-induced depression in individuals with alcohol use disorders may account for more than 30 percent of depressive episodes in that population. In the case of alcohol-induced depression, when a lasting abstinence is achieved, the depressive symptoms may resolve without further treatment. Finally, many medical conditions can manifest with symptoms of depression; these range from increased rates of depression following strokes or heart attacks to certain malignancies, such as pancreatic cancer to infectious diseases, such as mononucleosis.

For some with depressive episodes, there may be no identifiable psychosocial stress connected to the depression. For others, there will be a clear relationship between life events (breakups, financial stresses, housing problems, legal difficulties, etc.) that are associated with the mood episode.

In assessing individuals with co-occurring depressive and substance use disorders, it is important to not jump to conclusions about the nature or cause of the depression, but to keep an open mind and attitude of flexibility. Questions to be answered include the following:

- Has the person had other mood episodes, such as any prior periods of mania or hypomania? If yes, then the diagnosis by definition is in the bipolar spectrum (see Chapter 11).
- Does the person have a history of depressive episodes that predates the substance use problems?
- Is the person on medications that can cause depressive symptoms?
- Is the person in a withdrawal or post-intoxication state that can cause symptoms of depression?
  - o Opioid withdrawal
  - o Acute post-intoxication cocaine or stimulant states (crashes)
  - o Alcohol or benzodiazepine withdrawal
- Is there a family history of depression and/or other mood or mental disorders?
- Is a medical condition present that might be worsening or causing the symptoms of depression?
- What psychosocial stresses may be worsening, or even causing, the current depressive episode?

ASSESSMENT AND SCREENING TOOLS

Screening tools can be valuable assets in both the initial assessment and ongoing treatment of depression. Certain instruments, such as the ones described below, can be used to help clarify diagnosis and be followed over time to track changes over the course of treatment.

- **Beck Depression Inventory-II:** This widely used 21-item questionnaire is completed by the client; it takes approximately five minutes. It utilizes Likert-style severity ratings. It is copyright protected and available for purchase through Pearson Education, Inc. (www. pearsonassessments.com)

- **Hamilton Rating Scale for Depression:** Another frequently used 21-item assessment tool (versions with 17–27 items) is completed by clinicians. It uses ratings of 0–2, to 0–4. Downloadable copies are available online.

- **Patient Health Questionnaire 9 (PHQ-9):** The PHQ-9 is a widely used instrument that is completed by the client. As with all screening tools, it should be used in conjunction with a thorough clinical assessment before making a diagnosis. An adapted version of the PHQ-9 is available from the American Psychiatric Association (www.psych.org). In that version, the client is asked to rate symptoms over the past one, not two, weeks. In addition to the raw score, clinicians should note individual symptoms endorsed in the shaded boxes, especially the question related to suicidality. The PHQ-9 is in the public domain and can be freely copied.

PATIENT HEALTH QUESTIONNAIRE (PHQ-9)

Name:_____   Date:_____

Over the past 2 weeks, how often have you been bothered by any of the following problems?
(Use "√" to indicate your answer.)

		Not at all	Several days	More than half the days	Nearly every day
1	Little interest or pleasure in doing things	0	1	2	3
2	Feeling down, depressed, or hopeless	0	1	2	3
3	Trouble falling or staying asleep, sleeping too much	0	1	2	3
4	Feeling tired or having little energy	0	1	2	3
5	Poor appetite or overeating	0	1	2	3
6	Feeling bad about yourself—or that you are a failure or have let yourself or your family down	0	1	2	3
7	Trouble concentrating on things, such as reading the newspaper or watching television	0	1	2	3
8	Moving or speaking so slowly that other people could have noticed. Or the opposite—being so fidgety or restless that you have been moving around a lot more than usual	0	1	2	3
9	Thoughts that you would be better off dead, or of hurting yourself	0	1	2	3
Column totals					
Add columns together for total score					

Scoring the PHQ-9:

Total Score	Depression Severity
1–4	Minimal depression
5–9	Mild depression
10–14	Moderate depression
15–19	Moderately severe depression
20–27	Severe depression

PSYCHOSOCIAL TREATMENTS

A number of psychotherapies for depression have been shown to be efficacious, including cognitive behavioral therapy (CBT), interpersonal psychotherapy (IPT), and psychodynamic psychotherapy. However, little research has methodically assessed these same therapies in individuals who have both substance use disorders and depressive disorders.

One study, using a small sample size and no control group, did find positive outcomes for both depression and alcohol-related outcomes with CBT.

The clinical consensus is that psychotherapy, whether in group or individual format, be offered to patients with co-occurring depressive and substance use disorders. The selection of a particular therapy will be based on issues such as:

- Patient preference
- Availability
- Emerging evidence to support particular therapeutic approaches in individuals with co-occurring depressive and substance use disorders

From a pragmatic perspective, the inclusion of psychotherapy provides an ongoing relationship between the individual with depression and the therapist. Active stresses and problems are addressed, and connections and the interplay between negative mood states (depression, irritability, anxiety) and problem substance use can be made. In addition to psychotherapy, an overall attention to wellness strategies, including adequate sleep, nutrition, exercise and fostering important relationships, and sources of meaning (work, faith, and so forth) are associated with better outcomes.

PHARMACOLOGY

Most practice guidelines recommend the use of antidepressants in individuals with moderate or severe depression. However, few studies have looked at specific medications in people who have both mental and substance use disorders. Studies that have been done tend to have small numbers and often lack control groups.

There's a further finding, which is especially true when talking about depression, that response to antidepressant medications in people who are actively drinking and using other substances is less strong than for people who abstain. This is an important educational point to teach clients: Not only are their symptoms of depression worsened by their substance use, but while they continue to use, they are less likely to get the benefit, or the full benefit, of the medication.

In the past it was thought that prescribing antidepressants while people were still using drugs and alcohol was a bad idea. This approach may have been fueled both by earlier sequential paradigms for the treatment of co-occurring disorders (treat the drugs and alcohol first and only then address the mental illness) and by the relative risk involved with some of the older antidepressants, such as the tricyclic antidepressants, which, due to their effects on the heart, can easily be fatal in overdose situations. A third hypothesis as to why pharmacologic treatment for depression is sometimes held back is articulated in these questions: Is this a substance-induced mood disorder? And if it is, will it resolve when the problem substance is stopped?

The current consensus is to proceed with caution and to offer medication when a diagnosis of a depressive disorder has been clearly made and the person is not in an active withdrawal or intoxication state. The thinking is that the depressive symptoms increase the risk of relapse. To diminish that risk, it is important to begin treating the depression as soon as is safe.

In the absence of clear best choices of medications in clients with co-occurring depressive and substance use disorders, the prescriber needs to look at available medications for the treatment of depression and, based on an overall understanding of the client's specific situation and symptoms, make recommendations. Issues that might sway the decision for one agent over another include:

- Client preference and/or past experience. "That one worked for me before." "I tried that one, and it didn't do anything."
- Side-effect profile. Side effects can be both a positive and a negative. Certain agents might be avoided because of concerns of weight gain and metabolic syndrome (central obesity, development of Type II Diabetes, elevated cholesterol, etc.). Other agents might be useful because the client has trouble falling asleep and the medication is sedating, and can be given prior to bed.
- Cost. Will the person's insurance cover the medication, or will they have to pay out of pocket?
- Potential interactions with other medications the client is taking.
- Overall safety profile of the medication, especially if the person has a history of overdose.
- Safety of the medication if the person is likely to combine it with alcohol or illicit substances. For instance, sedating medications, when combined with opioids increase the risk of respiratory depression, coma, and death.
- Potential benefit/risk in other co-occurring conditions such as:
  - A patient who smokes might want to try bupropion, which also has the FDA indication for smoking cessation.
  - A person with a co-morbid anxiety disorder might benefit from an antidepressant that can treat both anxiety and depression.
  - Someone with weight loss and poor sleep as symptoms of their depression might be a good candidate for an agent that helps with sleep, such as mirtazapine/Remeron, which can also increase appetite.
  - A person with certain pain conditions might be a candidate for duloxetine/Cymbalta, which carries the FDA indications for fibromyalgia and diabetic peripheral neuropathy.
  - Someone with liver disease should avoid medications, such as duloxetine/Cymbalta, that have been associated with liver failure.

Antidepressants

Among numerous FDA-approved antidepressants, little data demonstrate that any one is superior. They all take at least two to four weeks, at times longer, to show clinical benefits. Some of the older antidepressants, the monoamine oxidase inhibitors, appear to have greater efficacy in the treatment of depression, but their side effects and potential for dangerous adverse reactions have relegated them to a rarely used status.

Choices of agents include:

- Selective serotonin reuptake inhibitors (SSRIs): fluoxetine/Prozac, sertraline/Zoloft, paroxitine/Paxil, citalopram/Celexa, escitalopram/Lexapro, vortioxetine/Brintellix, and fluvoxamine/Luvox (does not have the FDA indication for depression, but is an SSRI). Common side effects include sexual dysfunction in both men and women, weight gain (especially true for paroxitine/Paxil), headache, discontinuation syndromes, which can be severe, and manic activation.

- Serotonin norepinephrine reuptake inhibitors: venlafaxine/Effexor, desvenlafaxine/Pristiq, duloxetine/Cymbalta, levomilnacipran/Fetzima. Side effects are similar to the SSRIs, including sexual side effects and withdrawal syndromes. They can also be associated with elevations in blood pressure.

- Bupropion/Wellbutrin: Its mechanism of action is not well understood, but involves dopamine and norepinephrine. It is associated with decreased nicotine cravings. It should be avoided in people with certain eating disorders (bulimia and anorexia) and in individuals with a history of seizures.

- Trazodone/Desyrel: Trazodone has its effect on the serotonin system, but is not an SSRI or SNRI. It is infrequently used as an antidepressant due to sedation. It is often used off label to help with insomnia. It can rarely cause priapism—a sustained painful erection—which may require medical attention. In addition to sedation, common side effects include blurry vision, dry mouth, headache, and intense dreams.

- Mirtazapine/Remeron: Mirtazapine acts on both serotonin and norepinephrine. Its main side effects include sedation, increased appetite, and weight gain.

- Tricyclic antidepressants: Once popular, these medications, which include amitriptyline/Elavil, nortriptyline/Pamelor, and desipramine/Norpramin, are infrequently used as antidepressants in the United States due to their significant side effect burden and potential lethality in overdose situations. Typical side effects include dry mouth, urinary retention, constipation, and increased appetite. Because of their cardiac effects, they should be avoided in people with a history of coronary artery disease. An electrocardiogram should be obtained prior to starting treatment and monitored once a therapeutic level has been achieved. They should also be avoided in people with certain types of glaucoma.

- Monoamine oxidase inhibitors (MAOIs): Rarely prescribed, these include isocarboxazid/Marplan and phenelzine/Nardil. They are effective antidepressants that require adherence to a diet free from tyramine, a substance derived from the essential amino acid tyrosine. Tyramine is found in many foods, such as aged cheeses, Chianti wine, pickled and smoked meats and fish, chocolate, and soy sauce, to name a few. The potential interaction can lead to a hypertensive crisis, which can be life threatening. This same interaction can occur when MAOIs are combined with many other medications, including over-the-counter cold preparations and other antidepressants. Prior to going on an MAOI, there should be at least a two-week washout period for any other antidepressant, longer for those with longer half lives, such as fluoxetine/Prozac. Common side effects of the MAOIs include headache, insomnia, and weight gain.

Electroconvulsive Therapy (ECT), Transcranial Magnetic Stimulation (TMS), and Vagus Nerve Stimulation

Electroconvulsive Therapy

ECT is a highly effective treatment for severe depression. It is typically reserved for individuals who have not responded to multiple medication trials, and is especially effective for individuals with psychotic depressions. The treatment involves the creation of a seizure through the administration of a dosed electric current. Modern ECT includes the use of rapid-onset anesthesia and paralytic agents to prevent patients from having a physical seizure in which they could harm themselves. Side effects of ECT include memory loss, typically for the time surrounding the procedures, but some individuals report more sustained problems with memory. Other side effects include headache, nausea, muscle aches, and effects associated with the anesthetic agents used.

ECT requires a series of treatment, on average 6 to 12. When a response is achieved, the person may be offered a course of maintenance ECT (treatments less frequently) to help them sustain remission of symptoms. ECT can be offered on an inpatient or outpatient basis.

Transcranial Magnetic Stimulation

TMS involves the noninvasive exposure of the brain to brief electromagnetic pulses. It requires multiple treatments, typically 20–30 treatments over the course of four to six weeks. Side effects are minimal and mild, and include headache. There have been rare reports of seizure and manic switching with TMS.

Vagus Nerve Stimulation

Vagus nerve stimulation received FDA approval for refractory depression (at least four failed trials of medication) in 2005. It involves the surgical implantation of a device that stimulates the left vagus nerve. Common side effects include vocal changes, hoarseness, and cough. Adverse reactions include the development of obstructive sleep apnea, cough, and vocal changes.

Case Study: Joanne Mackey

Joanne Mackey is a 47-year-old divorced mother of two grown children and grandmother of one who is referred by her attending physician to an outpatient mental health practice for assessment and treatment of depression. Ms. Mackey, who is head nurse at a local skilled nursing home, states she has struggled with depression and some anxiety for most her of her life. "I'm just never happy."

She describes her current mood as moderately depressed (7–8/10), she has poor sleep, which she states is a chronic problem, with difficulty falling asleep, frequent middle of the night arousal, and early wakening. "I might get three or four hours a night." Her appetite is good, and she has recently put on five pounds, which concerns her and which she attributes to her current medication. She is able to go to work, which she describes as quite stressful. "I oversee 20 nurses and more than 50 patient care assistants." There is little that interests her or gives her pleasure, and she feels as though she has no energy and has to push herself just to make it through the day. Even spending time with her three-year-old granddaughter does little to brighten her mood. "I've just always felt defective, and try to hide it as best I can." She denies any thoughts of suicide but does admit, "I sometimes wish I just wouldn't wake up."

Her first episode of sustained depression was during her parents' divorce when she was 13. "I was angry and mad all the time. My father had an affair, and it was like he hadn't just cheated on my mom, but on all of us." She believes her mood remained depressed for more than a year, although she was able to function and excel in academics. Over the years she can recall more than eight episodes of sustained depression. She has been on multiple antidepressant medications including: fluoxetine/Prozac, sertraline/Zoloft, paroxitine/Paxil, bupropion/Wellbutrin, and has had trials of mood stabilizers (lithium and valproic acid/Depakote) both as monotherapy, and in attempts to augment the antidepressant. She is currently prescribed duloxetine/Cymbalta in combination with the tranquilizing medication aripiprazole/Abilify. The last was recently started, and she reports it's not been useful and she wants to stop taking it for fear of weight gain and metabolic syndrome.

She has been in individual therapy in the past, which she found useful. She does not currently have a therapist, and the one she last saw, and liked, has retired. She has never been hospitalized and denies any history of suicide attempts or self-injurious behavior.

As a part of the intake process the state's prescription monitoring program is accessed and reveals that over the past three years, Ms. Mackey has obtained numerous prescriptions for benzodiazepines (alprazolam/Xanax, lorazepam/Ativan, diazepam/Valium, and clonazepam/Klonopin) from five different physicians and APRNs, including the referring doctor. When presented with this information she becomes tearful and admits that for more than 15 years she has been taking benzodiazepine medications, both prescribed and purchased illicitly. She states she has never diverted medications from patients, but at times the temptation to do so has been intense, "It's only a matter of time, and I couldn't live with myself if I did that. I feel like a total criminal already, lying to my doctors." She quantifies her current usage of benzodiazepines as 15–20 mg/day of alprazolam/Xanax (75–100 mg equivalents of diazepam/Valium). "I know I'm addicted, but I can't stop taking them. And it's just gotten to be more and more. You have no idea how sick it makes me." She adds that if she goes for more than 12 hours without a benzodiazepine she gets acutely anxious, nauseas, and tremulous. In the past she has attempted to taper herself off of the benzodiazepines, but has never been successful. She denies any history of seizures, but is frightened of experiencing a serious withdrawal should she just stop taking the benzodiazepines.

She denies any significant use of other substances, including alcohol and nicotine.

Her medical history includes two vaginal births and a tubal ligation following the birth of her son. She has had work-related injuries, which resulted in lower back problems for which she was initially prescribed pain killers. She had a spinal fusion of L3–L5 10 years ago, which did not fully alleviate the problem. She denies active use of opioids and is aware of the dangers of combining them with benzodiazepines.

Her family psychiatric history includes her mother, who she reports was severely depressed around the time of her divorce, and Joanne's daughter has been treated for anxiety. She believes her father, who currently lives in Florida with his third wife, has a drinking problem.

Step One: Level of Care Determination

In this case study, Ms. Mackey's current level of benzodiazepine dependence, with symptoms of withdrawal when she attempts to cut down even for brief periods, necessitates a medically monitored detoxification. This recommendation is based on the potentially serious, even life-threatening withdrawal syndromes associated with both alcohol and benzodiazepine withdrawal (Chapter 16).

Where she has unsuccessfully attempted to self-taper on an outpatient basis, even the use of a partial hospital program, which might be able to provide the medical oversight, will likely be too low a level of care, at least initially. In this situation, an inpatient benzodiazepine detoxification will be the best fit. There, she can be safely tapered off the benzodiazepines, while simultaneously having depression and anxiety evaluated and treated. The length of the inpatient detoxification will be determined by severity of any withdrawal, and it's likely that the taper could be completed in a rehabilitation facility that provides both medical oversight and co-occurring treatment for depression and anxiety. Once she has been completely tapered, she would be stepped down to a less intensive level of care, which will be determined by her needs and preferences at that time.

As one can imagine, a person who presents for outpatient mental health treatment at the request of her doctor, and is then told she needs an inpatient detoxification, may struggle with this recommendation. Real-life issues related to work, child care, pet care, ability to pay, and so on need to be thought through, as well as the person's willingness and readiness to take definitive action.

Steps Two and Three: Constructing the Problem/Need List and Initial Goals and Objectives

Substance Use	Mental Health	Medical
On benzodiazepines for more than 15 years	Struggled with depression and anxiety most of her life	Poor sleep (chronic problem)
Has purchased medications illicitly	Depressed mood 7–8/10	Recent weight gain, possibly medication related
Has obtained benzodiazepines from multiple prescribers	Poor sleep (chronic problem)	Chronic pain problems
Uses 15–20 mgs of alprazolam/Xanax/day	Little interest or pleasure	
Experiences withdrawal symptoms if she doesn't use, even for brief periods	Thoughts of death	
Single class of drug use	No active suicidality	
Tolerance, as evidenced by dosage increasing over time	Feels "defective"/low self-esteem	
Feels guilty over usage and deception used to obtain benzodiazepines	Therapy has been helpful/therapist retired	
Concerned her addiction will lead to diverting medications from patients	Mother had depression	
	Daughter treated for anxiety	
	Chronic fatigue and low energy	

Using the preceding list, the patient and clinician will develop an initial problem/need list with measurable, realistic, behavioral, and desirable goals for treatment.

1. Severe benzodiazepine use as evidenced by (AEB) increased use over time, inability to stop or decrease use, withdrawal symptoms when dosage is decreased, and engagement in high-risk behaviors to obtain adequate supplies to keep from experiencing withdrawal.

   • Short-term goal(s): To safely taper off of benzodiazepine medication.

   • Long-term goal(s): To achieve a lasting abstinence from benzodiazepines.

2. Depression and anxiety AEB: a depressed mood, anhedonia, poor sleep, chronically low energy, low self-esteem, constant worry, frequent thoughts of death.

   • Short-term goal(s): To experience a 50 percent or greater decrease in depressive and anxious symptoms using 10-point self-rating scales and the Patient Health Questionnaire-9.

   • Long-term goal(s): To experience symptoms of depression and anxiety no greater than a 2 out of a possible 10.

3. Active medical issues: chronic insomnia, recent weight gain, and chronic pain.

   • Short-term goal(s): Complete an assessment of sleep and pain problems. If weight gain is secondary to medication, provide alternative treatment options.

   • Long-term goal(s): To be pain free, and able to get six hours (at least) of restorative sleep/night, and to maintain a desirable weight based on body mass index (BMI).

Step Four: Constructing the Treatment/Recovery Plan

TREATMENT/RECOVERY PLAN

Patient's Name: Joanne Mackey

Date of Birth: 2/15/1967

Medical Record #: XXX-XX-XXXX

Level of Care: Medically Supervised Inpatient Detoxification Unit

ICD-10 Codes	DSM-5 Diagnoses
F13.239	Benzodiazepine Withdrawal without perceptual disturbance with Benzodiazepine Use Disorder, Severe
F33.1	Major Depressive Disorder, recurrent episode with anxious distress

The individual's stated goal(s): "I want to be off all benzodiazepines. I don't want to be depressed or always feel so on edge."

1. **Problem/Need Statement:** Severe benzodiazepine use as evidenced by (AEB) increased use over time, inability to stop or decrease use, withdrawal symptoms when dosage is decreased, and engagement in high-risk behaviors to obtain adequate supplies to keep from experiencing withdrawal.

Long-Term Goal(s): To achieve a lasting abstinence from benzodiazepines.

Short-Term Goals/Objectives with target date:

To safely taper off benzodiazepine medication by 4/20/2014.

2. **Problem/Need Statement:** Depression and anxiety AEB a depressed mood, anhedonia, poor sleep, chronically low energy, low self-esteem, constant worry, frequent thoughts of death.

Long-Term Goal:

To experience symptoms of depression and anxiety no greater than a 2 out of a possible 10.

Short-Term Goals/Objectives with target date:

To experience a 50 percent or greater decrease in depressive and anxious symptoms using a 10-point self-rating scales and the Patient Health Questionnaire-9, by 4/20/2014.

3. **Problem/Need Statement:** Active medical issues: chronic insomnia, recent weight gain, and chronic pain.

Long-Term Goal(s):

1) To be pain free.

2) To be able to get six hours (at least) of restorative sleep/night.

3) To achieve and maintain a desirable weight based on body mass index (BMI).

Short-Term Goals/Objectives with target date:

1. Complete an assessment of sleep and refer for a sleep study, if necessary by 4/1/2014.

2. Complete an assessment of pain and address underlying causes by 4/1/2014.

3. If weight gain is secondary to medication, provide alternative treatment options by 4/1/2014.

Interventions					
Treatment Modality	**Specific Type**	**Frequency**	**Duration**	**Problem Number**	**Responsible Person(s)**
Medical and Psychiatric Assessments	History and physical, complete biopsychosocial assessment	Upon admission, and follow-up as needed	45–60 minutes	1,2,3	Physician/ APRN
Nursing Assessment	Nursing assessment	Upon admission, and as per the CIWA-B protocol* for benzodiazepine withdrawal	One hour on admission, and multiple times/ day as per the CIWA-B protocol	1,2,3	RN
Withdrawal Protocol	CIWA-B*	Based on symptom severity	Until patient has safely tapered off benzodiazepines, with a CIWA-B score of less than 5	1	RN, treating physician
Individual Therapy	Co-occurring focus CBT	3X/week	50 minutes for duration of admission	1,2	Ms. Mackey and primary therapist

Group Therapy	Substance abuse education	Daily	50 minutes for duration of admission	1,2	Ms. Mackey and group leader
	12-step groups	Daily	One hour for duration of admission	1	Ms. Mackey and AA/NA group leader volunteer.
	Relapse prevention	3X/week	One hour for duration of admission	1	Ms. Mackey and group leader
	Wellness and Recovery Group	Daily	One hour for duration of admission	1,2,3	Ms. Mackey and occupational therapist
	Mindfulness and Skills Training Group	Daily	One hour for duration of admission	1,2	Ms. Mackey and group leader
	Multiple family support and education group	1X/week	90 minutes	1,2	Ms. Mackey, her daughters, and group leader
Labs	Blood work/ electrocardiogram, other studies as indicated	Upon admission, and as needed	N/A	1,2,3	MD/APRN
Specimen Collection	Breath analysis/ urine drug screen	As ordered	For duration of admission	1,2	Clinician, or designee

Identification of strengths: Highly motivated to stop benzodiazepines. Has a strong work ethic, and finds current use of benzodiazepines to be in direct conflict with her moral beliefs. Identifies herself as a loving mother and finds meaning in her work as a nurse.

Peer/family/community supports to assist: Two adult daughters who have expressed an interest and willingness to be involved in treatment.

Barriers to treatment: Concerns that her medical leave benefit and health insurance will not adequately cover the necessary time and cost of treatment.

Staff/client-identified education/teaching needs: To understand the nature of her benzodiazepine use and how it may impact her overall mood and level of anxiety.

To develop healthier coping skills, including the use of psychosocial and possibly pharmacological treatments to more effectively manage her anxiety and depression.

Assessment of discharge needs/discharge planning: Ms. Mackey will have safely completed a taper from benzodiazepines and her mood and anxiety symptoms will be at a level where she will be able to continue her treatment at a less restrictive setting.

Completion of this treatment/recovery plan was a collaborative effort between the client and the following treatment team members:

SIGNATURES		Date/Time
Client:	*Joanne Mackey, RN*	3/18/2014 2pm
Physician:	*Louella Grant, MD*	3/18/2014 3:15pm
Primary Clinician:	*Gerald Singh, RN*	3/18/2014 2pm
Other Team Members	Blanche Crane, AT/OTR	3/18/2014 4pm
	George Pick, PCA	3/18/2014 4pm

* The CIWA-B (Clinical Institute Withdrawal Assessment for Benzodiazepines) is similar to the CIWA scale used to assess signs and symptoms of alcohol withdrawal (Chapter 16).

CHAPTER 11

Bipolar Disorder and Co-Occurring Substance Use Disorders

Overview

Genetics of Bipolar Disorder and the Development of Co-Occurring Substance Use Disorders

Diagnostic Dilemmas with Bipolar Disorder

Making the Diagnosis of Bipolar Disorder

Mood Charts

Screening and Assessment Tools for Bipolar Disorder

Psychosocial Treatment of Co-Occurring Bipolar and Substance Use Disorders

Pharmacotherapy

Case Study

OVERVIEW

Bipolar disorders (BD), characterized by disabling and sustained mood swings (mania, hypomania, and depression), are among the most common psychiatric disorders in people with substance use problems. The lifetime prevalence of non-tobacco substance use disorders in people with bipolar disorders range between 50–60 percent with many people having multiple substance use disorders. The three most common in bipolar disorder are alcohol, cannabis, and cocaine. This strong connection between substance use disorders and bipolar disorders is summed up well by Karen Kangas, Ed.D., a leader in the consumer advocacy movement, who observed, "I don't ask people with bipolar disorder if they ever used substances, instead I ask, 'What substances did you use?'"

The reasons why people with bipolar disorder are drawn to substances can include:

- Self-medication with alcohol, cannabis, and opioids to decrease symptoms of bipolar, such as using alcohol to combat the racing thoughts that make it impossible to sleep. Or using cannabis, alcohol, and other sedatives to obtain short-term relief from anxiety and depression. Some with bipolar disorder report they experience a paradoxical effect with cocaine, in that it helps them calm down (this is also seen in some individuals with ADHD).

- To maintain or increase the pleasurable (euphoric) experience of mania or hypomania with substances, such as cocaine, amphetamines, "bath salts" and other synthetic stimulants, and alcohol. The substance use can be symptomatic of the impulsivity seen when people are manic or hypomanic.
- To get high.
- To be social.
- To avoid withdrawal.

The clinical course and prognosis for people with co-occurring bipolar and substance use disorders are poorer than for people with just bipolar disorder. Findings for people with co-occurring bipolar disorder and substance use disorders include:

- Earlier onset of bipolar disorder
- More frequent mood episodes
- Longer time to recover between mood episodes
- Higher rates of rapid cycling (four or more mood episodes per year)
- More episodes with mixed features (presence of both depressed and manic/hypomanic symptoms at the same time)
- Greater frequency of psychotic symptoms (especially true for cannabis use)
- Higher rates of unemployment
- Higher rates of hospitalization
- Poorer response to medications, including lithium
- Higher rates of incarceration
- Higher rates of violence
- Lower treatment adherence
- Lower overall quality of life
- Roughly twice the number of suicide attempts
- Increased mortality from completed suicide and medical causes

GENETICS OF BIPOLAR DISORDER AND THE DEVELOPMENT OF CO-OCCURRING SUBSTANCE USE DISORDERS

Bipolar disorder (BD) has a strong genetic component with up to 80 percent of people with BD reporting a family history. This tendency, combined with genetic aspects of substance use disorders, place children of people with co-occurring bipolar disorder at tremendous risk.

When a strong familial component to BD is present, getting both a family psychiatric and substance use history is an important part of the assessment. This should also include family members the patient feels have severe mood episodes, with or without substance problems, that might never have been diagnosed.

Substance use disorders develop early in the course of bipolar disorder and peak between the ages of 14 and 20. In some cases individuals are able to identify mood episodes that preceded their substance use disorder; for others it appears the substance use disorder came first. Regardless, the earlier the onset of the bipolar disorder and the co-occurring substance use disorder, the worse the prognosis.

Early identification and intervention for children at risk for bipolar disorder, especially children of people with co-occurring BD and SUD, may decrease the likelihood that they will develop substance use problems and avoid the related worsening of their bipolar disorder.

DIAGNOSTIC DILEMMAS WITH BIPOLAR DISORDER

Bipolar disorders are among the most missed and misdiagnosed disorders in psychiatry. On average people do not receive an accurate diagnosis until they have had symptoms for a decade or more. Missed and misdiagnoses are compounded when co-occurring substance use disorders cloud the diagnostic picture, as do other comorbid psychiatric disorders, which run high (lifetime rates of 42%) in people with bipolar. Common co-occurring mental disorders include the anxiety disorders, such as generalized anxiety disorder, panic disorder, PTSD, and ADHD. There is also significant comorbidity with personality disorders, including borderline and antisocial.

People with bipolar disorder more commonly seek treatment when they are in a depressed phase of the illness, often with mixed features and intense anxiety and irritability. They may not consider their past episodes of mania or hypomania as abnormal, or they may not be flagged in the evaluation process. Many people with bipolar disorder view the increased energy, diminished need for sleep, and productivity that accompany hypomanic episodes as times they felt well.

When manic, people with bipolar disorder often have psychotic symptoms, and typically believe there is nothing wrong with them (anosognosia). They will not be interested in treatment, and only come to the attention of clinicians if their behavior is so extreme, risk taking, or potentially dangerous that they get brought in by family, friends, or police, for an emergency evaluation, and possibly hospitalization, or when they are arrested.

When people are manic, intoxicated, or in a withdrawal state, it's difficult to differentiate which symptoms are related to the substance use disorder and which are due to an underlying mental illness.

- Is the irritability and aggressiveness part of a hypomania with mixed features, or is it opioid withdrawal?
- Is the pressured speech and risk-taking behavior mania or intoxication with cocaine, bath salts, or other stimulants?

So too, if multiple psychiatric disorders are present, accurately teasing them apart is challenging.

- Is the hyperactivity from bipolar disorder or ADHD? Or both?
- Are the frequent mood swings evidence of a rapid-cycling bipolar or are they more consistent with borderline personality disorder, where a person's mood state can change rapidly and dramatically?

As a result of the at-times-confusing clinical picture, people with bipolar disorder are at great risk for receiving inaccurate diagnoses, unipolar depression (major depressive disorder) being the most frequent. The risk here is that certain treatments for unipolar depression, such as antidepressant medication, can worsen the symptoms of bipolar disorder through increased irritability and manic switching, which can include psychotic symptoms and increased frequency of mood episodes.

MAKING THE DIAGNOSIS OF BIPOLAR DISORDER

In order to accurately diagnose bipolar disorders, taking a careful history is crucial. What you need to find out is, over the course of this person's life, have they ever had a manic or hypomanic episode?

- **Manic episodes:** A period of sustained elevated or irritable mood that lasts at least one week, or any length if hospitalized. Untreated, manic episodes can last months, or in some cases years. When manic, individuals may not realize anything is wrong and in fact euphoria (feeling wonderful) can be among the symptoms. Along with this elevation in mood, mania can include:

  o Seemingly limitless energy.

  o Rapid/pressured speech and thought. This can be so extreme that it's impossible to carry on a conversation.

  o Tangential and circumstantial speech (thought) patterns. Here, it's hard to follow the person's train of thought as it moves rapidly from topic to topic. When asked to answer a question, they may start on topic, but quickly wander off to where the original question is never answered.

  o Decreased sleep, without complaints of tiredness.

  o Inflated sense of importance, or grandiosity. In mania, this state can become delusional to where the person believes he/she is an important figure, such as a prophet, Jesus, or the devil. They may believe they possess special powers and abilities (mind reading, being a wizard or prophet, etc.).

  o Increased goal-directed activity, such as writing a novel in three days, painting nonstop, or doing some other activity in a driven and relentless fashion. This behavior is often accompanied by tremendous enthusiasm, typically in excess of what is normal, for the activity.

  o Shifting enthusiasms and easy distractibility. Concentration may be impaired.

  o Risk taking and/or impulsive and unwise behaviors, including drugs, random sex, gambling, excessive shopping, maxing out credit cards, high-risk online investing, and spending retirement accounts, to give a few examples.

  o Irritability. When people are manic, they often don't take well to being questioned or challenged.

- **Hypomanic episodes:** Similar to mania, hypomanic episodes are less intense, but otherwise include the same symptoms (nondelusional grandiosity, rapid speech, racing thoughts, etc.). Where mania can include psychotic symptoms, such as delusions and even hallucinations, they are never present in hypomania. In the DSM-5, the duration criterion for a hypomanic episode is at least four days.

- **Depressed episodes:** In the DSM-5, depressed episodes in bipolar disorder are of at least two weeks' duration and include at least five of nine symptoms. One of these must be either a sustained depressed mood and/or persistent loss of interest or pleasure (anhedonia). Other symptoms include disturbances in sleep and appetite, guilt and feelings of worthlessness, poor concentration, low energy, apparent agitation or diminished movement, and thoughts of death and suicidality (thoughts, to actual attempts). Not included in the DSM-5 is the important predictor for suicide—hopelessness.

- **Mixed features:** A significant change between the DSM-IV-TR and the DSM-5 is the elimination of mixed episodes. In the current diagnostic manual both depressive disorders and bipolar disorders can have mixed features as a specifier. For instance, someone who is clinically depressed, but also is experiencing racing thoughts, distractibility, diminished sleep without complaining of feeling tired could be classified as having a depressed episode with mixed features.

In assessing for the presence of a bipolar disorder in someone who is currently depressed, it is useful to focus on their specific symptoms of depression, as there can be differences between a typical "unipolar" depression (people who have never had a manic or hypomanic episode) and what is sometimes considered an "atypical" depression, which is more associated with bipolar disorders. Symptoms in bipolar depressions are more likely to include:

- Excessive sleepiness and spending more time in bed (as opposed to insomnia and trouble sleeping)

- Constant feelings of tiredness, low energy; feeling heavy or weighted down

- Increased appetite (as opposed to the loss of appetite seen in more unipolar depressions)

- The presence of mixed features (racing thoughts, inability to concentrate, pressured speech, etc.)

- Anxiety

- Agitation

- Irritability

MOOD CHARTS

Having the client complete a mood chart where they recollect all significant mood episodes over the course of their lifetime can aid in diagnosis. Even though it is common for a first major mood episode (depressed, manic, or hypomanic) to occur in the setting of a major life stress, such as going into the military, going off to school, being pregnant, and so on, future mood episodes in bipolar disorder may not correlate to any identifiable stress.

In women, it is important to ask about mood episodes related to pregnancy, especially in the third trimester and postpartum. Women with bipolar disorder are at extremely high risk for severe mood episodes during these periods. Although not diagnostic on its own, the history of a peripartum depression or other mood episode should raise suspicion for the presence of a bipolar disorder.

MOOD CHART

Instructions: Please write down times in your life where you felt either moderately or severely depressed, as well as any periods where you had tremendous energy (were hyper). Include any significant events or stresses that were going on at this time, and whether you were using any substances, including alcohol. Use a 10-point scale for both periods of depressed mood and being hyper, with 10 being the most depressed or most hyper and 0 being not at all depressed or hyper. Write in your age on the bottom line (see sample) starting at the point you believe you first had a serious problem with your mood.

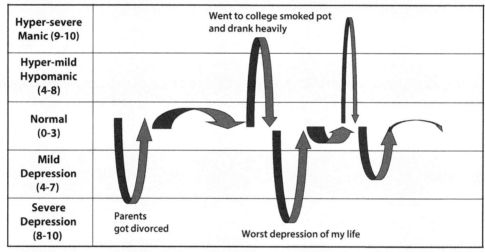

Hyper-severe Manic (9-10)	Went to college smoked pot and drank heavily
Hyper-mild Hypomanic (4-8)	
Normal (0-3)	
Mild Depression (4-7)	
Severe Depression (8-10)	Parents got divorced Worst depression of my life

12 13 14 15 16 17 18 19 20 21 22 23 24 25 26 27 28 29
Age (years)

Hyper-severe Manic (9-10)	
Hyper-mild Hypomanic (4-8)	
Normal (0-3)	
Mild Depression (4-7)	
Severe Depression (8-10)	

Age (years)

Screening and Assessment Tools for Bipolar Disorder

Screening tools and instruments that help quantify the severity of mood and behavioral symptoms in bipolar disorder can be useful adjuncts to clinical assessment and to measuring treatment progress. In particular, instruments that flesh out prior episodes of mania or hypomania can aid in arriving at an accurate diagnosis.

Frequently used tools for depressed episodes include:

- **The Beck Depression Inventory:** This 21-item patient-completed questionnaire uses severity ratings for symptoms of depression and is useful in terms of not only putting a number on the patient's current level of depression, but can be administered throughout treatment to chart progress.

- **The Hamilton Depression Scale (Ham-D):** Clinicians complete this 21-item tool (longer and shorter versions are available) that is widely used in studies of depression and can help track response to treatment. It takes approximately 20 minutes to complete.

- **The Patient Health Questionnaire 9:** This easily completed self-report screening tool corresponds to the symptoms of depression in the DSM. A copy is included on page 143.

Tools to assess mania and hypomania include:

- **The Young Mania Rating Scale:** This 11-item clinician-administered tool is used to evaluate the presence of current symptoms of mania or hypomania. It can be repeated to show changes in symptoms.

- **The Mood Disorder Questionnaire (MDQ):** The MDQ is the most widely used screening tool to assess the presence of prior mania or hypomania. Completed by the client, the MDQ, when combined with a careful history and clinical assessment, can aid in making an accurate diagnosis of bipolar disorder. When using the MDQ, it is important to spend time with a client to review his or her responses and to clarify the following:

  o How long did your symptoms last? Do their endorsed symptoms meet the DSM-5 duration for a manic (at least one week or any length of time if the symptoms are so severe the person requires hospitalization) or hypomanic (at least four consecutive days) episode?

  o Did these symptoms only occur in the setting of drug or alcohol use, or did they occur even when drugs and/or alcohol weren't involved?

  o Are the symptoms of hyperactivity, high energy, and poor concentration due to bipolar disorder, or are they more sustained and in keeping with possible attention-deficit/hyperactivity disorder? Conversely, do their shifting moods last on the order of hours, which might be more consistent with a personality disorder, such as borderline personality disorder?

Remember, a positive screening test is not diagnostic. It should however alert the clinician to take a thorough history and fully assess for the presence of a bipolar disorder.

THE MOOD DISORDER QUESTIONNAIRE (MDQ)

Instructions: Please answer each question as best you can.

1. **Has there ever been a period of time when you were not your usual self and…**

Place a check in each appropriate box	Yes	No
… you felt so good or so hyper that other people thought you were not your normal self or you were so hyper that you got into trouble?		
… you were so irritable that you shouted at people or started fights or arguments?		
… you felt much more self-confident than usual?		
… you got much less sleep than usual and found you didn't really miss it?		
… you were much more talkative or spoke much faster than usual?		
… thoughts raced through your head or you couldn't slow your mind down?		
… you were so easily distracted by things around you that you had trouble concentrating or staying on track?		
… you had more energy than usual?		
… you were much more active or did many more things than usual?		
… you were much more social or outgoing than usual, for example, you telephoned friends in the middle of the night?		
… you were much more interested in sex than usual?		
… you did things that were unusual for you or that other people might have thought excessive, foolish, or risky?		
… spending money got you or your family into trouble?		

2. If you checked YES to more than one of the above, have several of these ever happened during the same period of time? (circle one) Yes   No

3. How much of a problem did any of these cause you—like being unable to work; having family, money, or legal troubles; getting into arguments or fights? (Circle one response)

No Problem   Minor Problem   Moderate Problem   Serious Problem

4. Have any of your blood relatives (i.e., children, siblings, parents, grandparents, aunts, and uncles) had manic-depressive illness or bipolar disorder? (circle one) Yes   No

5. Has a health professional ever told you that you have manic-depressive illness or bipolar disorder? (circle one) Yes   No

Scoring the MDQ

The screen is considered "positive" if:

1. There are seven or more "yes" items in question number 1

And

2. "Yes" to question number 2.

And

3. "Moderate" or "Serious" to question number 3.

Psychosocial Treatment of Co-Occurring Bipolar Disorder and Substance Use Disorders

Limited studies look specifically at the treatment of co-occurring substance use and bipolar disorder. However, those studies that have been done, combined with common sense and clinical experience, show that combined/integrated treatments have better clinical outcomes than attempting to address one issue, treat it until it's resolved, and then move on to the next (sequential).

That said, there will be a prioritization based on a thorough clinical assessment, along with the patient's specific needs and goals. Where acute safety issues (withdrawal states, suicidality, and out-of-control behaviors that can be associated with manic and depressed states) are present, they will need to be immediately managed. Similarly, major social concerns that interfere with treatment (homelessness, unsafe housing, legal difficulties, custody, severe financial problems, lack of transportation, etc.) will need to be addressed early in treatment.

An integrated clinical approach for bipolar disorder and SUDs will include the following:

1. A thorough clinical assessment, as outlined in Chapters 2–4, and expanded in this chapter (use of screening tools, a careful history of mood episodes, and possibly the completion of a mood chart).

2. Patient education about both the substance use and bipolar disorder. This can be incorporated into both individual sessions and group therapies. Specific topics for bipolar that need to be covered include:

   • An overall education about bipolar disorder, geared to the education level and interest of the specific person. A diagnosis of bipolar disorder can be scary. Helping someone demystify the illness gives that person a greater sense of control and of being able to manage the illness. Steering clients to useful websites, pamphlets, and books is a good way to start. (See Resources and References for this chapter).

   • Medication education: Where medications are typically used in the treatment of bipolar disorder, it is critical that the person understand what each medication does, its risks, potential side effect and adverse reactions, and its hoped-for benefits.

   • Encourage the use of peer supports. These can be local groups or peer-run programs where they get a firsthand look at other people with bipolar disorder, who are successfully managing their illness and their lives. Having peers with bipolar disorder, often with a history of co-occurring substance use problems, who can share their experience, can be powerful and inspiring.

• Education around the importance of adequate restorative sleep. For many with bipolar disorder, changes in sleep patterns may be the first—and possibly only—warning sign of an impending mood episode: when manic or hypomanic sleep is diminished, and when depressed sleep and time spent in bed increases. Learning to regulate sleep can be one of the most effective strategies to prevent or decrease mood episodes. For some individuals, having discretion over whether or not to take a sedating medication if they are having difficulty sleeping can be effective.

• Help clients to identify their specific warning signs of an impending mood episode. In the early or prodromal stages of a mood episode, it is often possible to take action that can lessen the overall severity of the mood episode or head it off entirely. In addition to changes in sleep patterns, other warning signs can include:

  o Noticeable changes in mood. Feeling "too happy," depressed, anxious, or irritable.

  o Changes in thought and speech patterns. Becoming wired or racy.

  o Behavioral changes. This is often quite specific to the individual and can include shopping sprees they can't afford, impulsive decision making at home or work, and preoccupation with specific activities.

• The importance of daily routines in helping to regulate mood. Evidence indicates that sticking to a regular routine can decrease the frequency of mood episodes. On the flip side, frequent changes in schedule, such as rotating shift work, can contribute to mood destabilization. Probably most important, is the establishment of a regular bedtime and time of awakening.

• Education around the positive benefits of healthy habits (wellness) as part of a person's daily routine.

  o This includes teaching on nutrition and exercise (especially important when people are on medications that can cause weight gain and metabolic syndrome).

  o The importance of clean and sober supports in a person's life, which for some will involve significant changes in who they associate with.

• Education around specific linkages between substance use and bipolar disorder. Although clients may perceive real benefits from the use of cannabis, alcohol, and other substances, these positive effects are short term. The evidence is clear that people with bipolar disorder who use substances have worse outcomes (i.e., less response to medication, more frequent hospitalizations, more mood episodes, and greater incidence of suicide attempts).

3. Include other important supports, such as family or close friends, in treatment. This is to both provide education and to help increase the level of support for the person with bipolar disorder. These educational efforts could include directing family and friends to organizations, such as the National Alliance on Mental Illness (NAMI) at www.nami.org, which offer both support groups, as well as thoughtful and up-to-date trainings for family and peers.

4. Evidence-based psychotherapies for bipolar disorder:

• Integrated group therapy (IGT). Developed by Roger Weiss, MD, IGT is a cognitive-behavioral group therapy, specifically designed for people with co-occurring substance use and bipolar disorders. It is a manualized, 12-session therapy (was also studied in a longer

20-session format) used in conjunction with medication. It addresses both disorders simultaneously (i.e., "bipolar substance abuse"). Common features of both disorders are stressed. Thoughts and behaviors that aid recovery are encouraged, and conversely those that increase the risk of relapse with substance use or into a mood episode are discouraged. Connections between the two disorders are highlighted and clients learn how substance use worsens their bipolar symptoms and how going off their medications can lead to relapses with both mood episodes and substance use.

- Family-focused treatment (FFT). Developed by David J. Miklowitz and Michael J. Goldstein, FFT is a manual-driven, 21-session therapy that has both the person with bipolar and that person's family meet together. The emphasis is on education about bipolar disorder and on how to resolve family conflict. Family members are taught how to recognize symptoms of impending mood episodes, and problem-solving techniques are stressed. FFT is associated with decreased rate of relapse with mood episodes and improved family communication and problem solving.

- Interpersonal and social rhythm therapy (IPSRT). Developed by Ellen Frank, Ph.D., IPSRT helps people with bipolar disorder stabilize their mood through the establishment of healthy and regular routines and actively decreasing interpersonal conflict. It incorporates education around bipolar and helps the individual learn techniques to decrease conflict.

5. Other psychotherapies: A number of therapies can be adapted to incorporate both issues relevant to substance use and bipolar disorder. They include cognitive behavioral therapy (CBT), rational-emotive behavior therapy (REBT), dialectic behavior therapy (DBT), and others. Motivational interviewing techniques, can be incorporated into helping people change problem behaviors related to the substance use and the bipolar disorder, such as poor adherence to a medication regimen and continued problem substance use.

PHARMACOTHERAPY

Individuals with bipolar disorder should be offered initial, and ongoing, assessment for medication. This regimen will likely include the use of mood stabilizers, as well as medications to assist with cravings and other comorbid psychiatric disorders and symptoms.

There is a paucity of studies looking at specific medications in individuals who have both bipolar disorder and substance use disorders. Most drug studies exclude subjects with co-occurring disorders in an attempt to decrease confounding variables. In general, those studies that have looked at specific mood stabilizers in people with co-occurring SUDs and BD show a positive effect in both directions; that is, if you treat the bipolar disorder, the substance use disorder improves, and that when people are abstinent from substances their bipolar symptoms improve as well.

The primary goal for medication in bipolar disorder is to achieve mood stabilization, which means the person does not experience episodes of depression, mania, and/or hypomania. Common secondary targets for medication will include sleep disturbances (insomnia, hypersomnia, sleep apnea), anxiety, and irritability.

Many effective pharmacologic treatments are available for the symptoms of mania and hypomania. When people are manic, tranquilizers, often combined with mood stabilizers, are used to decrease the symptoms of excitement, agitation, and psychosis. However, far fewer medication options have been FDA approved for the treatment of the depressions associated with bipolar disorder. Antidepressants, which are used in unipolar depression and many of the anxiety disorders, are not first- or second-line treatments for bipolar depression, because they can be associated with triggering mania and hypomania, and may worsen the overall frequency and severity of mood episodes (rapid cycling).

Medications selected need to take into account the person's total presentation. If someone has a history of overusing/abusing anxiolytic medications, such as the benzodiazepines (clonazepam/Klonopin, diazepam/Valium, alprazolam/Xanax, etc.), or they are on opioid-replacement therapy (buprenorphine or methadone), these medications cannot be safely used. Benzodiazepines should also be avoided if someone is actively abusing alcohol, because the synergistic effects can lead to increased impulsivity, oversedation, and in extreme instances, respiratory depression and death. If someone is overweight, or is concerned about medications that can cause significant weight gain and metabolic syndrome, this will limit available options.

Medications for bipolar disorder include mood stabilizers (lithium, lamotrigine/Lamictal, valproate/Depakote), which are often augmented with tranquilizers/neuroleptics. Some of these, atypical neuroleptics (Quetiapine/Seroquel, Aripiprazole/Abilify, Ziprasidone/Geodon), have in recent years also received FDA approval as mood stabilizers, both as augmenting agents to lithium and valproate, but also as monotherapy. However, long-term studies demonstrating their effectiveness in preventing or diminishing the severity of mood episodes, especially when used as monotherapy, have not yet been conducted.

Patient education, both verbal and written (patient information sheets specific to the medication) should be provided for all medications. Special attention should be paid when using lithium, so that the patient is aware of expected side effects, as well as more dire—and potentially life-threatening—signs of lithium toxicity (worsening tremor, slurred speech, unsteady gate, nausea and vomiting, confusion).

When using lamotrigine/Lamictal, which involves a slow titration (up to a couple months), clients need to be alert to the signs of developing a serious, potentially fatal, allergic reaction, which takes the form of a severe rash and sores, Steven Johnson syndrome. If patients complain, or notice sores in their nose or mouth, or develop a significant rash on the trunk, thighs, and extremities, this warrants an emergency evaluation, and if the rash is thought to be caused by the medication it should be discontinued.

The atypical antipsychotics, while useful, carry significant risk for the development of metabolic syndrome, which includes substantial weight gain, elevations in lipids (cholesterol, triglycerides), and the development of type II diabetes, as well as hypertension and coronary artery disease. Some of these agents, such as olanzapine/Zyprexa, can be associated with weight gain on the order of one pound per week. Others such as risperidone/Risperdal and quetiapine/Seroquel have weight gain averaging half a pound per week. To date, the only atypical that appears not to be associated with significant weight gain is ziprasidone/Geodon.

Therefore, when using these medications, and any agent that is associated with significant weight gain, attention to a person's baseline health status, as well as changes in weight and laboratory values need to be included in the treatment. Medication education should discuss the risk for metabolic syndrome, combined with pragmatic nutritional counseling about portion control, healthy food choices, and getting adequate daily exercise. Patients should be weighed at regular intervals. Standard practice is to then calculate the body mass index (BMI), a number arrived at by dividing a person's weight by their height (there are a number of free smart phone and computer applications for this, including one through the National Institute of Health at http://www.nhlbi.nih.gov/guidelines/obesity/BMI/bmicalc.htm.)

Body Mass Index	
Underweight	Less than 18.5
Average	18.5–24.9
Overweight	25–29.9
Obese	30 or greater

The older antipsychotic medications, such as haloperidol/Haldol are commonly used in emergency room and inpatient settings when rapid tranquilization of an agitated mania is required, often in combination with a benzodiazepine, such as lorazepam/Ativan. The long-term use of this older group of antipsychotics is less common in maintenance therapy due to concerns of a potentially irreversible movement disorder, tardive dyskinesia (TD).

Mood-Stabilizing Medications			
Name	FDA-Approved Indications	Major Side Effects/ Adverse Reactions	Monitoring
Lithium	• Mania and maintenance treatment of bipolar disorder	• Weight gain, increased thirst, diarrhea, tremor, psoriasis • Dangerous/life-threatening toxicity if levels are too high • Can damage the thyroid gland and kidneys • Associated with increased rates of cardiac birth defects	• Lithium level • Renal function • Thyroid function tests • Weight/BMI
Lamotrigine/ Lamictal	• Bipolar I disorder in patients over age 18 • Maintenance treatment.	• Risk of a dangerous allergy/rash (Steven Johnson Syndrome) • Some concern about subtle birth defects	• Liver function tests
Valproic Acid/ Depakote	• Treatment of acute mania • Not FDA-approved as a mood stabilizer in the United States	• Weight gain, metabolic syndrome, sedation, mental sluggishness, hair loss, tremor • Birth defects/should be avoided in pregnant women, or women likely to become pregnant	• Liver function tests • Weight/BMI • Lipids Blood sugar • HgA1C
Carbamazepine/ Tegretol	• Not FDA-approved in the United States as a mood stabilizer	• Agranulocytosis (loss of white blood cell production)	• CBC Liver function tests

Second-Generation Tranquilizers/Neuroleptics/Antipsychotic Medications			
Name	FDA Indications	Major Side Effects and Adverse Reactions	Monitoring Requirements
Aripiprazole/ Abilify	• Schizophrenia (adults and adolescents) • Acute mania and mixed* episodes in bipolar I (ages 10 and up) • Maintenance treatment in bipolar I, both as monotherapy and adjunct with lithium or valproic acid (adults) • Adjunctive treatment in major depressive disorder	• Weight gain, metabolic syndrome	• Weight/BMI • Lipids Blood sugar • HgA1C
Asenapine/ Saphris	• Schizophrenia (adults) • Acute mania or mixed* episodes in bipolar I (adults)	• Weight gain, metabolic syndrome	• Weight/BMI • Lipids Blood sugar • HgA1C
**Clozapine/ Clozaryl	• Treatment-resistant schizophrenia • Reducing the risk of suicide in people with schizophrenia or schizoaffective disorder	• Agranulocytosis • Weight gain, metabolic syndrome • Hypotension	• Weekly, then biweekly, and then monthly • CBC Weight/BMI • Lipids Blood sugar • HgA1C
Iloperadone/ Fanapt	Schizophrenia (adults)	• Weight gain, metabolic syndrome	• Weight/BMI • Lipids Blood sugar • HgA1C
Lurasidone/ Latuda	• Schizophrenia • Depression associated with bipolar I	• Weight gain, metabolic syndrome • Sedation • Restlessness	• Weight/BMI • Lipids Blood sugar • HgA1C
Olanzapine/ Zyprexa	• Schizophrenia (ages 13 and up) • Bipolar I (both as monotherapy and adjunct to lithium or valproic acid) • Combined with fluoxetine/ Prozac for the treatment of depression associated with bipolar I	• Weight gain, metabolic syndrome • Sedation	• Weight/BMI • Lipids Blood sugar • HgA1C

Paliperidone/ Invega	• Schizophrenia (adult) • Schizoaffective disorder (ages 12–17) as monotherapy and adjunct to mood stabilizers and/or antidepressants	• Weight gain, metabolic syndrome	• Weight/BMI • Lipids Blood sugar • HgA1C
Quetiapine/ Seroquel	• Schizophrenia • Bipolar I disorder, mania and mixed* • Bipolar disorder depressive episodes • Adjunctive therapy in major depressive disorder	• Weight gain, metabolic syndrome • Sedation	• Weight/BMI • Lipids Blood sugar • HgA1C
Risperidone/ Risperdal	• Schizophrenia • Bipolar Mania • Irritability associated with Autistic Disorder (Pediatric indication)	• Weight gain, metabolic syndrome	• Weight/BMI • Lipids Blood sugar • HgA1C
Ziprasidone/ Geodon	• Schizophrenia (adults) • Bipolar I disorder acute mania or mixed* monotherapy (adults) • Adjunctive maintenance treatment with lithium or valproate (adults)	• Cardiac conduction problems, especially when combined with other medications	• Weight/BMI • Lipids Blood sugar • HgA1C

*Mixed episodes are not included in the DMS-5. Now noted with the specifier—mixed features.
**Clozapine is infrequently used in bipolar disorder due to the risks associated with this medication.

CASE STUDY: MELANIE HARDWICK

Melanie Hardwick, a 38-year-old, twice-divorced mother of two (sons, ages 16 and 18), is self-referred for treatment of an alcohol problem. She has been drinking heavily since she was a teenager, and reports that this has escalated over the past few years. "I need to stop, I know it's killing me. I went to my doctor and he says my liver has been damaged by the drinking. My supervisor at work has also made comments, and I think I'm in jeopardy of losing my job if I don't get help."

Her current alcohol consumption is a pint to a fifth of hard liquor daily. She has not gone more than three days in the past five years without a drink. She did drink last night, but has not had any alcohol this morning. She gets shaky in the morning, and on occasion has begun drinking early in the day to steady her nerves. She has never had an alcohol withdrawal seizure or symptoms of delirium tremens or withdrawal hallucinosis.

In addition to problems with alcohol she says she has always struggled with intense and severe mood swings, as well as anxiety. In completing the mood chart, she identifies a first period of sustained depression when she was 14. She thinks it was before she started to use alcohol. Over the course of her life she's had over six clinical depressions, including a severe postpartum episode following the birth of her second son. She describes this period as the lowest in her life. "I felt like the worst mother on the face of the planet, I didn't want to go near my baby. My mother said the same thing happened to her with one of her pregnancies." On the mood disorder questionnaire, she endorses nine symptoms of prior episodes of sustained and euphoric mood, although admits these incidents are rare. She currently scores a 17 on the Patient Health Questionnaire-9 (moderately severe). She believes the longest period of expansive and euphoric mood lasted "a few weeks" and was followed by a severe depression that lasted several months. She describes periods where she feels well and is able to accomplish a tremendous amount at home and work, but adds, "Usually I snap at everyone. I have a very short temper." She describes her current mood as anxious, depressed, and irritable. Her racing and anxious thoughts make it difficult for her to fall asleep. "It's one of the things booze does for me…it knocks me out."

In the past she has tried multiple medications for depression and anxiety. She reports that the antidepressants "make me worse. If you think I'm irritable now, you should see what I was like on Prozac." She has never been hospitalized for psychiatric or substance use reasons. She has had thought of suicide in the past, but has never made an attempt. She denies any current thoughts of suicide. She has never experienced delusions or hallucinations.

Her family psychiatric history includes her mother who has similar problems with her mood and was a heavy drinker in the past. Her oldest son is currently in counseling and was arrested last year for possession of marijuana. He has been on medication for ADHD and his current psychiatrist thinks he may have a bipolar disorder.

Her medical history includes two vaginal deliveries and a tubal ligation following her second child. She has no allergies and, other than the increased liver enzymes, has no active medical problems.

She describes her childhood as being a difficult one, where her mother's mood seriously affected both her and her two younger sisters. "Mom would fly into rages, and you knew to just stay out of her way when she was drinking." Her father left home when she was 8 years old, although her parents never divorced.

Melanie completed high school and got an associate's degree in accounting. She works doing tax preparation for a major accounting chain and has been with them for three years. She adds that it is the longest she's been able to hold a job; she often quits or is fired when she becomes too depressed to go to work and/or function on the job. She describes her first marriage as being to an alcoholic—"It's like I married my mother." It lasted four years and he is the father of her children. She states her second marriage ended on account of her drinking and having an affair with a man she met online. She admits that it was not the only occasion she had sex with relative strangers, and that this, along with "out-of-control shopping," is something she does during periods when she feels hyper.

On physical exam, she is found to be mildly tremulous (hands shake and tongue fasciculations), has a mildly elevated blood pressure of 140/90, with an elevated heart rate of 102. Despite not having had any alcohol this morning her breathalyzer test is slightly positive. Her dipped urine drug screen is negative. Her CIWA (Clinical Institute Withdrawal Assessment for Alcohol) score is 4 (see Chapter 16). Her body mass index is 22. Her Complete Blood Count shows a folate deficiency anemia, likely secondary to prolonged alcohol use.

Step One: Level of Care Determination

In this case study the most immediate, and potentially dangerous, concern is the presence of mild alcohol withdrawal symptoms. She will require a medically supervised detoxification from alcohol. Because she has no history of serious withdrawal syndromes or other pressing safety concerns (not suicidal, or engaged in high-risk activities) and her CIWA score is low, a range of appropriate levels of care is possible.

Her alcohol detoxification could be managed on an outpatient basis, such as in a co-occurring PHP or IOP equipped to manage an ambulatory detoxification. Depending on resources and her preference, this could also be managed with a brief inpatient detoxification admission followed by referral to either a residential co-occurring rehabilitation program or outpatient co-occurring program, such as an intensive outpatient program.

Step Two: Constructing the Problem/Need List

The pertinent findings (data) from the case study can be divided into three broad categories: substance use (alcohol and withdrawal), mental health, and medical. As is apparent, some information fits in multiple categories.

Although some uncertainty remains as to the psychiatric diagnosis, her history, family history, and current presentation provide adequate evidence to make a diagnosis of bipolar II disorder with mixed and anxious features. (She describes periods of hypomania, but not mania. Should there have been a single manic episode the diagnosis would then be bipolar I.) It would not be wrong to make a less definitive diagnosis, such as unspecified bipolar disorder and then clarify when she is no longer in alcohol withdrawal.

Substance Use	Mental Health (Bipolar II Disorder)	Medical
Drinking heavily since a teen	Intense mood swings	Elevated liver enzymes
Escalating use	Anxiety	Tubal ligation
Evidence of liver damage	Six episodes of clinical depression	Signs of alcohol withdrawal: shakes, elevated pulse and blood pressure
Family history of alcohol use disorder(s)	Postpartum depression	Negative urine toxicology screen
Morning drinking	Scores 9 symptoms on the mood disorder questionnaire related to periods of mania/hypomania, longest lasting a few weeks	Slightly positive breathalyzer
Gets the shakes	Scores 17 on the PHQ-9 (moderately severe depression)	CIWA score of 4
No history of seizures or DTs	Family history of postpartum depression	BMI 22 (normal range)
Never been in a substance abuse program or detox	Drinks to self-medicate and put herself to sleep	Folate deficient anemia likely secondary to alcohol

(Continued)

(Continued)

Job in jeopardy on account of drinking	Racing thoughts	
	Multiple trials of antidepressants, which made her worse	
Substance Use	**Mental Health (Bipolar II Disorder)**	**Medical**
	Son with cannabis use disorder, ADHD, and possible bipolar disorder	
	Past suicidal thinking but no attempts, not currently suicidal	
	Never hospitalized	
	Irritable	
	Has lost or quit jobs on account of her mood episodes	

Problem/Need list

1. **Alcohol withdrawal and severe alcohol use and dependence** AEB daily drinking, early morning drinking, withdrawal symptoms, unsuccessful attempts to cut down, folate deficiency anemia, and elevated liver enzymes from drinking.
2. **Recurrent and severe mood problems** AEB history of at least six episodes of depression, postpartum depression, and current depressed and anxious symptoms with mixed features. Current PHQ-9 score of 17.
3. **Active medical issues secondary to alcohol use and withdrawal** AEB elevated blood pressure and pulse, CIWA score of 4, folate-deficiency anemia, elevated liver enzymes, and tremulousness.

Step Three: Establishing the Initial Goals/Objectives for Treatment

In this case, the presence of alcohol withdrawal is the most-pressing issue and needs to be immediately, and appropriately, addressed.

1. **Alcohol withdrawal and severe alcohol use and dependence**
   - Short-term goal(s):
     1) Patient will be safely detoxified from alcohol, AEB a CIWA score of 0 and normal vital signs, following the completion of a detox protocol.
     2) Client will achieve early abstinence (three months) from alcohol, AEB negative breathalyzer, self-report, and negative alcohol metabolites in her urine.
   - Long-term goal(s): The client will achieve sustained (greater than one year) abstinence from alcohol, AEB self-report, negative breathalyzer, and negative alcohol metabolites.

2. **Recurrent and severe mood problems**

   • Short-term goal(s): Over four weeks, the client will experience at least a 50 percent reduction in her depressive and anxious symptoms as measured using the PHQ-9, self-report, and a 10-point anxiety scale.

   • Long-term goal(s): The client will be free from major mood episodes, AEB self-report, clinical impression, and the use of rating scales for depression and anxiety.

3. **Active medical issues secondary to alcohol use and withdrawal**

   • Short-term goal(s):

   1) See problem #1, safe and complete treatment of alcohol withdrawal.

   2) Resolution of abnormal liver function tests, AEB normal values on a repeat draw in four weeks.

   3) Reassessment of blood pressure and pulse following completion of the detox protocol. If still elevated, refer for further medical follow-up.

   • Long-term goal(s): The folate deficiency anemia will resolve AEB normal values on a repeat CBC in 3–6 months.

Step Four: Constructing the Treatment/Recovery Plan

In this case, the initial level of care needs to be able to provide a safe alcohol detoxification. Where this client's symptoms of withdrawal are mild, the least-restrictive option, if available in her community and with her insurance, would be a co-occurring PHP. However, should her symptoms worsen or she be unable to achieve abstinence, this approach would need reevaluation and a higher/inpatient level of care pursued.

TREATMENT/RECOVERY PLAN

Patient's Name: Melanie Hardwick

Date of Birth: 8/12/1976

Medical Record #: XXX-XX-XXXX

Level of Care: Co-occurring PHP

ICD-10 Codes	DSM-5 Diagnoses
F10.239	Alcohol withdrawal with severe alcohol use disorder
F31.81	Bipolar II Disorder with anxious distress and mixed features
Z56.9	Other problems related to employment

The individual's stated goal(s): "To stop drinking and to feel happy. To be someone my sons can be proud to call their mother. To keep my job."

1. **Problem/Need Statement: Alcohol withdrawal and severe alcohol use and dependence** AEB daily drinking, early morning drinking, withdrawal symptoms, unsuccessful attempts to cut down and elevated liver enzymes, and folate-deficiency anemia.

Long-Term Goal: The client will achieve sustained (greater than six months) abstinence from alcohol, AEB self-report, negative breathalyzer, and negative alcohol metabolites.

Short-Term Goals/Objectives with target dates:

1) Patient will be safely detoxified from alcohol, AEB a CIWA score of 0 and normal vital signs, following the completion of a detox protocol. (One week from today)

2) Client will achieve early abstinence from alcohol, AEB negative breathalyzer, self-report, and negative alcohol metabolites in her urine. (Two weeks from today)

2. **Problem/Need Statement: Recurrent and severe mood problems** AEB history of at least six episodes of depression, postpartum depression, and current depressed and anxious symptoms with mixed features. PHQ-9 score 17.

Long-Term Goal: The client will be free from major mood episodes, AEB self-report, clinical impression, and the use of the PHQ-9 rating scale.

Short-Term Goals/Objectives with target dates:

1) Over four weeks, the client will experience at least a 50 percent reduction in her depressive and anxious symptoms as measured using the PHQ-9, self-report, and a 10-point anxiety scale. (Four weeks from today)

---

3. Problem/Need Statement: Active medical issues secondary to alcohol use and withdrawal

Long-Term Goal: The folate deficiency anemia will resolve AEB normal values on a repeat CBC in 3–6 months.

Short-Term Goals/Objectives with target dates:

1) See problem #1, safe and complete treatment of alcohol withdrawal. (One week from today)

2) Resolution of abnormal liver function tests, AEB normal values on a repeat draw in four weeks.

3) Reassessment of blood pressure and pulse following completion of the detox protocol. If still elevated, refer for medical follow-up. (Two weeks from today)

Interventions					
Treatment Modality	**Specific Type**	**Frequency**	**Duration**	**Problem Number**	**Responsible Person(s)**
Pharmacological Management of Alcohol Withdrawal	CIWA protocol	Daily	One week, or until symptom free	1	MD/nurse practitioner and RN
Nursing Assessment	CIWA protocol	Daily	One week, or until symptom free	1	RN
Psychiatric Assessment	Comprehensive assessment	Once and with ongoing follow-up and reassessment	Once for one hour, and then as needed	1,2,3	MD/nurse practitioner
Ongoing Pharmacological Management	Medication evaluation and management	Initially weekly, then as needed	For the duration of the admission	1,2,3	MD/nurse practitioner
Labs	Labs/blood work, urine toxicology, breathalyzer, other studies	As ordered	As needed	1,2,3	MD/nurse practitioner

PHP Group Therapy	Integrated group therapy	5X/week	12 sessions (to begin in PHP and then continue at next level of care)	1,2,3	Clinician or designee, client

Interventions					
Treatment Modality	**Specific Type**	**Frequency**	**Duration**	**Problem Number**	**Responsible Person(s)**
	Chemical dependency education	5X/week	One week	1,2	Clinician or designee, client
	Relapse prevention	5X/week	One week	1,3	Clinician or designee, client
	Family education group	1X/week	One week	1,2,3	Clinician, client, her mother
Individual Counseling	1:1 CBT therapy	2X/week	For the duration of the PHP and then ongoing at the next level of care	1,2	Clinician or designee
Peer Support	AA attendance	At least twice weekly	Ongoing	1,3	Client

Identification of strengths: Insightful with a high level of motivation to stop drinking. She identifies her children and her role as a mother as being two of the most meaningful things in her life. Has a strong work ethic and doesn't want to lose her current job.

Peer/family/community supports to assist: She identifies her sons as major supports. Her mother is currently in recovery, and she views her as a support, as well. Her mother has agreed to provide transportation for the client to and from the program while she is going through the detox process. The client has also expressed a willingness to attend local 12-step groups.

Barriers to treatment: Significant risk of relapse. Job-related concerns (being able to get adequate time off).

Staff/client-identified education/teaching needs: To understand the nature of her alcohol use disorder and how it affects her problems with anxiety and mood swings. As medications are recommended and trialed, she will require ongoing education about them as well.

Assessment of discharge needs/discharge planning: Once she has successfully completed an alcohol detoxification and has achieved early abstinence, she will be able to transition to a less-intense treatment modality, such as a co-occurring intensive outpatient program.

Completion of this treatment/recovery plan was a collaborative effort between the client and the following treatment team members:

SIGNATURES		Date/Time
Client:	Melanie Hardwick	3/15/2014 3 p.m.
Physician:	Artem Baranski, MD	3/15/2014 3:10 p.m.
Treatment Plan Completed By:	*Kayla Herrington, RN, LADC*	3/15/2014 3:10 p.m.
Primary Clinician:	**Louise Jefferson, LPC**	3/15/2014 2:30 p.m.

CHAPTER 12

Anxiety Disorders and Co-Occurring Substance Use Disorders

OVERVIEW

All of the anxiety disorders carry high rates of co-occurrence with substance use disorders (more than threefold higher than the general population). In a large study of people seeking treatment for alcohol use disorders, more than 30 percent were found to also have an anxiety disorder. This finding makes both intuitive and factual sense when one thinks about the nature of sedating/depressive medications, such as alcohol and the benzodiazepines (diazepam/Valium-type drugs) and the short-term relief they can provide for symptoms of excessive worry and anxiety. The self-medication hypothesis in co-occurring disorders takes on particular significance when discussing anxiety. Research shows that the majority of the anxiety disorders, with the notable exception of posttraumatic stress disorder (PTSD), develop years before the substance use disorder(s).

Tremendous symptom and syndrome overlap may occur among the anxiety disorders. Most adults with anxiety disorders can trace their origins back to childhood, with symptoms of separation anxiety, school avoidance, specific phobias, and generalized anxiety. For many, their anxiety symptoms seem to "morph" over the course of time, with periods of increased stress generating exacerbations, which might include altogether new symptoms.

The connection between substance and anxiety disorders makes tremendous sense. Someone with obsessive-compulsive disorder might experience panic attacks and periods of agoraphobia (fear of leaving the house), and start to use alcohol as a way to muster up the courage to go to the grocery store. So too, someone with social phobia, renamed social anxiety disorder in the DSM-5, may have panic attacks triggered by the fear of public speaking or even by thinking of having a meal in a college cafeteria.

This somewhat fluid nature of the anxiety disorders becomes even more complex when substance use disorders co-occur. Not only can substances provide temporary relief from symptoms of anxiety, they can also cause anxiety syndromes, at times severe, especially when people are going in and out of withdrawal states from alcohol or other sedating medications. What the person identifies as an anxiety disorder may, in fact, be an alprazolam/Xanax withdrawal that has worsened the underlying condition.

There's an interesting relationship between substance use and anxiety disorders in that having one both increases the probability of having the other, as well as hastening its development. The age of onset of anxiety disorders is up to seven years earlier in people with substance use disorders than those without. From a public health perspective, identifying children and adolescents with anxiety disorders, and knowing their increased risk for developing problem drug and/or alcohol use, represents an opportunity for early intervention.

Individuals with co-occurring anxiety and substance use disorders, versus those with one or the other, have poorer outcomes, including higher rates of other psychiatric disorders (mood disorders in particular), increased rates of hospitalization, higher rates of disability, increased medical comorbidity, and higher rates of suicide. Patterns of alcohol and substance use in people with anxiety disorders also tend to be more severe.

It's important to carefully assess an individual's specific symptoms and syndromes, as clarification of anxiety diagnoses, substance use diagnoses, and other co-occurring medical and psychiatric disorders will guide treatment. A few points to remember in the assessment process include the following:

- If someone is experiencing a withdrawal state (alcohol, opioids, benzodiazepines) this may worsen symptoms of anxiety, irritability, and depression. In the absence of a clear history, definitive diagnosis of a nonsubstance-induced anxiety disorder may need to be deferred until after the withdrawal has been fully treated.

- Following a binge with certain substances (cocaine, PCP, other stimulants), anxiety symptoms may be exacerbated and confuse the diagnostic picture.

- In taking the history, it is important, although not always possible, to identify which came first, the problems with anxiety, even if never formally diagnosed, or the substance use disorder(s).

ASSESSMENT TOOLS AND RATING SCALES

It is useful, both diagnostically and moving forward into treatment, to create a common language between the client and the therapist for evaluating symptoms of anxiety. This can involve the use of screening and evaluation tools, as well as numeric scales, such as:

- The Yale-Brown Obsessive-Compulsive Scale (Y-BOCS), which helps to put a number and severity on current symptoms of OCD, based on the amount of time an individual spends involved in OCD thoughts and actions on a daily basis.

- Subjective Units of Distress (SUDs). This is a useful scale, where the client rates their overall level of distress from 0 (no distress) to 100 (the most distress imaginable). Not only does this aid in quantifying distress at the time of evaluation, but can also be used to assess clinical interventions moving forward.

  o "Before you gave the talk, what was your SUDs? What was it during the talk? And what was it after?"

  o "What was your SUDs before looking at the picture of the spider? What was it during? Did it change as you sat with the anxiety and practiced mindful breathing? What was it after?"

- Likert scales. Likert scales are the most widely used technique to put a number on a symptom. These involve the use of five-point scales, typically 0–4 or 1–5. The highest number will represent most severe/extreme, or all of the time/constant, and the lowest number stands for none of that symptom or never.

0	1	2	3	4
(None)	(Mild)	(Moderate)	(Severe)	(Extreme)
1	2	3	4	5
(Never)	(Rarely)	(Often)	(Most of the time)	(Constant)

Likert scales comprise the bulk of many other assessment tools and can be applied to most symptoms.

- Ten-point scales. Similar to Likert scales, asking a patient to rate their symptoms on a 10-point scale, can be a useful way to both quantify the severity of a particular problem, and to track progress over time. When using a 10-point scale, it is important to define the parameters for your client. "Using a 10-point scale, where 0 is none and 10 is the worst anxiety anyone could ever have, rate your current level of anxiety."

- The Patient-Reported Outcomes Measurement Information System (PROMIS) Emotional Distress short form for anxiety is a seven-item screening instrument/ assessment tool completed by the client. It utilizes five-point Likert scales. The copyright is held by the PROMIS Health Organization, but can be reproduced without permission by clinicians for use with their patients. Copies, along with scoring guidelines, are available from the American Psychiatric Association at www.psychiatry. org/practice/dsm/dsm5/online-assessment-measures#Disorder, along with many other recommended assessment tools.

ANXIETY DISORDERS WITH CO-OCCURRING SUBSTANCE USE DISORDERS

The following are some brief descriptions of the anxiety disorders, their associations with substance use disorders, and other common comorbid disorders. PTSD and trauma, which frequently include anxious symptoms, will be addressed in the next chapter. Also the specifier "with anxious distress" can be applied to numerous non-anxiety disorders, such as the psychotic and mood (depressive and bipolar) disorders.

Generalized Anxiety Disorder (GAD)

Generalized anxiety disorder (GAD) includes protracted (more than six months) and excessive anxiety that is directed toward various situations and settings in a person's life (school, work, family, finance, health, etc.). In addition to anxiety, GAD can include irritability, poor concentration, muscle tension, and general and pervasive feelings of being "keyed up" and "on edge." The nervousness and worry often lead to significant problems with sleep.

GAD carries more than a twofold lifetime risk for developing a substance use disorder and nearly a sixfold risk for having a mood disorder. Alcohol use disorders, followed by other depressant substances, are the most common substance problems with GAD. People with co-occurring substance use and generalized anxiety disorders have poorer treatment outcomes, with increased levels of disability, more suicide attempts, and higher rates of hospitalization.

The majority of people with GAD will describe the anxiety predating the substance use. As teens, people with GAD are at great risk for developing problems with alcohol and other drugs that provide a temporary relief from their excessive worry and anxiety. On average, people with GAD develop problematic substance use earlier than those who just have substance use disorders.

Heavy drinking and misuse of anxiolytic medication can complicate the diagnostic picture in working with people who have GAD, especially if the substance use is not reported, minimized, or not adequately assessed. There can be tremendous symptom overlap between alcohol or benzodiazepine withdrawal and GAD.

Studies that have looked at the treatment of substance use and generalized anxiety disorders show superior outcomes when both are adequately assessed and addressed in treatment.

Social Anxiety Disorder (Social Phobia)

Social anxiety disorder is characterized by intense, at times incapacitating, fear, and dread of being in social situations. People with social anxiety disorder are often profoundly worried and ruminative about how others negatively perceive and judge them. Social anxiety disorder carries high rates for comorbid, and severe, alcohol and drug use disorders. Individuals are also at greater risk for both unipolar and bipolar depressive disorders.

Social anxiety disorder typically develops first, followed by the substance use disorder. Studies have shown that the age for developing substance use problems is somewhat later for social anxiety disorder than the other anxiety disorders. One explanation is that people with social anxiety disorder avoid peer situations where drugs and/or alcohol will be available.

However, as with the other anxiety disorders, patterns of substance use, especially alcohol and other depressant medications, can be severe.

Panic Disorder

While all of the anxiety disorders can include panic attacks, panic disorder is characterized by recurrent panic attacks and persistent symptoms of either intense fear or worry that the attacks will recur and/or efforts to avoid situations and settings that might precipitate an attack. In many instances, this fear of having a panic attack, or of losing control, can lead to agoraphobia, where the individual is frightened to leave their house. In the DSM-5, agoraphobia has been separated out from panic disorder, and where people meet criteria for panic disorder and agoraphobia, both diagnoses are given.

Panic disorder is associated with a fourfold increase in rates of alcohol dependence, and the 12-month comorbidity rates for mood disorders is over eightfold. As opposed to most other anxiety diagnoses, panic disorder more frequently develops after the substance use disorder.

Agoraphobia

Agoraphobia is the intense, and out-of-proportion to the situation, fear of specific situations, typically being in public, or even just being out of the home or going to a store. This fear and anxiety lead to avoidance where people refuse to leave the home, or do so only in the company of someone else. As with all anxiety disorders, it carries increased rates of co-occurring substance use problems.

Obsessive-Compulsive Disorder (OCD)

OCD involves obsessive and intrusive thoughts, typically accompanied by intense urges to perform specific actions or think certain thoughts (compulsive behaviors or thoughts) in an effort to make the anxiety associated with the obsession go away.

Substance/Medication-Induced Anxiety Disorder

While many with anxiety disorders turn to various substances to try and relieve their symptoms, there are also people who develop anxiety disorders as a result of using substances. This can include the presence of panic attacks and generalized anxiety. There are a broad range of substances that can cause anxiety disorders to develop, including caffeine, cocaine, opioids, other stimulants (such as those used to treat ADHD, and methamphetamine), alcohol, and benzodiazepines.

TREATMENT FOR CO-OCCURRING ANXIETY AND SUBSTANCE USE DISORDERS

Psychotherapies

Many studies validate psychosocial and pharmacological treatments for anxiety disorders, but few have systematically studied anxiety disorders that co-occur with substance use disorders. In recent years, however, studies that looked at cognitive behavioral therapy (CBT) and motivational interviewing (MI), both separate and combined, have observed positive benefits for both the anxiety and substance use disorders. So too mindfulness, based in Zen meditation, and other contemplative practices have also proved to be of benefit.

Other forms of therapy, such as psychodynamic and eclectic, while not thoroughly studied in these populations, may help as well, but the practitioner and client will need to address both problems. A tremendous amount still remains to be studied on the efficacy of particular therapies and approaches to the treatment of co-occurring anxiety and substance use disorders, the following interrelated points appear to be true.

- Abstinence from the problem substance(s) is associated with improvement in the anxiety disorder.
- Decreased symptoms of the anxiety disorder(s) increase the likelihood of abstinence from the problem substance(s). The anxiety symptoms are often triggers for drug craving and for use.

Cognitive Behavioral Therapy. Cognitive behavioral therapy (CBT) (Chapter 8) has a long and well-established track record for treating the entire range of anxiety disorders and symptoms, from panic attacks to targeting specific phobias (spiders, snakes, small spaces, heights, etc.), to helping people manage obsessive-compulsive disorder. Specific techniques are employed based on the individual's symptoms, such as graded exposure to a feared event, situation, or thing, combined with response prevention, such as not letting a person with OCD and germ-contamination fears wash their hands after touching a feared object. CBT is typically a time-limited therapy with 10–12 weekly sessions. Less frequent 'booster' sessions may be helpful to maintain and reinforce gains made in therapy.

Motivational Interviewing Techniques. Motivational interviewing (MI) techniques (Chapter 8) have been shown effective in helping people change problem behaviors and can be delivered alone or in combination with CBT techniques. MI can also be used in a "step-wise" fashion where one or two motivational interviewing sessions could then be followed by a longer 10-to-12-week course of CBT.

Wellness

While easily incorporated into specific psychotherapies, such as CBT, attention to an individual's overall wellness can have a dramatic positive effect on both the anxiety and substance use problems. The trick here is to create workable strategies with the client that builds on that person's existing strengths and preferences. Key components to a wellness routine include:

- Adequate restorative sleep
- Daily exercise (Studies have been generally positive in terms of improving both mood and anxiety symptoms. It appears less important the type of exercise, but at least 45 minutes daily is desirable. This can be anything from going to the gym, to taking the dog for a long walk.
- Healthful eating
- Treatment of any active medical issues
- Restriction of caffeine
- Attention to important social relations, spending time with sober family and friends

- Contemplative practices: Mindfulness meditation, yoga, prayer, tai chi
- Hobbies, especially those where people get the experience of being completely involved. This may be experienced as losing "track of time," and the list is extensive, from gardening, painting, playing and/or listening to music, to writing/journaling, puzzling, playing games, and all forms of handicraft, such as knitting, sewing, and so forth.

Pharmacology

Few well-controlled studies directly assess particular medications for people with co-occurring substance use and anxiety disorders. So the prescribing clinician must combine information from available studies, many of them on older medications, with standard of care practice for each of the disorders being addressed. In addition, the prescriber needs to ask the following question: Does this medication intended for the one disorder, potentially make the other worse or more problematic?

A few points to keep in mind include the following:

- If benzodiazepines are to be used, they must be carefully prescribed and monitored. If at all possible, their use should be avoided in this population, and when used, avoid short-acting agents, such as alprazolam/Xanax. Benzodiazepines should be avoided altogether in people on opioid replacement therapy (buprenorphine and methadone). Their combined use is associated with negative psychological and physical outcomes, including death. The vast majority of unintentional fatal overdoses (greater than 90%) involve opioids combined with other central nervous system depressants, most notably the benzodiazepines.
- Antidepressant medications typically take at least two to four weeks to get any response, possibly two to three times that long when being used for anxiety disorders. Effectiveness of antidepressant medications is hindered by active substance use. For people with bipolar disorders with anxious and/or mixed features, antidepressants may worsen irritability and precipitate mania or hypomania.

Antidepressants. The mainstay of treatment for anxiety disorders are the antidepressants. Studies that have looked at the antidepressants in people with substance use problems have been few and have shown mixed results. Older medications, such as the tricyclic antidepressants may be more effective in treating both depression and anxiety in people with co-occurring substance use disorders, however their toxicity, risk in overdose (cardiac conduction delays, heart block, and death), need for blood monitoring, and side-effect profile make them less attractive to both clients and prescribers.

The current standard of care is to use selective serotonin reuptake inhibitors (SSRIs) and serotonin-norepinephrine reuptake inhibitors (SNRIs) first. For individuals with both depressive and anxious symptoms, this strategy makes tremendous sense, but if some improvement is not seen after six to eight weeks (of note, this is somewhat longer than when using antidepressants for just depression) of an adequate trial of a medication at an adequate dose the clinician needs to consider dose adjustment, augmentation with another medication, or switching to another agent altogether.

Selective Serotonin Reuptake Inhibitors

Compound	Trade Name	Dose Range (mg/day)
citalopram	Celexa	10–40
escitalopram	Lexapro	10–20
fluoxetine	Prozac	10–60
fluvoxamine	Luvox	50–200
paroxitine	Paxil	10–60
sertraline	Zoloft	50–200
Vilazodone	Viibryd	20-40

Serotonin-Norepinephrine Reuptake Inhibitors

Compound	Trade Name	Dose Range (mg/day)
duloxetine	Cymbalta	40–60
desvenlafaxine	Pristiq	50
levomilnacipran	Fetzima	40–120
venlafaxine	Effexor, Effexor XR	75–375

Tricyclic Antidepressants

Compound Name	Trade Name	Dose Range (mg/day)
amitriptyline	Elavil	50–300
amoxapine	Ascendin	200–400
clomipramine	Anafranil	150–250
desipramine	Norpramin	100–300
doxepin	Sinequan	150–300
imipramine	Tofranil	150–300
maprotiline	Ludiomil	75–150
nortriptyline	Pamelor	50–150
protriptyline	Vivactil	30–60

Benzodiazepines. All of these medications are potentially habit forming and can be misused for their sedating, disinhibiting, and euphoric properties. For people with anxiety disorders, the benzodiazepines can provide prompt relief from symptoms of anxiety, as opposed to the SSRIs and SNRIs that will take weeks to months to achieve their maximum benefit.

Once someone is physiologically dependent on a benzodiazepine they may be at risk for significant withdrawal syndromes, similar to those seen in alcohol. People who have been taking these medications consistently for more than a couple weeks should be tapered off, with careful follow-up to assess for withdrawal. Medications in this class with shorter half-lives, such as alprazolam/Xanax and lorazepam/Ativan are associated with more severe and rapid onset of withdrawal symptoms and syndromes.

Benzodiazepines

Compound	Trade Name	Half-life (hours)	FDA Indications
alprazolam	Xanax	6.3–14	• GAD • Panic disorder
chlordiazepoxide	Librium	5–30	• Anxiety and anxiety disorders • Preoperative anxiety • Alcohol withdrawal
clonazepam	Klonopin	18–30	• Panic disorder • Some forms of seizure disorders
clorazepate	Tranxene	40–50	• Anxiety • Alcohol withdrawal
diazepam	Valium	20–80	• Anxiety and anxiety disorders • Alcohol withdrawal • Muscle spasm • Protracted seizures (status epilepticus)
flurazepam	Dalmane	50–90+	• Insomnia
lorazepam	Ativan	10–20	• Anxiety and anxiety associated with depressive symptoms • Protracted seizures
oxazepam	Serax	5–20	• Anxiety and anxiety associated with depression • Alcohol withdrawal
temazepam	Restoril	5–17	• Short-term treatment of insomnia
triazolam	Halcion	2–4	• Short-term treatment of insomnia

Other Medications with FDA Indications for Anxiety Disorders. Hydroxyzine/Vistaril/ Atarax is an antihistamine that can be used in an as-needed manner (prn) for the treatment of anxiety and, per the package insert, "tension associated with psychoneurosis." It is somewhat sedating and has some off-label benefit as a nonaddictive sleep aid. Typical doses range from 50–100 mg up to four times per day as needed for anxiety. Some patients report significant relief with this medication and use it daily.

Buspirone/Buspar is a medication that binds to serotonin receptors in the brain. It has the FDA indication for generalized anxiety disorder (GAD). Typical dose range begins at 7.5 mg twice per day and can be titrated up to 60 mg per day. Benefits from buspirone may take two to four weeks, or longer, to be felt.

CASE STUDY: DENNIS JONES

Dennis Jones is a 38-year-old married father of two with no history of any treatment for either substance abuse or mental illness. He presents cleanly shaved, dressed in jeans and a polo shirt, and appears physically fit. He speaks with animation, seems nervous, and makes frequent clearing sounds in his throat. He is seeking treatment for his daily marijuana use. He states, "I've been smoking pot since I was a teenager, and I have to stop."

When asked "Why now?"

He replies, "I work as a welder, and they've started to drug test us. I gave two dirty urines. They told me if I want to keep my job I have to get into a treatment program, stop smoking pot, and give clean urines. I can't lose my job. My wife stays home with the boys, and to be honest I'm spending too much money on pot and it's time to give it up. I also don't want my sons to grow up thinking it's okay or that their dad is a pothead."

In the course of the interview, he also admits to the use of alcohol, but adds, "It's not a problem…I don't black out or anything." When he was in his early twenties, he did receive a DUI/DWI, for which he had to attend two months of court-mandated driving classes. Since being told he had to stop smoking marijuana, his alcohol consumption has increased from a couple times a week to at least "a few beers after work" nightly. He adds, "I know I'm just replacing one drug with another," but states, "I haven't had anything for the last four days." He has no history of any form of alcohol withdrawal and has none at the time of this evaluation.

He denies other drug use, although he reports he tried synthetic cannabis (K-2/Spice) because he knew they wouldn't test for it. He says it made him feel paranoid, and he'd never do it again. He doesn't smoke cigarettes.

When asked about his childhood and school history, he initially says, "It was fine." When pressed for details, the clearing noises in his throat become more pronounced and at times he stutters. His parents divorced when he was four and he had little contact with his father growing up. He explains that his father's absence is one of the reasons it's important for him to be a good father to his young children. He says he was always shy and easily embarrassed. In school he was frequently teased about his stutter, which improved as he got older. He completed high school, but had frequent absences and would often fake being sick to avoid going to school. Social settings make him profoundly nervous and he avoids them altogether unless he's had "a couple beers or a joint." He describes situations where his anxiety spikes, accompanied by racing pulse, palpitations, drenching sweat, light-headedness, and the feeling that something horrible is about to happen. In the past he's felt like he was having a heart attack and has sought treatment twice in emergency rooms, and both times told he was having a panic attack. These attacks have increased (2–3 times/week) and he is sometimes frightened to leave the house for fear of having an attack. He admits that one of the reasons he likes both marijuana and alcohol is that they relieve his stress and his anxiety.

When asked to rate his current level of anxiety on a 10-point scale (10 being the worst possible) he states it's an 8, and that on any given day it ranges from no less than a 4 to a 9 or 10. Using the same scale he reports his feelings of depression are much lower, although the current threat to his job has increased them from a 1 or 2, to a 4.

His family history is significant for his mother who's been treated for anxiety and has been taking diazepam/Valium for decades.

He has been married for 14 years. He describes his wife as being the one "who wears the pants in the house." She has made it clear that if he were to lose his job on account of his drug use, she would take their two children, ages 7 and 9, and move in with her parents.

He has no active medical issues, is on no medication, and has no reported allergies.

Step One: Level of Care Determination

In this case, the client has no pressing safety or medical concerns (no history of any alcohol withdrawal and no visible symptoms of withdrawal after four days without a drink) and an outpatient level of care is appropriate. When the client states he needs "to be in a program" in order to keep his job, this should be clarified. Has his workplace stipulated the type of program he needs to complete? What kinds of documentation will they require, and how is this to be handled?

Possible options will include a co-occurring intensive outpatient program (IOP), a co-occurring outpatient clinic, or referral to an outpatient therapist able to address both the substance use and psychiatric disorders. He will also need access to a psychiatrist or psychiatric nurse practitioner.

Step Two: Constructing the Problem/Need List

Dennis Jones's significant data can be grouped into two large categories, one related to his substance use and the other covers his mental health issues.

Substance Use	Mental Health
Daily cannabis use since he was a teen	Anxious as a child
History of alcohol use	School avoidant
Has tried synthetic cannabis to avoid positive drug screens	Stuttered as a child, frequently teased
DUI in his twenties	Panic attacks 2–3/week
Job in jeopardy because of "dirty urines"	Socially avoidant (phobic)
Wife has said she'll move out and take the children if he loses his job	Anxiety predated substance use: turned to cannabis and alcohol to medicate away anxiety
Doesn't want his children to view their father as a "pothead"	Frightened to leave the house for fear of having a panic attack
Increased use of alcohol since having to stop cannabis	Anxiety 8–10/10
No history of any withdrawal symptoms when he stops drinking	Mild situational increase in feelings of depression 4/10
Action stage of motivation to change his behavior	Mother with anxiety

Problem/Need list:

1. **Active substance use problems** as evidenced by (AEB) daily cannabis use, resulting in risk for termination from work. Recent increase in alcohol consumption with a past history that has included a DUI.

2. **Severe and persistent problems with anxiety** AEB panic attacks and daily anxiety ranging 8–10 out of 10. Recent increase in situational depression (mild). Lifelong problems with anxiety that predated use of drugs and/or alcohol.

Step Three: Establishing the Initial Goals/Objectives for Treatment

1. **Active substance use problems**

   • Short-term goal(s) with target date:

      1) To be in early abstinent recovery from cannabis and alcohol, AEB by negative toxicology screens and negative alcohol metabolites. (4/1/2014)

      2) To be able to return to work by 4/14/2014.

   • Long-term goal(s): To be in a sustained (greater than six months) abstinent recovery from all illicit drugs and alcohol, AEB self-report and negative urine toxicologies.

2. **Severe and persistent problems with anxiety**

   • Short-term goal (s) with target date:

      1) To clarify the nature of his anxiety problems by undergoing a thorough psychiatric assessment (completion by 4/7/2014).

      2) To reduce his current level of anxiety by at least 40% using a 10-point scale by 4/14/2014.

      3) To address situational stressors (threat of job loss) by 4/7/2014.

   • Long-term goal(s):

      1) To be free from anxiety symptoms of greater than 2–3 on a 10-point scale.

      2) To be free from depressive symptoms by self-report and by completion of a follow-up Patient Health Questionnaire-9 (See page 143) with a score of no greater than a 7.

TREATMENT/RECOVERY PLAN

Patient's Name: Dennis Jones

Date of Birth: 9/14/1978

Medical Record #: XXX-XX-XXXX

Level of Care: Outpatient

ICD-10 Codes	DSM-5 Diagnoses
F12.20	Cannabis use disorder, severe
F10.10	Alcohol use disorder, mild
F41.1	Generalized anxiety disorder with panic attacks
Z56.9	Other problems related to employment
Z63.0	Relationship distress with spouse

The individual's stated goal(s): "To finally do something about my anxiety without trying to drug it away. To not have to worry about losing my job. To be a better role model to my kids and to not have to keep trying to hide my pot smoking from my wife. To decrease the tension in my marriage."

1. Problem/Need Statement: Active substance use problems AEB daily cannabis use, resulting in risk for termination from work. Recent increase in alcohol consumption with a past history that has included a DUI. Marital stress related to substance use.
Long-Term Goal: To be in a sustained abstinent recovery from all illicit drugs and alcohol, AEB self-report and negative urine toxicologies.
Short-Term Goals/Objectives with target dates:
1. To be in early abstinent recovery from cannabis and alcohol, AEB by negative toxicology screens and negative alcohol metabolites. (4/1/2014)
2. To be able to return to work by 4/14/2014.

2. Problem/Need Statement: Severe and persistent problems with anxiety AEB panic attacks and daily anxiety ranging 8–10 out of 10. Recent increase in situational depression (mild). Lifelong problems with anxiety that predated use of drugs and/or alcohol.

Long-Term Goals:

1. To be free from anxiety symptoms of greater than 2–3 on a 10-point scale.

2. To be free from depressive symptoms by self-report and by completion of a follow-up Patient Health Questionnaire-9 with a score of no greater than a 7.

Short Term Goals/Objectives with target dates:

1. To reduce his current level of anxiety by at least 40% using a 10-point scale by 4/14/2014.

2. To clarify the nature of his anxiety problems by undergoing a thorough psychiatric assessment (completion by 4/7/2014).

3. To address situational stressors (threat of job loss and marital stress) by 4/7/2014.

Interventions					
Treatment Modality	**Specific Type**	**Frequency**	**Duration**	**Problem Number**	**Responsible Person(s)**
Psychiatric Assessment	Complete diagnostic assessment	Upon admission	One to two hours	1,2	MD/nurse practitioner and RN
Individual Therapy	Integrated CBT	Weekly	12 weeks (50 minute sessions)	1,2	Primary therapist
Family Therapy	Couple's counseling	Weekly	Two sessions (50 minutes) and then reassess	1,2	Primary therapist, client, and his wife
Ongoing Pharmacological Management	Medication evaluation and management	Initially weekly, then monthly, or as needed.	For as long as the client is in treatment.	1,2	MD/nurse practitioner
Labs	Urine toxicology, breathalyzer, alcohol metabolites, other studies, as needed	As ordered	As needed	1,2	MD/nurse practitioner
Peer Support	AA/NA attendance	At least twice weekly	Ongoing	1	Client

Wellness	Exercise/play time with children	Daily for at least one hour	Ongoing	1,2	Client
Communication	Liaison with human resources for patient's job	As needed and always with signed consent	Ongoing	1	Client, clinician

Identification of strengths: High level of motivation to address both anxiety and substance use problems. Identifies being a good father and being the family "breadwinner" as meaningful and important to him. Loyal to friends and family.

Peer/family/community supports to assist: His wife, his boss.

Barriers to treatment: Minimal sober supports.

Staff/client-identified education/teaching needs: To understand the relationships between his substance use and his anxiety disorder. To learn new ways to manage anxiety and negative emotions. To develop a sober support system.

Assessment of discharge needs/discharge planning: When stated goals have been achieved, will require a less-intensive treatment plan, possibly all peer based with ongoing medication management if medications are being used.

Completion of this treatment/recovery plan was a collaborative effort between the client and the following treatment team members:

SIGNATURES		Date/Time
Client:	Dennis Jones	3/28/2014 2 p.m.
Physician:	Lydia Sweet, MD	3/28/2014 4:45 p.m.
Treatment Plan Completed By:	Margaret Able & Dennis Jones	3/28/2014 2 p.m.
Primary Clinician:	Margaret Able, LCSW	3/28/2014 2 p.m.

CHAPTER 13

Posttraumatic Stress Disorder and Co-Occurring Substance Use Disorders

---

Overview

Symptoms of PTSD

Assessment and Screening Tools for PTSD

Treatment of Co-occurring PTSD and Substance Use Disorders

Psychotherapies

Enhancing Resiliency, Safety, and Wellness

Pharmacological Treatments

Case Study

OVERVIEW

Posttraumatic stress disorder (PTSD) affects more than 5 million Americans in any 12-month period, and has a lifetime prevalence of over 7 percent. It is somewhat unique among mental disorders, as its presence is predicated on a person having experienced or witnessed a traumatic event, or series of events. It is common among victims of child abuse/neglect, sexual assault survivors, war veterans, prisoners, ex-convicts, and people who've been through devastating man-made and natural disasters.

Rates of co-occurring posttraumatic stress disorder (PTSD) in people seeking treatment for substance use disorders (SUDs) are five times higher than those found in the general population, and range between 20 and 50 percent. On the flip side, more than one-third of people with PTSD have had at least one non-tobacco substance use disorder. Histories of exposure to trauma (not necessarily with the development of PTSD) are found in the vast majority of people with substance use disorders (90%). And 80 percent of women seeking treatment for substance problems report histories of physical or sexual assault.

The clinical course for people with co-occurring PTSD and substance use disorders is poorer than for either condition alone. PTSD is associated with increased drug/alcohol craving, poor adherence to treatment, decreased time to relapse, as well as higher relapse rates. People with both PTSD and substance use disorders have higher rates of multiple psychiatric diagnoses, more severe symptoms, poorer physical health, and overall worse social functioning.

Some people, such as those with histories of childhood sexual abuse and/or neglect, may present with complex symptoms including frequent suicidality, profound emotional vulnerability, and self-injurious behaviors (cutting, burning).

The good news is that symptoms of PTSD respond positively to treatment when substance use problems are in remission. Conversely, when PTSD symptoms are well controlled people are less likely to engage in problem substance use. One study that looked at the correlation between abstinence from cocaine and/or alcohol showed a modest, but significant reduction in PTSD symptoms, anxiety, and depression, especially during the first two weeks of abstinence. Also encouraging are studies that have looked at treatment for both PTSD and substance use. Some of these studies have used sequential treatment, with the substance disorder being addressed first. Others have used parallel treatment, where one provider helps with the substance use problem and the other with the PTSD, and some have used integrated models where both issues are addressed simultaneously. Overall, the results for both the substance use and PTSD have been positive. Studies that have then gone on to examine whether combined treatment for both disorders is superior to treatment for the substance use alone have not shown clear superiority for any particular treatment. What those comparison studies have revealed is that addressing the substance use component will generate improvement in the symptoms of PTSD.

PTSD more commonly precedes the substance use problem and increases the likelihood that a person will go on to develop problem substance use. This relationship lends credence to the self-medication hypothesis, where people turn to substances to try and relieve painful and negative emotions and thoughts. Certain symptoms of PTSD, such as flashbacks and cues to past traumas, can increase craving for alcohol and other substances of abuse. From a behavioral perspective this makes sense, as the substance becomes associated with rapid relief from negative emotions (a reinforcer). Studies show that when PTSD symptoms are high, so too are drug cravings, relapse rates, and substance use.

Symptoms of PTSD

The symptoms of PTSD can be broken into the following clusters, and in the current diagnostic manual (DSM-5), a critical number need to have been present for at least one month to make a PTSD diagnosis. The related diagnosis of acute stress disorder is applied for those with symptoms lasting from three days to one month. Symptoms may manifest immediately following exposure to trauma, or may be delayed for weeks, months, and even years:

- Intrusive thoughts
  - Intense, and unwanted, remembering of traumatic experience
  - Nightmares
  - Flashbacks, where the person relives the event as though it is currently happening
- Avoidance
  - Deliberately avoiding situations and places that trigger memories of the traumatic event(s)
    - A rape victim who was attacked in a park now avoids all parks.
    - A resident of Manhattan who experienced 9/11 moves away and refuses to visit.

- Arousal
  - o Hypervigilance—the feeling of always needing to be watchful and alert to the presence of danger
  - o Easily startled
    - A combat veteran hears a loud noise and dives for cover.
    - A victim of a home invasion hears a knock on the door and has a panic attack.
  - o Easily angered/hair-trigger temper
- Negative emotional (mood) states
  - o Depression
  - o Irritability
  - o Anger
  - o Guilt and shame
  - o Helplessness
  - o Feeling numb
- Disturbances in thought (cognition)
  - o Feelings of derealization and/or depersonalization; feeling disconnected from the world, oneself, and from others
  - o Amnesia related to the traumatic event(s)
  - o Unrealistic and/or exaggerated beliefs about the traumatic event, in which the person blames herself and/or others
    - "I shouldn't have been walking alone."
    - "Why didn't I get an electrician in to check the wiring?"
    - "If I'd gotten home 10 minutes earlier, this would never have happened."
    - "Someone should have known what he was up to."

ASSESSMENT AND SCREENING TOOLS FOR PTSD

In addition to completing a comprehensive assessment (see Chapters 2–4), which includes a screening module for trauma, as well as assessments of dangerousness to self or others, specialized screening tools can be helpful in clarifying a PTSD or other trauma-related diagnosis. Tools that capture a particular period of time, such as symptoms experienced over the last month, can be used to document response to treatment and be incorporated into treatment/recovery plans.

Recommended screening tools include:

- **Clinician-Administered PTSD Scale for the DSM-5 (CAPS-5):** This 30-item structured interview has been widely used in research and is considered the "gold standard" for the assessment of PTSD. It has recently been revised to incorporate the changes to the PTSD criteria in the DSM-5. It utilizes a Likert scale rating (0–4) for symptom severity. It takes 45–60 minutes to complete, and assesses PTSD symptoms for the prior month. While primarily used in research, it can be used clinically by appropriately trained clinicians. A separate version is available for children and adolescents. Copies of this instrument can be requested and obtained from the VA, at www.ptsd.va.gov/professional/assessment/ncptsd-instrument-request-form.asp.

- **The Short Screening Scale for PTSD:** Designed for trauma survivors, this is a brief seven-item "yes" or "no" questionnaire that includes items related to hyperarousal and avoidance. A score of 4 or more is considered positive and should warrant further clinical evaluation.

- **Trauma Screening Questionnaire:** This 10-item screen is used with trauma survivors. It includes five items related to re-experiencing and five related to arousal. A score of 6 or more is considered positive and should lead to a more detailed assessment of symptoms.

- **PTSD Symptom Checklist (PCL):** This 20-item self-report checklist can be used as a screening tool, to aid in the diagnosis of PTSD, and to follow up response to treatment. It takes 5–10 minutes to complete, and utilizes a 1- to 5-point rating scale. An updated version—the PCL-5—incorporates criteria changes in the DSM-5.

Copies of the PCL-5 as well as other screening tools for PTSD, can be requested by master's level, or higher, clinicians free of charge through the Department of Veterans Affairs: www.ptsd.va.gov/professional/pages/assessments/ncptsd-instrument-request-form.asp.

TREATMENT FOR CO-OCCURRING PTSD AND SUBSTANCE USE DISORDERS

Among the well-validated psychotherapies for PTSD, few have been systematically studied in people with co-occurring substance use disorders. To date, reviews looking at studies of specific psychotherapies for people with co-occurring PTSD and substance disorders have shown that many do indeed reduce symptoms of both, even months after the completion of treatment. What is not clear is whether these treatments are superior, or greatly superior, to treatment for substance use alone. While this finding may appear discouraging, it needs to be taken in the context of research that is extraordinarily difficult to conduct—that is, evaluation of a specific therapy against a control group that doesn't inadvertently provide elements of the therapy being studied, while simultaneously trying to find a large enough patient group that meets all necessary criteria. Beyond that, when selecting the group to be studied, do you include all substances, or just alcohol or cocaine or opioids or…?

On the pharmacological side of treatment, few studies look at specific drugs for PTSD and fewer still for the treatment of co-occurring PTSD and SUDs. At the time of this book's publication, only two agents have an FDA indication for PTSD, sertraline/Zoloft and paroxitine/Paxil.

Psychotherapies

The therapies selected for inclusion in this book are those that have either been widely disseminated and/or have been studied in people with co-occurring disorders.

Nonexposure–Based Treatments

- **Seeking Safety:** Developed by Lisa Najavits, Ph.D., this nonexposure, cognitive-behavioral treatment is the most extensively studied of the nonexposure/present-based therapies for co-occurring PTSD and substance use disorders. Seeking Safety has five central principles:

  1. Safety—An overall focus on increasing safe behavior and decreasing and eliminating unhealthy ones, such as using drugs and alcohol and being in abusive relationships.

  2. Integrated treatment of PTSD and substance use problems—In all modules both the PTSD and substance(s) are addressed (i.e., the treatment is fully integrated).

  3. Focus on ideals—Enhance the establishment/reestablishment of positive ideals, including self-worth, integrity, honesty, and responsibility.

  4. Four content areas:

     i. Cognitive—Use of cognitive restructuring, challenging of beliefs, especially as they relate to the PTSD and the substance use, such as "I need to drink so I don't feel so much pain"

     ii. Behavioral—The implementation of coping skills and commitment to positive action

     iii. Interpersonal—Attention to improving relationships and positive supports, including the option of inviting significant people to attend a session to help support the person in recovery

     iv. Case management

  5. Therapist process—There is an emphasis on enhancing the therapist's skills, supporting them in the work, and respecting their individual styles.

Seeking Safety is a highly flexible, yet structured, therapy that consists of 25 modules that can be provided in any order, based on need and preference. It can be used in a group or individual format, and the actual number of sessions can vary. Seeking Safety can be provided both as a stand-alone therapy or with other treatment modalities, such as 12-step, pharmacotherapy, case management, relapse prevention, and exposure therapy. It has been studied in rape victims, incarcerated women, veterans, adolescent girls, and other populations.

Overall, Seeking Safety has been shown to decrease both symptoms of PTSD and substance use disorders. Recent studies have also looked at including an exposure (imaginal) component to Seeking Safety. Early results, appear promising.

- **Target:** This gender-specific group-based therapy (eight to nine sessions) can be offered within substance use treatment. Target utilizes psychoeducation, cognitive restructuring techniques (CBT), and teaches emotion regulation skills.

- **Transcend**: This 12-week partial hospital–based program includes 10 hours of group therapy per week. It was studied in war veterans with PTSD and substance use disorders. It uses a manual, which includes a workbook for participants and guidelines for therapists. It is provided following the completion of a substance abuse program.

It includes concepts from a variety of therapeutic disciplines (CBT, psychodynamic, 12-step, relaxation training, and structured exercise). It does include some in-group sharing of traumatic experiences. Groups are cohort based (i.e., the same participants start and finish together).

- **Trauma Recovery and Empowerment Model (TREM):** A 33-session group-based treatment for women that is offered within substance use treatment, TREM includes psychoeducation, cognitive restructuring (CBT), and teaches emotion regulation skills. The manual includes brief trauma exposure. There is also an adapted gender specific version for men, M-TREM.

- **Integrated CBT**: This has been studied as an 8- to 12-session protocol that includes psychoeducation, CBT skills, such as cognitive restructuring, breathing retraining, coping strategies, and relapse prevention. It is provided within substance treatment.

- **DART** for co-occurring disorders: DART includes psychoeducation and skills training during nine hours per week for 12 weeks. It is provided within substance use treatment.

- **Substance dependency posttraumatic stress disorder therapy (SDPT).** This is an individual, cognitive-based therapy that focuses on coping skills and relapse prevention.

Exposure-Based Treatments. In all of the exposure-based therapies, by definition, the individual will re-experience some degree of their trauma. All of these therapies prepare the client with a variety of grounding and/or cognitive-behavioral training prior to the exposure components, to minimize re-traumatization. Proper training and supervision for these therapies is highly recommended prior to attempting their use.

- **Prolonged Exposure (PE):** Developed by Edna Foa, Ph.D., prolonged exposure is an effective individual CBT-based treatment for PTSD. There have been multiple positive studies using PE with people who have co-occurring PTSD and substance use disorders. Its efficacy as a treatment for PTSD is endorsed by the Institute of Medicine. In 2013 results of a large study of PE in male and female veterans with PTSD (substance disorders were not specifically addressed) showed significant improvement in reducing symptoms of PTSD and depression.

    Prolonged exposure includes: CBT elements, education regarding the nature of PTSD, and exposure to the trauma, which includes both imaginal remembering of the event, and repeated in vivo (real life) exposure to feared situations and other cues the person has avoided since the trauma.

- **Cognitive Processing Therapy (CPT):** Developed by Patricia Resick, Ph.D., CPT is an 11- or 12-session manual-based treatment that has been used with sexual assault survivors and refugees, and the Veterans Administration has adopted it for use with veterans. It has been used in both group and individual therapy formats. It includes education about trauma and how it changes a person's thoughts and beliefs. Cognitive processing therapy utilizes cognitive-behavioral principles of identifying thoughts and feelings, how they are connected, and then has the client challenge distorted beliefs. The exposure portions of this therapy involve writing exercises (homework assignments) where the traumatic event(s) are recalled and written down with as much detail as possible, and then reviewed with the therapist. Erroneous beliefs are challenged using CBT/Socratic–style reasoning. Specific issues of safety, trust, power, and intimacy are addressed.

- **Eye Movement Desensitization and Reprocessing (EMDR):** Developed by Francine Shapiro, EMDR utilizes exposure-based recollections of traumatic events in conjunction with deliberate and repetitive lateral eye movements. Its efficacy has been demonstrated in multiple clinical trials, and it is included in several practice guidelines as an evidence-based therapy.

- **Concurrent Treatment of PTSD and Cocaine Dependence (CTPCD)/Concurrent Treatment of PTSD and Substance Use with Prolonged Exposure (COPE):** This individual therapy includes 16 hour-and-a-half sessions. The therapy uses CBT, coping skills, psychoeducation, relapse prevention, and imaginal and in-vivo exposure to past trauma (an adaptation of prolonged exposure). It is provided as a stand-alone therapy. Study results were positive for both PTSD and substance use outcome measures.

Enhancing Resiliency, Safety, and Wellness

A growing body of research underscores the importance of resiliency. These are the factors that make people more able to handle the stress that life throws their way. It is what allows one person to endure and survive a horrific experience, which leaves someone else destroyed. From clinical and wellness perspectives, the literature on resiliency provides a wealth of strategies that can be applied when working with people who have PTSD and related disorders.

But first, it is important to address issues of safety. Is your client currently in a situation that is stressful or traumatizing?

- Is the home environment a safe one?
- Is the home environment sober, or are people actively using?
- Is the person in a significant relationship where they are being abused physically, emotionally, or sexually?
- Is someone staying with her partner for fear of negative consequences should she leave? This can involve financial, custodial, or personal safety concerns. People in abusive relationships are at the greatest risk for harm when they attempt to leave their abuser.
- Is someone's job, such as being combat deployed in the military, an ongoing source of stress and possibly traumatization?
- Is someone currently undergoing legal difficulties that include the threat of incarceration?
- Is someone currently incarcerated?

For clinicians, understanding a client's active sources of distress and helping that person diminish, manage, and/or possibly eliminate them will be an important focus of treatment.

There are many strategies to help foster resiliency and wellness, many of which are incorporated into the therapies just reviewed. These include:

1. Establish, reestablish, and strengthen positive supports and role models.
   a. Positive family relations
   b. Sober mentors, such as 12-step sponsors
   c. Attendance and participation in mutual self-help
2. Address basic wellness needs.
   a. Healthful nutrition
   b. Physical activity and exercise
   c. Attention to medical problems
   d. Adequate restorative sleep
   e. Pleasurable activities and hobbies
3. Address issues of religion and spirituality. People are often able to draw strength from their faith, which includes finding meaning in the adversity they have had to endure.
4. Promote cognitive flexibility and growth.
   a. The importance of acceptance (This does not imply that one approves or endorses the experiences they have been through, but that they acknowledge they occurred. Acceptance becomes an important step in allowing forward movement and growth.)
   b. The use of humor to gain a sense of control over negative experiences
   c. Finding meaning, and possibly purpose, in having survived the experience
   d. Enhanced optimism (When life hands you lemons, make lemonade.)
5. Enhance meaningful activities.
   a. Work
   b. Volunteerism/giving back to others

Pharmacological Treatments

As with all co-occurring disorders, few studies have adequately evaluated specific agents with people who have both substance use disorders and PTSD. Therefore, prescribers need to evaluate both halves of the equation—the PTSD and the substance problem(s)—and weigh the relative pros and cons of both on-label (FDA indicated) and off-label (has not received FDA indication for a particular use) medications.

Pharmacologic Treatment of PTSD

- **Selective-serotonin reuptake inhibitors:** The only two medications (at the time of this publication) receiving an FDA indication for the use in PTSD are the selective-serotonin reuptake inhibitors sertraline/Zoloft and paroxetine/Paxil. Even though these agents have shown themselves to be superior to placebo, their overall effect on decreasing symptoms is modest.

- **Other antidepressants:** Other antidepressant medications that may be of benefit in PTSD include:

   o Other SSRIs

   o SNRIs, such as venlafaxine/Effexor and duloxetine/Cymbalta

   o Other antidepressants, such as the more-sedating mirtazapine/Remeron

- **Alpha-adrenergic agents:** These older blood pressure medications have been studied in PTSD. They can decrease symptoms of hyperarousal and distressing dreams. Frequently used agents include prazosin/Minipress and clonidine/Catapres.

- **Atypical antipsychotics:** These agents are sometimes used off-label to target specific symptoms such as hyperarousal. However, their potential benefit must be weighed against significant risks for adverse events including weight gain, and the development of metabolic syndrome.

- **Anticonvulsants:** There have been numerous studies looking at the potential benefits of agents like valproic acid/Depakote, carbamazepine/Tegretol in PTSD. The overall results have been mixed.

- **Benzodiazepines:** While often prescribed for their short-term relief of anxiety, studies looking at these in PTSD have not shown them to be of benefit. Because of their risk for abuse and dependence—especially in a person with co-occurring substance problems—they should be avoided.

Pharmacologic Treatment of Substance Use Disorders in People with PTSD. In looking at the use of potential medications for the substance disorder in a person with PTSD, there are a few considerations: what is the substance being targeted? Are there specific agents that have been shown to be effective for that substance? Are those agents FDA approved? Have they been studied in people with co-occurring PTSD?

Once we get beyond alcohol, opioids, and tobacco, there are no FDA approved medications targeting specific substance use disorders.

For people who have co-occurring opioid dependence and PTSD, replacement therapy is a likely option (buprenorphine/Suboxone, methadone). Similarly if someone has an alcohol use disorder, medications such as the opioid antagonist naltrexone/Revia or acamprosate/Campral could be considered.

Off-label studies of SSRIs, atypical antipsychotics, and anticonvulsants (valproic acid/Depakote, topiramate/Topamax) have shown some possible benefit.

CASE STUDY: JIM LATHROP

Jim is a 30-year-old, recently divorced father of one, and a state trooper. He presents for treatment with a two-year history of severe mood swings, explosive rage, insomnia, and nightmares. He's dressed neatly in jeans and a flannel shirt, he's clean shaven and carries a faint odor of alcohol.

When asked about the symptoms that bring him in for his first encounter with a mental health professional, he is wary and wants reassurance that whatever he says will not get back to his place of work. "They wanted me to see the state shrink after it happened. No way in hell was I going to do that."

After the rules, and potential exceptions, to confidentiality are explained, he seems poised to leave. "What the hell …I've got to do something. I need you to fix me, because I can't go on like this. It's like living in hell…I can tell you exactly when it started." He describes a horrific and well-publicized multiple homicide/suicide, where he was a first responder and was present when a recently laid-off man killed his three young children, his wife, and then himself. "I've been a trooper for nine years and I've seen bad stuff," he chokes up. "It was seeing the kids.…

At first I was just kind of numb, like there was a fog in my head, like things weren't real, like it was a movie or something. I figured it was normal and it would go away. It got worse. It's like my brain wouldn't shut up and I kept seeing them, and couldn't stop thinking about what they must have felt, how terrified they had to be."

As he speaks, Jim is visibly distraught, his mood shifts rapidly from profound sadness to anger. "You go through life thinking you're normal, and suddenly something happens and it's like my brain just won't shut up. When I try to relax, it's even worse. Like there's something waiting for me to let down my guard, and there they are. I should have gotten there faster. I heard the shots. I should have broken in. We should have saved them …at least the baby." At times he has difficulty speaking, and sobs when he describes how he unsuccessfully attempted to resuscitate the youngest child.

"It all went to shit after that. It's all I can do to show up to work, and being a trooper is all I ever wanted to do. Anything can set me off. Any kind of loud noise and I feel like I'm jumping out of my skin. It destroyed my marriage. I don't blame Kaitlin for leaving, and if something doesn't happen…I just can't go on feeling like this. Becky—she's three—she deserves a dad, and if I don't get fixed, it's not going to be me. I can't focus. I can't do anything right."

When asked specifically about suicidal thoughts or plans, he says, "Yeah, I think about it. But I'd make it look like an accident. That's the weird thing…before this happened, I'd never thought about offing myself. Now, a day doesn't go by where I at least wonder if I wouldn't be better off dead. Just turn the wheel hard to the right on the highway, and go off a cliff…get it over with." Upon further questioning, he admits that he doesn't want to end his life, "I couldn't do that to my little girl." As a state trooper, he does own and carry a firearm. He states he has had no changes in his behavior toward his weapon, and that after every shift he removes the bullets and places the gun in a safe. He has no history of past suicidal thoughts or behaviors. He has no thoughts of harming anyone else.

As the interview shifts to the substance abuse history, Jim is frank about the increase in his alcohol consumption. "It used to be a couple beers after work, go out with the guys, nothing hard core. Now, I don't go out with anyone, and beer is too slow." He quantifies his daily consumption as at least a fifth, sometimes a quart or more of whiskey. In the past few months it's progressed from drinking after work, to starting the day with a "slug or two in my coffee" to steady the shakes. He admits he had "a couple hits before coming here." He is a nonsmoker and denies any other drug use. He has never been in treatment for an alcohol use disorder. He has no history of seizures or delirium tremens.

He denies any known family history of mental illness, but thinks his father and grandfather, both deceased, had problems with alcohol. He describes his suburban childhood as a happy one. He had friends, graduated high school, and received a bachelor's degree in criminal science. Prior to two years ago he was active in his church, played league baseball, and considered himself to be in a happy marriage, and had been overjoyed at the birth of his daughter. He and his estranged wife had planned on having three children, "that won't be happening now." He still talks with his ex-wife and has feelings for her. He is close with his mother and visits at least weekly. He views both of them as supports.

He denies having any active medical problems and is on no medications. His tonsils were removed as a child.

His breathalyzer shows a level of .08 (the legal limit in his state for driving), his pulse is mildly elevated at 102 beats per minute, and his blood pressure is 120/90. He does have a slight tremor when he holds his hands out. His CIWA score (Chapter 16) is 4, mostly based on his level of anxiety. He has no symptoms of a withdrawal hallucinosis.

Step One: Level of Care Determination

The client in this case study displays a typical interplay between trauma and substance abuse. Because it has progressed to include signs and symptoms of physiological alcohol dependence, as seen by the mild withdrawal symptoms, even while still under the influence, this individual will require a medically supervised detoxification. Additionally, his reports of daily thoughts of ending his life, accompanied by a plan, will need to be explored thoroughly. He has multiple risks for making a suicide attempt, which include access to firearms, active and heavy drinking, depressive and PTSD symptoms, and recent major losses.

Options for the initial level of care will include an inpatient detoxification unit or psychiatric unit that is equipped to manage an alcohol detoxification, followed by a less-restrictive treatment program, based on Mr. Lathrop's preferences, resources, availability, and clinical appropriateness. Or if Mr. Lathrop is able to put together a solid safety plan, a partial hospital program that can provide a medically supervised detoxification, substance abuse treatment, and treatment to address his suicidality and PTSD might also be an option.

In this instance, Mr. Lathrop expresses a strong desire to pursue outpatient treatment, at least initially. He is fearful that being on a locked inpatient unit will worsen his PTSD. He is, however, willing to take a leave from his job and involve family (his mother and ex-wife) in the construction of a safety plan, which will include immediate removal of firearms from the home.

Step Two: Constructing the Problem/Need List

Substance Use	Mental Health	Medical
Alcohol use has escalated since the trauma	Severe mood swings	Shaky hands when he doesn't have a drink
Daily drinking (one-fifth to a quart of whiskey)	Rage attacks	Mildly elevated pulse and blood pressure
Morning drinking	Insomnia	CIWA score of 4
Shakiness in the morning	Nightmares	Positive breathalyzer
Has had alcohol prior to coming in for the evaluation	Symptoms started following intimate involvement with a horrific tragedy	
No prior treatment for drugs or alcohol	Daily thoughts of suicide, thoughts of vehicular suicide to make it look like an accident	
Nonsmoker	Sadness and depression	
Does not use other drugs	Relates the loss of his marriage to his drinking and mood swings	

Substance Use	Mental Health	Medical
Family history of alcohol use disorders	Hyperstartle response	
	Feelings of depersonalization and derealization	
	Flashbacks to the traumatic event	
	Guilt over not having been able to get there earlier and do more	
	No known family history of mental illness	
	Owns and carries a firearm	

In this instance, where there is significant active suicidal thinking, it is reasonable, and in many organizations expected, to address this as a separate problem/need. Where the medical issues appear to be related to the alcohol, those could be included in that problem/need statement.

1. **Active suicidality with daily thoughts of ending his life**, as evidenced by (AEB) thoughts of vehicular suicide. Other major risk factors include access to firearms, severe PTSD symptoms, and active alcohol use. Protective factors include his desire to be part of his daughter's life and to be able to return to a job that he loves.
2. **Active and severe alcohol use** with increased daily drinking and signs of early withdrawal.
3. **Severe posttraumatic symptoms**, with daily flashbacks, nightmares, hyperstartle, mood swings, depression, anxiety, and rage attacks.

Step Three: Establishing the Initial Goals/Objectives for Treatment

1. **Active suicidality with daily thoughts of ending his life**
   - Short-term goals (with target dates):
     1) To craft a safety plan with specific contingencies that includes his mother's involvement, to be done by the end of the day.
     2) To assess the presence of any suicidal thoughts or behaviors (daily).
   - Long-term goals: To have no suicidal thoughts.
2. **Active and severe alcohol use with daily drinking and signs of early withdrawal**
   - Short-term goals (with target dates):
     1) To safely complete a detoxification from alcohol (7–10 days from today).
     2) To achieve early abstinence from alcohol (starting today).
   - Long-term goals: To be in a sustained abstinence from alcohol.

3. **Severe posttraumatic symptoms**

- Short-term goals (with target dates): To experience a 50 percent or greater reduction in PTSD symptoms by six weeks from today, as evidenced by self-report and using the PTSD checklist.

- Long-term goals: To be as free from symptoms of PTSD, as possible. No more than 30 percent of current levels as measured on the PTSD checklist.

TREATMENT/RECOVERY PLAN

Patient's Name: James Lathrop
Date of Birth: 12/2/1984
Medical Record #: XXX-XX-XXXX

Level of Care: Partial Hospital Program

ICD-10 Codes	DSM-5 Diagnoses
F10.239	Alcohol withdrawal without perceptual disturbances with alcohol use disorder, severe
F43.10	Posttraumatic stress disorder with dissociative symptoms (derealization)
Z63.5	Disruption of family by separation
Z56.9	Other problems related to employment

The individual's stated goal(s): To feel better. To not be so on edge and jumpy. To be able to control my anger. To not feel like my thoughts are so out of my control. To like my job again. To get back with my wife and to be a part of my daughter's life again. To not have so many nightmares and flashbacks.

---

1. Problem/Need Statement:
Active suicidality with daily thoughts of ending his life, including thoughts of vehicular suicide.

Long-Term Goal: To have no thoughts of suicide.

Short-Term Goals/Objectives (with target dates):
1. To craft a safety plan, with specific contingencies, that will include involving the patient's mother in his treatment (by the end of today).
2. To assess the presence of any suicidal thoughts or behaviors (daily).
3. To remove all firearms and ammunition from the home (by the end of today).

---

2. Problem/Need Statement:
Active and severe alcohol use with increased daily drinking, and signs of early withdrawal.

Long-Term Goal: To be in a sustained abstinence from alcohol.

Short-Term Goals/Objectives (with target dates):
1. To safely complete a detoxification from alcohol by one week to 10 days from today.
2. To be in early abstinence from alcohol (starting today).

---

3. Problem/Need Statement:
Severe posttraumatic symptoms, with daily flashbacks, nightmares, hyperstartle, mood swings, depression, anxiety, and rage attacks.
Long-Term Goal:
To be as free from symptoms of PTSD, as possible. No more than 30 percent of current levels as measured on the PTSD checklist (PCL-5).
Short-Term Goals/Objectives (with target dates):
To experience a 50 percent or greater decrease in symptoms of PTSD by self-report and using the PTSD checklist (six weeks from today).

Interventions					
Treatment Modality	**Specific Type**	**Frequency**	**Duration**	**Problem Number**	**Responsible Person(s)**
Pharmacological Management of Alcohol Withdrawal	CIWA protocol	Daily	3–14 days	2	MD/APRN, RN, client, client's mother
Nursing Assessment	Comprehensive nursing assessment	Upon admission	One to two hours	1,2,3	RN
Psychiatric Assessment	Complete psychiatric assessment	Upon admission	One to two hours over the course of the first two weeks	1,2,3	MD/APRN, client
Ongoing Pharmacological Management	Medication management	Weekly for the first two weeks, then as needed	Over the duration of the admission	1,2,3	MD, client
Labs	Complete metabolic profile, CBC, urine drug analysis, breathalyzer, and alcohol metabolites	Upon admission, urine screens ongoing	Over the course of the admission	1,2,3	MD
Safety Assessment	Suicide assessment	Daily	As long as the patient continues to experience suicidal thoughts or behaviors	1	Primary clinician or designee, client
PHP Group Therapy	Relapse prevention	Daily	50 minutes	2	Group leader, client

(Continued)

(Continued)

Interventions					
Treatment Modality	Specific Type	Frequency	Duration	Problem Number	Responsible Person(s)
	Seeking Safety—integrated CBT for PTSD and SUDs	Daily	50 minutes	1,2,3	Group leader, client
	Psychoeducation	2X/week	50 minutes	1,2,3	Group leader, client
	Mindfulness	2X/week	50 minutes	1,2,3	Group leader, client
Individual Counseling	Integrated CBT with exposure	2X/week	50 minutes	1,2,3	Primary therapist, client
Peer Support	AA	On all days client is not in program	1–2 hours	2	Client

Identification of strengths: Wants to feel better, and be able to participate more fully at work. Has a strong sense of morality. Has a strong work ethic and sense of duty to his family and his job.

Peer/family/community supports to assist: Client's mother will drive patient to and from program while he is undergoing the detoxification component, and will have the patient stay with her until he is feeling well enough, and safe enough, to return to his own home. She will keep his firearms securely locked in a gun safe at her home.

Barriers to treatment: The client is not sure how long he can remain out of work without going on a formal leave of absence. He is worried how being in treatment might hurt his ability to return to work.

Staff/client identified education/teaching needs: To understand the relationship between his PTSD symptoms and his drinking and how they influence one another, in both positive and negative ways.

Assessment of discharge needs/discharge planning: To be substance free and free from thoughts of self-harm.

Completion of this treatment/recovery plan was a collaborative effort between the client and the following members of the treatment team:

SIGNATURES		Date/Time
Client:	James Lathrop	6/12/14 2 pm
Physician:	Carlton Blaise, MD	6/12/14 4:15 pm
Treatment Plan Completed By:	James Lathrop & Debra Hayes, LCSW	6/12/14 2 pm
Primary Clinician:	Debra Hayes, LCSW	6/12/14 2 pm
Other Team Members	Mary Lathrop, (Jim's Mom)	6/12/14 4 pm

Schizophrenia, Other Psychotic Disorders, and Co-Occurring Substance Use Disorders

OVERVIEW

Worldwide, the prevalence of schizophrenia and other psychotic disorders (schizoaffective disorder, schizophreniform disorder, etc.) is roughly 1 percent. This does not include people who experience psychotic symptoms in response to substance-induced or medically induced psychotic disorders, such as the hallucinations associated with alcohol and benzodiazepine withdrawals, or intoxication with PCP, hallucinogens, and many other substances.

Lifetime rates of co-occurring substance use disorders in people with schizophrenia range from 47 to 70 percent, not including tobacco. Substance use in this population is associated with increased rates of hospitalization, violence, incarceration, homelessness, HIV and hepatitis infections, and poor adherence to treatment. The most common drugs of abuse for people with schizophrenia are nicotine and alcohol, followed by cannabis and cocaine. Tobacco use is especially prevalent with rates ranging between 70 to nearly 90 percent. Heavy smoking (more than 40 cigarettes/day) is also extremely high.

Even though people with psychotic disorders run the spectrum in terms of overall functioning, the schizophrenia spectrum disorders are chief among those considered as severe/serious and persistent mental illness (SPMI), severe/serious and persistent illness (SPI), or severe/serious mental illness (SMI).

With regards to co-occurring disorders, people with schizophrenia and other SPMI are among those that have received the most attention and study. It is in this group that the movement for integrated treatment took root, based on the realization that traditional substance use programs and mental health programs were not adequately addressing clinical and psychosocial needs. This push for integrated treatment is now moving to include primary care (medical care), as well through the creation of behavioral health–enhanced person-centered medical homes/behavioral health homes. The hope and intent here is to decrease the significant lifespan disparity (15–24 years) between people with severe mental disorders and the general population. Causes for this abysmal health outcome are multifactorial and include several preventable causes of morbidity and mortality, such as high rates of smoking, obesity, drug and alcohol use, elevated cholesterol and other lipid abnormalities, and sedentary lifestyle. Much interest and concern surrounds the question of what role medications that are associated with weight gain and metabolic syndrome may be doing to worsen this lifespan-disparity statistic.

Integrated treatment (psychiatric and substance use) for people with schizophrenia and other SPMI is now included as an evidence-based practice in medicine. The recommendation, to enhance adherence, is that treatment be located within a single facility and team of providers. Core components of integrated treatment for people with schizophrenia-spectrum and substance use disorders may include:

- Psychosocial interventions
  - o Motivational enhancement
  - o Harm reduction strategies
  - o Skills training
  - o Dual-focused self-help and other 12-step community-based supports
  - o Peer supports
- Medication
  - o To manage the symptoms of schizophrenia
  - o To manage withdrawal syndromes
  - o To try and decrease substance use
- Case management strategies.
  - o Assertive community treatment (ACTT)
  - o Targeted case management

Treatment for people with schizophrenia-spectrum disorders is often located in community mental health centers and not-for-profit clinics. Some of these may be state run, while others will receive a mixture of state and federal funding combined with fee-for-service payment.

In addition to the integration of substance use and mental health services is the growing awareness that routine medical evaluation and follow-up is crucial to improve overall health outcomes. New models of integrating the medical component of treatment are currently emerging, including behavioral health person-centered medical homes, which can be colocated within a mental health clinic.

SPECIAL CONSIDERATIONS

There is a tremendous range of functioning for people with schizophrenia-spectrum disorders. This continuum includes people who will have fully realized lives with rich work, home, and social connections, and others who may live in the margins of society, where pressing concerns involve poverty, homelessness, exposure to violence, and involvement with the legal system.

Cognitive Deficits

At present, there are no medical markers for schizophrenia, and it is likely that what is currently included in the spectrum represents multiple conditions. These are neuropsychiatric disorders, which often include cognitive and functional impairments that can range from subtle to severe. Problem areas can include difficulty with focus, attention, and the ability to switch between tasks, as well as with processing multistep undertakings, negotiating social situations, and dealing with complex systems (housing, health care, disability, legal, etc.).

For clinicians unfamiliar in working with people with cognitive impairments and the negative symptoms of schizophrenia, it is easy to label client behavior as non-adherent or willfulness when they habitually miss appointments or don't follow through with the things they said they'd do in session. Strategies to address cognitive deficits and the negative symptoms of schizophrenia may include:

- Neuropsychological testing to identify and clarify strengths and deficits and assist in developing effective interventions
- Use of case management/care management services, such as targeted case management (TCM) and assertive community treatment teams (ACTT), especially for people with frequent hospitalization who struggle to maintain their basic needs in the community
- Use of peer mentors and mutual self-help
- Family psycho-education and enhancing the person's natural supports, including use of the faith communities and wellness programs
- Identification of particular skills the person needs, such as drug refusal
- Skills training that works with identified cognitive processing issues, such as breaking down tasks into their component parts, and practicing until the skill is learned.
- Careful attention to the selection of medications to enhance functioning and minimize side effects that could negatively impact memory, focus, level of alertness, and other cognitive processes

Social Issues

People with schizophrenia-spectrum disorders experience high rates of social problems. These issues run the gamut from family disintegration and limited, or absent, social support networks, to homelessness, poverty, and legal problems. In addition, because of cognitive deficits that may be associated with the individual's disorder, negotiating complex systems, such as obtaining and maintaining disability, low-income housing, and adequate food, may prove impossible for some.

Engagement with Treatment

For people with co-occurring substance use and schizophrenia, engaging them in treatment can be challenging. This process is often complicated by the person's inability to acknowledge that he or she has a mental illness (anosognosia). Anosognosia is often cited as the reason why a person discontinues their medication, "I'm not sick. I don't need this. Why would I take it?" One strategy/approach to address the difficulties with both the overall engagement process and anosognosia is to identify what it is the person wants, versus what it is you as a clinician thinks they need. If they are homeless and they want help with that, but not with their drinking or drug use or with the voices they're hearing, then assistance with housing is the best way to start. This "meeting the person where they're at" approach provides the possibility, using motivational and harm-reduction strategies (Chapter 8), to help the person move forward in all areas of recovery.

Diagnostic Issues

As with other co-occurring substance use and mental disorders, teasing apart the history is essential for clarifying diagnoses. In particular, the clinician wants to know which came first, the use of alcohol and/or drugs, or the development of psychotic symptoms. In theory, one would think this is straight forward. In practice, it is often unclear, even after a thorough assessment. Schizophrenia, which has its typical onset in the late teens and early twenties, can have a significant prodromal phase, free from any evidence of psychosis. One study used childhood home movies and asked viewers to identify which child would go on to develop schizophrenia. Based on withdrawn and odd behaviors, the viewers were able to accurately do this, well above what could be expected from chance alone.

It can be difficult to identify the underlying cause of psychotic symptoms, as they can be attributed to a psychotic disorder, such as schizophrenia, the effects of drugs, alcohol, and various medical conditions, or a combination of the above. The importance of clarifying what may be substance or medically related is both challenging and important. People with psychotic disorders, when they are in crisis, can easily have serious medical conditions, such as dangerously low blood sugar or alcohol withdrawal, overlooked or attributed to their mental disorder.

Historical, clinical, and physical findings can help clarify the diagnoses:

- Did the psychotic symptoms precede the substance use problem?
- At what age did the person first experience psychotic symptoms?
- Does the person have psychotic symptoms when they are not using substances?
- Are the psychotic symptoms typical for a schizophrenia-spectrum disorder?
  - Auditory hallucinations are by far the most frequent hallucinatory experience in schizophrenia.

- o Visual and tactile hallucinations, while they can occur in schizophrenia, are more suggestive of a substance-induced psychosis, withdrawal state, or other medically induced delirium.
- o Substance-induced psychotic symptoms more frequently include positive symptoms of schizophrenia, such as hallucination, delusions, and disorganized speech and behavior. Negative symptoms (low motivation, diminished speech, lack of interest, blunted emotional range) are less typical.
- Are the timing and onset of psychotic symptoms directly related to the ingestion of or withdrawal from drugs or alcohol?
- Does the person have an underlying medical condition that could cause the psychotic symptoms?
- Are the symptoms compatible with syndromes related to medications the person takes, such as a lithium toxicity delirium, or anticholinergic delirium, as can be seen from overtaking many psychiatric medications, or can even occur with prescribed dosages?
- Screening tests:
  - o Urine toxicology can detect substances that can account for the psychotic symptoms.
  - o Liver function tests may indicate the presence of chronic alcohol use or the presence of infectious disease related to intravenous drug use, such as Hepatitis C.
  - o Elevated ammonia levels seen in heavy drinkers can account for confusion and delirious states.
- Do physical findings indicate an altered physiological (medical or drug-induced) state?
  - o Dilated or pin-point pupils
  - o Nystagmus (visible rhythmic movements of the eyes, often seen in certain intoxication states, such as with PCP and ketamine. This can also be associated with serotonin syndrome.)
  - o Flushed or bone-dry skin
  - o Elevations in blood pressure and pulse
  - o Elevated temperature
  - o Hyperexcitable reflexes
  - o Muscle rigidity
- Does the patient, family, or other reporters provide information that the symptoms are typical for the person's psychiatric disorder, or do they indicate that something different is going on?
- Has the person been using substances that can cause psychotic symptoms? In the case of this question, this is a growing and rapidly changing list, which will include many substances that may not show up on typical toxicology screens, such as synthetic cannabis (K-2, Spice), and various amphetamine-type stimulants, "bath salts," which are sold under a broad variety of names. This also includes the misuse of prescription medications, as well as many over-the-counter sleep and cold medications.

Drugs That Can Cause Psychotic Symptoms

Drug	Comments
Alcohol	Psychosis possible when intoxicated, as well as common in severe withdrawal states (i.e., hallucinosis and delirium tremens). Rarely associated with persistent psychosis, as seen in some instances of alcoholic dementia (Korsakoff's dementia).
Barbiturates	Psychosis possible when intoxicated and in withdrawal states.
Benzodiazepines	Psychosis possible during intoxication, and in withdrawal states.
Cannabis and synthetic cannabis (K-2, Spice)	Psychosis possible, rare cases of persistent psychosis. Synthetic cannabis is associated with more extreme psychosis. Also cannabis is frequently treated or "dipped" in substances such as formaldehyde, which can cause a prolonged delirium (up to six months).
Hallucinogens (LSD, psilocybin/magic mushrooms, peyote)	Hallucinations and delusions while intoxicated. Rare cases of persistent psychosis that can last for weeks to months.
Inhalants (nitrous oxide, toluene, other solvents)	All associated with psychotic symptoms while intoxicated. Solvents implicated in persistent psychotic states.
MDMA (Ecstasy)	Psychosis common.
NMDA antagonists (PCP, Ketamine)	Psychosis during intoxication that may persist for weeks. PCP is often combined with cannabis.
Opioids (heroin, methadone, oxycodone)	Hallucinations during intoxication. Rare cases of persistent psychosis with smoked heroin (chasing the dragon). Rare cases of withdrawal-related psychosis, which can be protracted (weeks to months).
Steroids	Psychosis possible, along with typical behavioral and mood changes. "Roid rage."
Stimulants (cocaine, ADHD medication, bath salts, methamphetamine)	Psychosis possible while intoxicated, all forms of hallucinations and delusions, including extreme paranoia and grandiosity. Psychosis can persist for weeks after the last use.

Medical Conditions That Can Cause Psychotic Symptoms

Medical Condition	Symptoms
Infectious diseases	HIV/AIDs, bacterial or viral meningitis, high fever states, Lyme disease, syphilis, urinary tract infections.
Neoplasms (tumors/cancers)	Certain hormone-secreting tumors, certain lung cancers.
Electrolyte abnormalities	Many disturbances in electrolyte balance can manifest as confusion or delirium, such as dangerously low sodium.
Metabolic and nutritional abnormalities	B12 deficiency, hypoglycemia (low blood sugar), hyperglycemia (elevated blood sugar), hypoxia (inadequate oxygen in the blood), hypercarbia (increased CO_2 levels).
Medication toxicities	An extensive number of medications can cause toxic and delirious states, both alone and in combination with other medications, illicit drugs, and alcohol. This includes: lithium, anticholinergic medications, sedative hypnotics, opioids, anticonvulsants, anti-Parkinson's medications, antivirals, antiarrhythmics, steroids, and many others.
Endocrine abnormalities (hormonal)	Hyper- or hypothyroidism, hyperadrenalism.
Dementia (neurocognitive disorders)	All of the dementias, such as Alzheimer's disease, can be associated with delusions and hallucinations. In some, such as Lewy body disease, this is common.
Autoimmune disorders	Lupus, multiple sclerosis
Renal disorders (kidney)	Uremia (elevations in waste products in the blood due to renal failure)
Hepatic disease (liver)	Hepatic encephalopathy. Elevated ammonia levels due to liver disease.
Neurologic conditions	Stroke, seizures (postictal confusion and delirium), multiple sclerosis, head trauma.

There is also a growing body of evidence that in some cases, substance use may hasten, or even bring on the development of schizophrenia and related syndromes. Cannabis, in particular, has been implicated in susceptible individuals, who carry a particular gene variant and protein involved in the synthesis of dopamine (cyclic O-methyl transferase/COMT).

One study that followed 45,000 Swedish army conscripts for 15 years showed that those that smoked cannabis on a regular basis were six times more likely to have a follow-up diagnosis of schizophrenia. Similar results have been found in other studies.

THE DSM-5 AND SCHIZOPHRENIA-SPECTRUM DISORDERS

In the current DSM-5 diagnostic system, psychotic disorders are characterized by abnormalities in the following areas:

- Delusions. These are fixed false beliefs and can take many forms.
  - Paranoid (persecutory) delusions. The false belief that known, or unknown, persons or entities wish to cause you harm.
  - Grandiose delusions. The belief that a person has special powers or abilities that they do not have. This can include the belief that you are a famous person, God, the devil, or have supernatural powers and/or abilities.
  - Erotomanic delusions. The erroneous belief that another person—often a famous person—is in love with you. In some instances the person may have met the object of their delusion, but often they have not.
  - Thought insertion and thought broadcasting. The belief that you can read another person's mind or vice versa.
  - Thoughts of reference. The belief that there are special messages just for you coming through the television, the newspaper, or other medium.
- Hallucinations. In schizophrenia-spectrum disorders, hallucinations are most frequently auditory (hearing voices), but can also be visual, and less frequently tactile (touch) or olfactory (smell).
- Disorganized thinking. This abnormality will be evidenced in the person's speech patterns and may include:
  - Tangential thoughts and looseness of associations. There is a connection between thoughts, but the overall train rambles and does not come to conclusive points. It's difficult for a listener to follow what the person is trying to say.
  - Word salad. This is where there is a seeming disconnect from one utterance to the next. Speech may appear jumbled and completely nonsensical.
  - Unusual patterns of enunciation, rhyming, echolalia (the repeating of words), echopraxia (the repeating, or parroting, of another person's behaviors).
- Disorganized behavior. These can run the range from idiosyncratic and odd mannerisms to catatonia.
- Negative symptoms. Observers note diminished emotional range and response, often referred to as a flat or blunted affect. Negative symptoms can include symptoms of depression, such as loss of interest, inability to experience much pleasure, apathy, amotivation, and ambivalence. A person with negative symptoms may have no interest in doing anything more than staying at home watching TV while chain-smoking cigarettes for hours, even days, on end.

In the DSM-5 the psychotic disorders include delusional disorder, brief psychotic disorder (symptoms last from one day to one month), schizophreniform disorders (symptoms last from one month to six months), schizophrenia (symptoms have been present for more than six months), schizoaffective disorder (there is both evidence of a psychotic disorder and a mood disorder, where for at least a two-week period there have been psychotic symptoms without a mood episode). There are also designations for psychotic disorders that can be due to medical conditions, and substance/medication-induced psychotic disorders.

Schizophrenia-Spectrum Disorders

Disorder	Criterion A*	Time Frame	Other Key Features
Delusional Disorder	Delusions only	At least one month	Never meets criteria for schizophrenia, typically able to function. Not due to another medical, substance, or mental disorder.
Brief Psychotic Disorder	Presence of one or more: delusions, hallucinations, disorganized speech	One day to one month	Not due to another medical, substance, or mental disorder.
Schizophreniform Disorder	Presence of two or more criterion A, one must be: delusions, hallucinations, disorganized speech	One month to six months	Not due to another medical, substance, or mental disorder.
Schizophrenia	Presence of one or more: delusions, hallucinations, disorganized speech	At least six months	Not due to another medical, substance, or mental disorder.
Schizoaffective Disorder	Presence of two or more criterion A, one must be: delusions, hallucinations, disorganized speech	Not specified	• Major mood episode (depressive or manic) concurrent with criteria A symptoms of schizophrenia. • Delusions or hallucinations without a mood episode must be present for at least two weeks at some point in the illness. • Not due to another medical, substance, or mental disorder.

*Criterion A: Delusions, Hallucinations, Disorganized Speech, Disorganized Behavior, Negative symptoms

ASSESSMENT AND SCREENING TOOLS

Clinician-Rated Dimensions of Psychosis Severity

This eight-item, Likert-type (0 = not present, 4 = present and severe) assessment tool that covers the five core symptoms of schizophrenia. Three additional items assess for the presence and severity of cognitive impairment, depression, and mania. It is available through the American Psychiatric Association (www.psychiatry.org/practice/dsm/dsm5/online-assessment-measures#Disorder) and can be used freely by researchers and clinicians as a recommended assessment tool in the DSM-5.

The Positive and Negative Syndrome Scale (PANSS)

A 30-item clinician-administered instrument, this scale measures the positive and negative symptoms of schizophrenia. It is widely used in studies evaluating the efficacy of medication and non-medication therapies for people with psychotic disorders. It takes 45–50 minutes to complete.

The Brief Psychiatric Rating Scale (BPRS)

Developed in the early 1960s, the BPRS is one of the most widely used clinician-administered screens for psychiatric disorders, including the presence of psychotic symptoms. The BPRS is based on the clinician's interview and interactions with a client. Most versions contain 24 items, which are rated on a scale of 0 (not present) to 7 (extremely severe). It can be given over the course of treatment and used to mark clinical progress. It takes approximately 20–30 minutes to complete.

SPECIFIC PSYCHOSOCIAL TREATMENT APPROACHES

Psychotherapies

Assertive Community Treatment. ACT (see Chapter 7) is a widely disseminated, evidenced-based treatment approach to working with people with severe mental illness, especially those who have difficulty engaging in treatment and who have had multiple hospitalizations. It involves the use of a multidisciplinary team, which provides integrated treatment and support to clients. ACT teams meet frequently to review cases and share responsibility among team members. Caseloads are kept low (10:1 ratio for case managers) on account of the intensity of services to be delivered. The majority (ideally 80% or more) of services are delivered in the community versus an office-based setting. ACT provides 24/7 availability. Positive outcomes from ACT include decreased rates of hospitalization and improved psychosocial outcomes.

Integrated Dual Diagnosis Treatment. Although this book focuses on integrated treatment across all diagnoses, the concept of integrated treatment first took root in working with people with severe and persistent mental illness (SPMI). Integrated dual diagnosis treatment (IDDT), as studied in the SPMI population, is considered an evidence-based approach for working with people who have severe mental illness and co-occurring substance use disorders. IDDT is typically provided through agencies and mental health clinics that employ multidisciplinary treatment approaches, often through the use of assertive community treatment teams. Key components to the IDDT model include:

- Stage-specific treatment
  - o Engagement—This involves the establishment of a relationship with the client. With people with schizophrenia-spectrum disorders, this may include various forms of community outreach, and literally "meeting the person where they are at." This could be in a coffee shop, the person's apartment, or on a park bench.
  - o Establishment of treatment goals with the client.
  - o Interventions that are specific to the person and where they are in their recovery.
  - o Attention to the person's immediate, intermediate, and longer-range goals.
- Attention to basic needs, such as housing and finances
- Motivational interviewing (Chapter 8)
  - o Attention to the person's level of motivation to change high-risk behaviors, including substance use.
  - o Typically done in 1:1 sessions of varying lengths. Various studies have found three 1-hour sessions associated with positive outcomes.
  - o Emphasis on empowerment and responsibility.
  - o Evaluation of the risks and benefits of continued drug and alcohol use. Weighing the pros and cons.
- Cognitive behavior therapy (CBT)
  - o CBT strategies assist with recognizing thoughts, emotions, and behaviors associated with craving and relapse.
  - o CBT, through cognitive restructuring, can help people identify healthier ways to manage their mental illness, real-life stresses, and cravings. Cognitive restructuring can be used to challenge beliefs about the positive benefits of drug/alcohol use.
  - o CBT can help normalize relapses and get the person back on track. "It's not the end of the world. Today's a new day."
  - o CBT can be used to model and practice skills through techniques such as role playing, which can be especially helpful in developing drug refusal skills.
  - o CBT can be used to improve overall problem-solving skills.
- Principles of harm reduction and "meeting the person where they are at"
  - o Empowering the person in recovery.
  - o Supporting all positive change.
- Assertive community outreach, including homeless outreach teams, the use of peer engagement specialists, and other case management approaches
- Comprehensive and multidimensional services and supports that might include:
  - o Psychiatric assessment and ongoing treatment, including medication.
  - o Housing assistance.
  - o Vocational training, assistance, and support.

- Peer supports.
- Wellness programs.
- Enhancement of natural social supports (family, friends, faith community.)
- Utilization of mutual self-help (12-step, Double Trouble in Recovery).
- Liaison with other providers.
- Liaison with the criminal justice system.
- Access to specialized programs for individuals with particular diagnoses and needs (i.e., dialectic behavior therapy, eating disorder treatment, CBT for specific anxiety disorders, etc.).

Behavioral Treatment for Substance Abuse in Serious and Persistent Mental Illness (BTSAS): Developed by Alan Bellack, MD, and colleagues, this small-group approach (4–6 members, although with some individual components) consists of manualized treatment that includes several integrated features. BTSAS emphasizes the over-learning of a few important skills, such as drug refusal, and adapts the treatment to the individual's specific needs and cognitive abilities.

BTSAS has several core components:

- Individual motivational interviewing, in which a specific drug to address is identified.
- Contingency management, which uses the results of urine drug screening to provide monetary rewards.
- Collaborative goal-setting in which realistic short-term goals are identified.
- A harm reduction approach, which works with people at all stages of their drug use.
- Social skills training to teach drug refusal and to enhance sober social supports.
- Psychoeducation regarding drug use, unsafe behaviors and their consequences. This includes education about mental disorders and specific risks for people with co-occurring substance use problems.
- Relapse prevention training, to help people identify high-risk situations, how to avoid them, and how to manage urges and lapses.

BTSAS is a structured treatment where clients learn the format, which includes a urinalysis, review of goals and goals setting, a review of the prior session, and presentation of new material, which typically includes didactic, discussion, and role playing around important skills to be learned.

Case Management. While included as part of the ACT model and many others, case management as an add-on to other treatments has been shown to be effective in improving overall care integration and adherence to treatment. People with schizophrenia often have severe problems with motivation, as well as other specific cognitive deficits that can easily lead to treatment failure, especially when the individual is faced with having to navigate multiple complex systems, such as mental health and substance use agencies, the legal system, welfare and disability agencies, and even managing basic needs such as housing and grocery shopping.

Case managers, through the use of a comprehensive needs/goals assessment, help coordinate and monitor their client's treatment. Specific roles of the case manager can include:

- Identification of needed/desired services, and then helping the client navigate systems to put them in place, such as obtaining a primary care physician or nurse practitioner.
- Care coordination, from the setting up of appointments, to helping the client arrange transportation.
- Assistance and skills training in budgeting so that critical services, such as the rent and utilities, get paid, and that there is adequate food in the house.
- Working with the client's specific goals to help them more fully realize their lives in the community. This could include assistance with vocational, educational, spiritual, social, and recreational goals.

Peer and Natural Supports

- Mutual self-help: Even though 12-step groups (AA, NA, etc.) are considered a mainstay of substance abuse treatment, they may not always be welcoming, or feel welcoming, to people with co-occurring schizophrenia-spectrum disorders. Helping the person in recovery find a home group where they feel comfortable, and connecting them with a suitable sponsor, may be a particularly helpful and meaningful intervention.
- Double Trouble in Recovery Groups and Dual Diagnosis Anonymous: These 12-step mutual self-help groups are specifically designed for people with both mental illness and substance use disorders. These targeted groups allow individuals to address both their issues with mental illness and their substance abuse. Hundreds of groups meet nationwide, but the organization currently has no central website. For those interested in starting a group, a low-cost electronic manual is available: *Double Trouble in Recovery: Basic Guide* by Howard Vogel. To find a group, one should contact 211 or the local mental health authority.
- Peer support specialists: Over the past decade, the use of peer specialists has grown, often embedded within assertive community treatment teams (ACTT) as well as in other case management–type services. Peer specialists are people in recovery with mental illness, and possibly substance use disorders as well, who help clients. Peer support specialists differ from traditional case managers in that their role is more directly focused on engaging with a client as one person in recovery to another. It is common for peer support specialists to focus on particular human interactions, such as going to a movie or eating a meal together, or doing some other more social and less typically treatment-type activity.

Pharmacology

Among the few studies that look at specific antipsychotic medication for people who have both schizophrenia and substance use disorders, those done generally show improvement in both the symptoms of schizophrenia and the severity of the substance use disorder. These findings, which include decreased substance use and improved functioning, support the importance of offering pharmacologic treatment, even when people are actively using. That said, important factors need to be considered when medications are prescribed for people with co-occurring schizophrenia-spectrum and substance use disorders.

- Assess the potential for drug interactions and adverse reactions between any medication and the person's substance(s) of abuse.
  - o Sedating antipsychotics such as quetiapine/Seroquel will increase the overall risk of respiratory depression in a person who abuses central nervous system depressants such as opioids and alcohol.
  - o Someone who misuses amphetamines or goes through intermittent alcohol or benzodiazepine withdrawal while taking certain antidepressants or antipsychotics will be at an increased risk for seizures.
  - o Cocaine is associated with increased adverse cardiac events, which could be worsened with the use of medications associated with cardiac-conduction delays, such as the prolongation of the QT interval (a measurement of the heart's electrical conduction, which if it becomes too long can lead to dangerous arrhythmias and sudden death) with medications like ziprasidone/Geodon and even methadone.
  - o Cigarette smoking, through its effects on the liver, can decrease the blood levels of certain antipsychotic medications by more than 50 percent.
- Keep medication regimens as safe and streamlined as possible. Less is often more. And the other truism in prescribing is "start low and go slow." The risk of suicidal behavior increases when someone is intoxicated, and so limiting the amounts of medications people have and their potential lethality in overdose should be considered.
- Limit the prescribing of medications that can be abused, misused, and/or diverted, such as the benzodiazepines and stimulants.
- Consider strategies that will increase adherence, such as once-a-day or long-acting injectable medications. Where needed, case managers and in-home nursing supports can assist with community-based medication management.
- Assess how medications are stored and kept secure. Does the person need a lockbox? Would daily medication delivery improve the chances that the person's medications would not be misused or diverted? This precaution could be achieved through the use of an ACT team, other case management model, through the use of an in-home nursing agency, or with a responsible family member.
- Educate patients as to which medications are to be taken even if they have lapsed into substance use.

Antipsychotic Medications. The mainstay pharmacologic treatments for schizophrenia are the antipsychotic medications, also termed neuroleptics and major tranquilizers, which are divided into two broad classes: the first- (typical) and second- (atypical) generation antipsychotics.

First- and Second-Generation Antipsychotics

First-Generation/ Typical Antipsychotics	Available as a Long-Acting Decanoate	Second-Generation/ Atypical Antipsychotics	Available as a Long-Acting Decanoate
Chlorpromazine/ Thorazine	No	Aripiprazole/Abilify	Yes
Fluphenazine/Prolixin	Yes	Asenapine/Saphris	No
Haloperidol/Haldol	Yes	Clozapine/Clozaryl	No
Loxapine/Loxitane	No	Iloperadone/Fanapt	No
Molindone/Moban	No	Lurasidone/Latuda	No
Perphenzaine/Trilafon	No	Olanzapine/Zyprexa	Yes
Thioridazine/Mellaril	No	Paliperidone/Invega	Yes
Thioxithene/Navane	No	Quetiapine/Seroquel	No
Trifluoperazine/ Stelazine	No	Risperidone/Risperdal	Yes
		Ziprasidone/Geodon	No

Both classes of antipsychotic medication carry significant risks for numerous side effects and serious adverse reactions, including potentially fatal ones. Concerning, too, is the development of movement abnormalities with the older medications and obesity and metabolic syndrome with the newer ones.

All these medications are available in pill or capsule form, and several can be given as a rapid-acting injectable (haloperidol/Haldol, olanzapine/Zyprexa). These agents are typically used in situations where rapid tranquilization is required to help someone who is severely agitated.

Long-acting decanoate-injectable medications (every two to four weeks) are also available for several medications. Decanoate medications, because they are dosed infrequently, are associated with higher rates of adherence to medication. They carry all the risks and benefits associated with the shorter-acting version of the medication and can be associated with local reactions at the injection site (pain, redness, swelling). At the time of this book's publication these injectables include two of the first-generation antipsychotics and several of the second-generation medications.

Side Effects and Adverse Reactions Common with the First-Generation/Typical Antipsychotics

- **Movement abnormalities and dystonias**
  - Parkinsonism. This involves the shortening of a person's gait "the thorazine shuffle," accompanied by diminished arm swing, rigidity in the body, and a flattened and often depressed appearing facial expression.
  - Akathisia. An uncomfortable feeling of restlessness, which can be severe and may be manifested by anxious and fidgety behavior and an inability to stay still, including

foot and arm tapping and rocking. It can easily be mistaken for the hyperactivity and inattention seen in attention deficit hyperactivity disorder (ADHD).

o Acute dystonic reactions. These are involuntary contractions or spasming of muscles. They can come on suddenly after administration of an antipsychotic. They are rarely life threatening but can be profoundly disturbing, and even painful. They often require emergency treatment with the use of anticholinergic medications such as diphenhydramine/Benadryl, benztropine/Cogentin, or trihexyphenidyl/Artane. Opisthonic reaction is an involuntary reaction in which the eyes roll back. Torticollis is contraction of the muscles of the neck.

o Tardive dyskinesia (TD) is a common and potentially irreversible involuntary movement abnormality mostly associated with the older antipsychotics. TD typically affects the muscles around the mouth and tongue and can include lip smacking and the unintended protrusion of the tongue. TD can include the major muscle groups of the arms, legs, and trunk as well. Although most frequently limited to the face and tongue, it can affect all muscle groups and become disfiguring and disabling.

- **Anticholinergic Side Effects**

  o Dry mouth.

  o Urinary retention.

  o Decreased ability to sweat (especially worrisome in warm weather when it puts people at risk for heat exhaustion and stroke).

  o Confusion. In severe instances anticholinergic side effects can progress to confusion and delirium and easily be confused with a worsening of the underlying psychotic illness.

- **Orthostatic changes** involve drops in blood pressure, at times without an adequate increase in pulse, when a person goes from lying down to seated, or seated to standing. It results in light-headedness and in more severe instances the person could fall or pass out.

- **Sedation** can be caused by any of the antipsychotic medications, but it is most significant with chlorpromazine/Thorazine and thioridazine/Mellaril.

Side Effects and Adverse Reactions Common with the Second-Generation/Atypical Antipsychotics

- **Metabolic syndrome** is caused by the increased appetite and alterations in insulin and glucose metabolism seen with the atypical antipsychotics. It encompasses serious health conditions, characterized by weight gain, increased abdominal girth, and elevations in blood pressure, cholesterol, and triglycerides. These changes predispose the person to obesity, type 2 diabetes, hypercholesterolemia, coronary artery disease, and stroke. Metabolic syndrome represents a major health concern and is one factor in the overall poor mortality statistics for people with schizophrenia-spectrum disorders.

  Significant weight gain has been reported with all the atypical antipsychotics with the exception of ziprasidone/Geodon. With some medications, such as clozapine/Clozaryl and olanzapine/Zyprexa, weight gain can be a pound, or more, per week. Other medications such as risperidone/Risperdal and quetiapine/Seroquel can have weight gain more on the order of half a pound per week.

- **Sedation:** Especially significant with clozapine/Clozaryl and quetiapine/Seroquel.

- **Blood pressure changes:** Can be profound with clozapine/Clozaryl.

Clozapine, Special Considerations, Monitoring, and Concerns. Clozapine/Clozaryl/Fazaclo was the first of the second-generation antipsychotics. It is considered the "gold standard" because a significant number of patients who have not responded or have had an adequate improvement with other medications will show clinical improvement, in some instances substantial, on clozapine.

Clozapine carries the risk for a potentially life-threatening condition, agranulocytosis, in which the bone marrow stops producing white blood cells that are necessary to protect the body from infection. Because of this risk, clozapine is not used as a first-line treatment for schizophrenia, but is reserved for individuals who do not respond to other agents. Rates of agranulocytosis run as high as 1 percent, and individuals on clozapine need to be registered and have regular blood counts (CBC) drawn. Initially, draws are weekly, then biweekly, and after six months, if all the results are normal, monthly. Pharmacies are required to verify the blood work results before filling prescriptions.

In addition to the risk of agranulocytosis, clozapine carries a heavy side effect/adverse reaction burden, which can include:

- Seizures, especially when the dose is greater than 600 mg/day.

- Sialorrhea, extreme salivation and drooling. It's not uncommon for people to complain of pillow-drenching drool.

- Weight gain and metabolic syndrome, which can be severe with clozapine, averaging roughly one pound per week.

- Orthostatic blood pressure changes. This is often experienced as light-headedness, and in severe cases can predispose to falls.

- Tachycardia—rapid heart rate. It is common for people on clozapine to have resting heart rates greater than 100 beats per minute.

- Sedation. Often severe, and requires a slow titration of the medication for the person to be able to tolerate it.

Monitoring for Tardive Dyskinesia

People on antipsychotics, both first- and second-generation, should be monitored for the development of tardive dyskinesia. The standard of care includes the use of the Abnormal Involuntary Movement Scale (AIMS). An AIMS examination should be completed prior to starting or switching antipsychotics and then every six months thereafter. The AIMS exam takes 5–10 minutes to perform and can be completed by the prescriber or, with training and adequate supervision, other providers. The AIMS examination is in the public domain and may be freely copied.

The Abnormal Involuntary Movement Scale (AIMS) Examination

Performing an AIMS examination follows these steps:

1. At some point before, or after, the examination, observe the patient when they are unaware, for signs of involuntary movement, for instance in the waiting room.

2. Ask the client to remove their shoes and socks. (This will allow visualization of movement in the toes.)

3. Have the patient sit in a firm chair without arms.

4. Ask the client if they have anything in their mouth (gum, tobacco). If they do, have them remove it, as the chewing could be mistaken for symptoms of tardive dyskinesia (TD).

5. Ask the client if they wear dentures and/or have problems with their teeth. Loose fitting dentures can lead to mouth movements that look like TD.

6. Ask the client if they notice any involuntary movements in their mouth, face, lips, hands, feet, or other parts of their body. Ask them to describe these movements, and whether they are distressed and/or impaired by them.

7. Have the client sit in the chair with their hands resting on their legs or knees and their feet shoulders-width apart. Visually scan the client from head to toe for any signs of movement.

8. Ask the client to let their arms and hands hang unsupported by their legs. Observe the body for movement.

9. Ask the client to open their mouth, and observe the tongue for movements. Do this twice.

10. Ask the client to stick out their tongue. Observe the tongue for unusual movements, such as thrusting, or crossing the midline of the mouth.

11. Ask the client to tap their thumb against each of their fingertips in rapid succession. Have them do this for ten to fifteen seconds with one hand, and then the other. Observe movements throughout the body, as they do this. This strategy is called activation and will bring out or worsen movements of tardive dyskinesia.

12. Extend and flex the client's left and right arms. Notice signs of rigidity or cog-wheeling (where the arm has a jerky ratchet-like quality as it is moved). This type of cog-wheel rigidity can be associated with the adverse reaction of parkinsonism.

13. Ask the client to stand. Observe the body for signs of movement.

14. Ask the client to extend their arms in front of their body with palms facing down. Observe the entire body for movement.

15. Have the client walk a few paces, turn, and then walk back. Observe for normal arm swing and for gait. In people with parkinsonism the gait may be shuffling in nature, and have a restricted, or absent, arm swing. This may also activate movement associated with tardive dyskinesia.

Scoring the Abnormal Involuntary Movement Scale Examination

• The AIMS examination is considered positive if there is a score of two on any two movements, or a score of three or four on any single movement.

• The score is not summed (i.e., a score of one on five separate movements does not equal five).

• Add one to a score if the client is aware and/or distressed by the movement.

THE ABNORMAL INVOLUNTARY MOVEMENT SCALE (AIMS)

Client name:_____   Date:_____

ID number:_____   Examiner:_____

Code: 0 = None 1= Minimal 2 = Mild 3 = Moderate 4 = Severe

Instructions: Complete the examination prior to scoring.

Facial and oral movements:

1. Muscles of facial expression (forehead, around the eyes, cheeks, grimacing, smiling, blinking).	0	1	2	3	4
2. Lips and around the mouth (puckering, lip smacking, pouting).	0	1	2	3	4
3. Jaw (biting, grinding, lateral movements, clenching).	0	1	2	3	4
4. Tongue (rate only movement increases in and out of the mouth).	0	1	2	3	4

Extremity movements:

5. Upper: Arms, wrists, hands, and fingers. Include slow and rapid movements, snake-like movements. Do not include tremor.	0	1	2	3	4
6. Lower: Legs, feet, toes, ankles. Lateral movements of the knee, foot tapping, inward and outward movements of the feet, flexing and contracting of the feet.	0	1	2	3	4

Trunk movements:

7. Neck, shoulders, hips, torso (rocking, twisting, squirming, pelvic gyrations).	0	1	2	3	4

Overall severity of movements:

8. Severity of abnormal movements.	0	1	2	3	4
9. Incapacitation of abnormal movements.	0	1	2	3	4

Client's awareness of movements:

No awareness = 0 Aware, no distress = 1 Aware, mild distress = 2 Aware, moderate distress = 3 Aware, severe distress = 4

10. Client's awareness of movement	0	1	2	3	4

Dental status

11. Current problems with teeth and/or dentures?	Yes	No
12. Are dentures usually worn?	Yes	No

Comments:_____   Examiner's signature:_____   Date/Time:_____

Monitoring for Metabolic Syndrome

With the serious risk of metabolic syndrome associated with the second-generation antipsychotics, it is crucial that routine monitoring—prior to starting or changing medication and then ongoing—is done. There are a number of monitoring guidelines and the following are those recommended by the American Diabetes Association and the American Psychiatric Association:

- Personal and family history of obesity, diabetes, high blood pressure, cardiovascular disease, and lipid abnormalities, obtained at baseline and updated annually.
- Weight and height.
- Calculation of body mass index (BMI) done at baseline (before starting the medication) and then monthly for the first three months, and then quarterly. Greater frequency may be required if the BMI is increasing. Free applications for calculating BMI are available, including this one through the Centers for Disease Control: www.cdc.gov/healthyweight/assessing/bmi/index.html.
- Waist circumference at baseline, monthly for the first three months, and then quarterly.
- Fasting lipids (cholesterol, triglycerides, HDL, LDL) at baseline, then at three months, and every five years. If there are elevations, the frequency would be adjusted.
- Fasting Blood glucose at baseline, three months, and then annually.

In addition to the above, it's common for practitioners to also obtain a Hemoglobin A1C, which is a marker for the development of diabetes.

Strategies to Address Weight Gain and Metabolic Syndrome. For people on medications that carry the risk of weight gain and metabolic syndrome, education and early intervention are crucial.

- Address modifiable cardiovascular risk factors and unhealthy lifestyle habits such as tobacco use, elevated lipids, lack of adequate exercise, and unhealthy and high-calorie diets.
- Educate family and involved supports about the risk of metabolic syndrome and efforts that can be done to prevent it, and reverse it should it occur.
- Maintain active medical follow-up and liaison between the psychiatric prescriber and the primary care practitioner. Should someone develop weight gain, elevations in lipids, hypertension, and so forth, these will need to be followed, and addressed, medically. This might include the use of medications for elevated lipids (statins) or for type 2 diabetes (oral antidiabetic agents, such as metformin.)
- Consider the use of antipsychotic agents less associated with metabolic syndrome (i.e., ziprasidone/Geodon and possibly aripiprazole/Abilify).

CASE STUDY: DAVID GRAY

David Gray is a 23-year-old single, Caucasian man who is initially evaluated in the emergency room where he has been brought by police on an emergency hold/police request for psychiatric evaluation. His mother, Lillian Gray, with whom he lives, called 911 after he threatened to kill himself. She is present for the evaluation. She reports that her son has been drinking heavily and using other substances as well. She has several empty packages of a substance her son has been purchasing over the Internet, which claims to be "plant food."

In the emergency room, David is extremely agitated, red-faced, and aggressive toward staff. He swears and when the police remove the handcuffs, he lunges for a nurse. A security code is called, and with the assistance of his mother, David agrees to take a shot of haloperidol/Haldol and lorazepam/Ativan. He calms noticeably, but appears distracted and admits to hearing the voice of the devil telling him to end his own life. His mood fluctuates rapidly, at times sobbing, and then in a matter of minutes laughing and talking rapidly with an odd punctuated cadence, where he repeats certain words. His blood alcohol level is 0.12 (legal limit for driving: 0.08) and his urine toxicology is positive for cannabis. His blood pressure and pulse are both elevated and return to normal range with the administration of an additional dose of lorazepam/Ativan.

His mother describes how David has always had emotional problems and how he started to drink, smoke cigarettes, and use cannabis when he was in middle school. "He was always very shy, never made friends, and told me that pot was the only thing that calmed him down." He dropped out of school in the tenth grade, "He just stopped going." He has been hospitalized twice (both times involuntary) with similar presentations and has had two additional emergency room evaluations where he was discharged home with his mother and referrals to outpatient treatment. "I tried to get him to keep those appointments, but he won't. He insists there's nothing wrong with him and that all he needs is marijuana." She states he's taken deliberate overdoses in the past, and she's frightened that one day he will take his life.

The family history is significant for a maternal uncle with schizophrenia who committed suicide, and David's father died from cirrhosis after decades of heavy drinking. His mother does not use substances and reports that other than anxiety over her son, she has no mental health problems.

David's medical history is unremarkable, although he's not been to see a physician, other than in the emergency room evaluations, for years. He has no allergies. Blood work obtained in the emergency room is normal with the exception of elevated liver enzymes and an elevated mean corpuscular volume (MCV) on his complete blood count (CBC).

As David's blood alcohol level drops, he continues to display bizarre behavior with pressured speech and rapid shifts in his mood. When asked about suicide, he replies, "I'm a waste of space. What's the point?" He continues to report hearing voices, and eventually falls asleep after a dose of tranquilizing medication. He is placed on a CIWA protocol for alcohol withdrawal, and the emergency room psychiatrist makes the determination to hospitalize David on an involuntary basis based on his imminent risk for self-harm and that he is gravely disabled, based on his current level of psychosis, auditory hallucinations telling him to kill himself, agitation, and substance use.

Part Two

Three days later David is on an inpatient psychiatric unit. His symptoms of alcohol withdrawal are well-controlled with Lorazepam/Ativan combined with a medication for blood pressure. He has been prescribed risperidone/Risperdal for his hallucinations and delusional thinking but has refused most doses of this medication. He states, "There's nothing wrong with me. All I need to do is smoke pot. It's the only thing that helps."

He is calmer, overall, and no additional emergency doses of injectable tranquilizers have been required. He is able to be interviewed and answers most questions. He states he's been hearing voices since he was 14. It is usually the voice of a man he doesn't recognize, but thinks it's the devil. It often tells him to harm himself or carries on a narrative of derogatory comments about David: "You're worthless, a piece of shit. …" He states when he's tried to harm himself in the past, it's been at the urging of the voice. He admits to frequent thoughts of self-harm, but states he currently has no intention of acting upon them. He denies any thoughts of harming others. He rates his mood as severely depressed: 10/10. He rates his level of anxiety as between an 8–10/10. He reports that his goal is to get out of the hospital and go back to smoking "as much pot as I can." He does, however, agree that his drinking has become excessive. "But I didn't need to be in a hospital to stop, I do that all the time on my own."

His mother visits daily. She provides additional information, as well as prior records from his two earlier hospitalizations. She states that her son's mood fluctuates between extreme depression to where he won't leave his room for weeks, and even months, at a time, to periods of manic agitation often accompanied by heavy drug and alcohol use. During those periods he stops sleeping, becomes loud and hyperverbal, and talks about having special powers. During these episodes she calls the police because his behavior becomes frightening and at times dangerous, such as getting behind the wheel of a car and driving at high speeds while intoxicated. She believes that even when he is not depressed or manic, he continues to hear voices. He has been arrested on multiple occasions for possession of cannabis and breach of peace. He's received two DUIs, and does not currently have a license. As far as she is aware, he has no history of violence toward anyone but himself, although he has "trashed his room and punched holes in the wall" on multiple occasions. She states that David has never hit her, but has threatened to do so multiple times.

Step One: Level of Care Determination and Discussion

This case study involves a fairly typical story of a person with a psychotic disorder who presents to an emergency room with grossly disorganized behavior, hallucinations, delusions, and severe substance use, with imminent risk of a withdrawal from alcohol. He requires inpatient hospitalization both for treatment of alcohol withdrawal and to stabilize his symptoms of mania and psychosis.

Beyond the immediate situation, the larger question will be how to engage this individual in treatment moving forward. The history of repeated failed referrals to outpatient levels of care will need to be explored and new strategies pursued. His inability to see that anything is wrong (anosognosia) coupled with his stated goal of continuing to smoke cannabis (precontemplative stage of change) creates a challenging and common scenario.

For this client, it is useful to think in terms of staged treatment and short-term, intermediate, and longer-range goals. In cases of imminent safety issues, the short-term goals are focused on crisis stabilization and inpatient hospitalization is indicated. Once he is out of danger of a serious withdrawal and his behavior and thoughts no longer represent an imminent danger to himself or others, he will need to transition to a less-restrictive setting.

Currently in the United States, the average inpatient psychiatric hospitalization is about one week long. Far too short a period to do more than stabilize the immediate crisis. The risk here is that without adequate aftercare plans and linkages to treatment, this individual will quickly relapse and require rehospitalization or suffer the consequences of his more out-of-control behaviors.

So in a sense, inpatient psychiatric units have to do aggressive crisis management and aftercare planning that starts during the intake. In this case, treatment could go in a number of directions. Clearly, David would meet admission criteria for a longer post-acute rehabilitation stay, ideally in a facility that has treatment for people with serious co-occurring disorders. However, with his stated goal of leaving the hospital and his lack of motivation to be abstinent from cannabis, this is unlikely to happen on a voluntary basis. Depending on the state David lives in, his mother, the hospital, or an outside agency might decide to pursue a longer inpatient hospitalization on an involuntary basis; this is typically done through a process of going before a judge to obtain a commitment, or commitment to treatment, order.

A less restrictive option that might be acceptable to David would be the referral to a state agency or to a private not-for-profit mental health agency that can provide community-based services such as an ACT team. Ideally this team would also include a peer-engagement specialist, case manager/coordinator, substance abuse counselor, psychiatrist or prescribing advanced practice nurse, and other specialty services, including group and individual therapies for people with co-occurring disorders. In order for this kind of outpatient linkage to work, it is best that the initial stages of engagement occur while he is still on the inpatient unit. In an ideal circumstance this would include completion of the application with first contacts with the peer specialist and case manager occurring on the inpatient unit. This would allow David to have a chance to meet the people he would be working with and hopefully find some benefit—other than his desire to get out of the hospital—to enter into treatment.

Step Two: Constructing the Problem/Need List

Substance Use	Mental Health	Medical
Heavy use of alcohol	Threatened to kill self	No allergies
Use of synthetic cannabis and other substances	Agitated and aggressive	Only medical contact has been through emergency rooms and on psychiatric units
Blood alcohol level 0.12 hours after last drink	Labile mood	Blood pressure and pulse elevated
Urine toxicology positive for cannabis	Always "shy" and withdrawn	Elevated liver enzymes and MCV
Cannabis calms him down	Cannabis calms him down	
Began to drink and use cannabis in middle school	Since age 14 hears the devil telling him to kill himself	
Father was a heavy drinker who died of cirrhosis	Speaks in an odd cadence	
Two DUIs	Depression rated 10/10	
Multiple arrests	Uncle with schizophrenia committed suicide	
High-risk behaviors when manic and intoxicated	Two prior involuntary hospitalizations	

Substance Use	Mental Health	Medical
Wants to keep smoking cannabis daily	Episodes of manic agitation	
	Episodes of sustained depression	
	Hears voices even when not having a mood episode	
	Believes nothing is wrong with him (anosognosia)	
	High-risk behaviors when manic and intoxicated	
	History of overdoses	
	Does not follow up with aftercare plans.	

In this case study both the substance use and mental health problems/needs will meet criteria for an inpatient admission. Deciding which diagnosis goes first may have more to do with the type of the unit this person gets admitted to and how they need to document in order to get reimbursed (i.e., a predominantly detoxification unit would list the substance use issue first, versus a predominantly psychiatric unit, which would likely list the mental health problem/need statement first). The few issues in the medical column could constitute a separate problem/need statement or be subsumed in the substance use statement.

1. **Active and severe substance use with imminent risk of alcohol withdrawal** AEB daily drinking, elevated vital signs, daily use of cannabis and synthetic drugs purchased via the Internet. Blood alcohol level of 0.12 hours after last drink and urine toxicology positive for cannabis. Abnormal labs consistent with heavy drinking.

2. **Severe and disabling psychosis and depression with command auditory hallucinations telling him to kill himself**, delusional thinking, disorganized speech, agitation, high-risk behaviors, and severe depression (10/10) and anxiety (8–10/10).

3. **Inadequate medical care**, only contact with medical care has been in acute settings. Has been on high-risk medications and has multiple high-risk behaviors (i.e., tobacco use, heavy drinking).

Step Three: Establishing the Initial Goals/Objectives for Treatment

1. **Active and severe substance use with imminent risk of alcohol withdrawal**

   - Short-term goals (with target dates):

     1) Client will be treated for signs and symptoms of alcohol withdrawal using a CIWA protocol (immediately).

     2) The patient will be free from all signs of alcohol withdrawal within 5 days.

   - Long-term goals:

     1) The patient will be abstinent from alcohol.

     2) The patient will be abstinent from cannabis and other substances.*

2. **Severe and disabling psychosis and depression with command auditory hallucinations telling the patient to kill himself**

- Short-term goals (with target dates):

    1) Provide a safe environment (immediately).

    2) Decrease symptoms of manic agitation to where the patient gets at least seven hours of sleep/day and reports a 50 percent or greater reduction in auditory hallucinations (by the third day of admission).

    3) The patient will identify at least one positive reason to continue taking medication for his mood and psychotic symptoms (by day of discharge).

- Long-term goals: The patient will achieve full remission from his symptoms of psychosis and mood swings.

3. **Inadequate medical care**

- Short-term goals (with target dates):

    1) Complete a history and physical, including AIMs examination, and obtain routine screening tests, including screens for metabolic syndrome (within 24 hours of admission).

    2) Identify any active medical issues (within 3 days of admission).

- Long-term goals: The patient will have a regular outpatient primary care provider and receive regular follow-up for any active problems.

TREATMENT/RECOVERY PLAN

Patient's Name: David Gray

Date of Birth: March 3, 1991

Medical Record #: XXX-XX-XXXX

Level of Care: Adult inpatient detoxification and acute psychiatric

ICD-10 Codes	DSM-5 Diagnoses
F10.239	Alcohol withdrawal with alcohol use disorder, severe*
F25.0	Schizoaffective disorder bipolar type
F12.20	Cannabis use disorder, moderate
F17.200	Tobacco use disorder, moderate
Z91.19	Nonadherence to medical treatment

The individual's stated goal(s): "To get out of the hospital and be able to smoke as much pot as I can get my hands on, and to not get thrown back in here."

1. Problem/Need Statement: Active and severe substance use with imminent risk of alcohol withdrawal
Long-Term Goal: Abstinence from alcohol. Decrease in cannabis and tobacco consumption and use of other illicit substances.
Short-Term Goals/Objectives (with target date):
1. Client will be treated for signs and symptoms of alcohol withdrawal using a CIWA protocol. (8/13/17)
2. The patient will be free from all signs of alcohol withdrawal within 5 days. (8/17/2014)

2. Problem/Need Statement: Severe and disabling psychosis and depression with command auditory hallucinations telling the patient to kill himself.
Long-Term Goal: The patient will achieve full remission from his symptoms of psychosis and mood swings.
Short-Term Goals/Objectives (with target date):
1. Provide a safe environment. (8/12/14)
2. Decrease symptoms of manic agitation to where the patient gets at least seven hours of sleep/day and reports a 50 percent or greater reduction in auditory hallucinations. (by third day of admission)
3. The patient will identify at least one positive reason to continue taking medication for his mood and psychotic symptoms. (by day of discharge)

3. Problem/Need Statement: Inadequate medical care.
Long-Term Goal: The patient will have a regular outpatient primary care provider and receive regular follow-up for any active problems.
Short-Term Goals/Objectives (with target date):
1. Complete a history and physical, including AIMS examination, and obtain routine screening tests, including screens for metabolic syndrome. (within 24 hours of admission)
2. Identify any active medical issues. (within 3 days of admission)

Interventions					
Treatment Modality	**Specific Type**	**Frequency**	**Duration**	**Problem Number**	**Responsible Person(s)**
Alcohol Detoxification	CIWA protocol	Every shift	Until CIWA score is less than 5, his vital signs have normalized, and the patient has been tapered off medication	1	MD/RN staff
Medical	Medication management, including evaluation and management of medical issues	Daily	Daily meeting with prescribing physician	1,2,3	MD
Safety Checks	Monitor for self-harm, high-risk, or worsening of withdrawal	Every 15 minutes	To be reassessed daily	1,2	Nursing and patient-care staff
Individual Therapy	Motivational interviewing	Daily	30–60 minutes	1,2	Primary clinician
Group Therapy	Goals setting	Daily	50 minutes	1,2,3	Occupational therapist
	Skills group	Daily	50 minutes	1,2	Activity therapist
	Psychoeducation	Daily	50 minutes	1,2	Nurse practitioner
	Double Trouble in Recovery	Daily	50 minutes	1,2	Peer specialist

(Continued)

(Continued)

Interventions					
Treatment Modality	**Specific Type**	**Frequency**	**Duration**	**Problem Number**	**Responsible Person(s)**
Family	Counseling and liaison	Daily in person or phone contact with patient's mother	15–30 minutes, longer if needed	1,2	Social worker, primary nurse
Discharge planning and coordination	Referral to local ACT team	As required throughout the admission	As required, with the goal of having at least two meetings between David and a member of the ACT team while he is on the unit	1,2,3	Social worker

Identification of strengths: Intelligent and creative, with some willingness to stop drinking.

Peer/family/community supports to assist: His mother and the local mental health authority.

Barriers to treatment: Risk for relapse after discharge. Past history of not connecting to outpatient providers.

Staff/client-identified education/teaching needs: To help Mr. Gray identify potential advantages to using community supports, and to help him understand the connections between his substance use and problems at home and in the community.

Assessment of discharge needs/discharge planning: To be free from any signs of alcohol withdrawal and to have no active suicidal urges. To have a clear discharge plan in place with a completed referral to the ACT team.

Completion of this treatment/recovery plan was a collaborative effort between the client and the following treatment team members:

SIGNATURES		Date/Time
Client	I agree with maybe half of what's on here, but I'm signing anyway so I can get out of here, David Gray.	8/12/2014 2:15pm
Physician	Mellissa Croft, MD	8/12/2014 2:20pm
Treatment Plan Completed By	*Jeanette Grace, RN*	8/12/2014 2:22pm
Social Worker	*Tracey Thrall, LCSW*	8/12/2014 3:10pm
Other	*Lillian Gray—David's mother*	8/12/2014 3:30pm

* In this instance the code for alcohol withdrawal with alcohol use disorder severe <u>without</u> perceptual disturbances has been selected, even though the patient clearly has psychotic symptoms. The rationale is that his psychotic symptoms are likely related to his psychotic disorder and not to an alcohol withdrawal syndrome.

CHAPTER 15

Personality Disorders and Co-Occurring Substance Use Disorders

---

Overview

The Personality Disorders

Treatment of Co-Occurring Substance Use Disorders and
  Personality Disorders

  Dialectic Behavior Therapy

  Pharmacotherapy

Case Study

OVERVIEW

Studies place the overall prevalence of personality disorders in the United States at over 9 percent, with the majority of those never seeking or receiving, treatment. Cluster A disorders (paranoid, schizoid, schizotypal) rates range from 2.1 percent to 6.8 percent, Cluster B (borderline, antisocial, narcissistic, histrionic) 1.5–6.1 percent, and Cluster C (avoidant, dependent, obsessive-compulsive) 2.6–10.6 percent.

All the personality disorders have high rates of co-occurring substance use disorders, as well as other mental disorders. Co-occurrence is especially true for people with borderline and antisocial personality disorders, where it is common for them to have multiple (three or more) comorbid substance use and mental disorders. While relatively fewer in number, people with cluster B personality disorders are among those most likely to seek and receive treatment in any 12-month period (nearly 50%). The reason is likely that these disorders include more severe symptoms (e.g., frequent suicidality, impulsivity, and emotional and behavioral dyscontrol). Of all the personality disorders, borderline and antisocial have received the most research attention.

THE PERSONALITY DISORDERS

In order to meet DSM-5 criteria for a personality disorder, a person must have a pervasive (stemming back to adolescence or early adulthood) and maladaptive pattern that involves impaired interpersonal relationships, ways of viewing themselves and the world around them (misperceptions), and may include problems with impulsivity and emotion regulation. Tremendous overlap can occur between the personality disorders as they are defined in the DSM, and individuals will often have traits of more than one (i.e., someone with borderline

241

personality disorder may have antisocial and narcissistic features). In addition to overlap between personality disorders, there is significant comorbidity with substance use disorders and other mental disorders, especially the mood, anxiety, and impulse control disorders.

Cluster A Personality Disorders

- Paranoid Personality Disorder

  Suspicious, has trouble trusting and suspects and misperceives the intentions of others, holds grudges, and quick to anger.

- Schizoid Personality Disorder

  Emotionally detached, flat, and isolative. Avoids interpersonal relationships. Minimal interest in sex or other pleasurable pursuits. Seems indifferent to praise or criticism.

- Schizotypal Personality Disorder

  Trouble forming relationships/lack of close relationships, eccentric beliefs and presentation (dress, style of speech), prone to distortions. Ideas of reference (nondelusional), odd thoughts and beliefs, unusual sensory experiences, suspiciousness, anxiety in social settings.

Cluster B Personality Disorders

- Antisocial Personality Disorder

  Disregard for the rights, safety, property and feelings of others. Deceitfulness, impulsivity and illegal activities. Lacks empathy. Frequent fights/assaults. May be predatory.

- Borderline Personality Disorder

  Emotionally vulnerable, impulsive, with self-injurious behavior (cutting, burning). Recurrent suicidality, transient paranoia and dissociation. Black-and-white thinking (people, things, and situations, are either all good or all bad).

- Histrionic Personality Disorder

  Excessive expressed emotions/dramatic speech and dress. Provocative and seductive. Requires/seeks to be center of attention. Dramatic. Suggestible.

- Narcissistic Personality Disorder

  Grandiose sense of self. Requires/insists upon admiration. Believes rules do not apply to special people, such as themselves. Fantasizes about power and importance. Lacks empathy. May appear arrogant. Takes advantage of others to achieve own ends.

Cluster C Personality Disorders

- Avoidant Personality Disorder

  Avoids interpersonal relationships and situations. Feels inadequate, inferior, and judged. Rejection sensitive and believes others think negatively of them. Risk avoidant.

- Dependent Personality Disorder

    Needs to be taken care of. Submissive and clingy. Fearful of rejection and abandonment. Feels helpless and in constant need of nurturance. Becomes frantic when relationships end.

- Obsessive-Compulsive Personality Disorder

    Rigid, orderly, and perfectionistic. Intolerant of other ways of doing things. Often unable to complete tasks secondary to perfectionism. Morally inflexible. "The rules are the rules." Has trouble discarding even worthless items, and prone to hoarding.

TREATMENT FOR CO-OCCURRING SUBSTANCE USE AND PERSONALITY DISORDERS

When discussing personality disorders, we are looking at a broad range of clinical, and at times extreme, presentations. The spectrum of personality disorders runs from people who are socially isolative, emotionally restricted, and globally avoidant to people whose lives are like living in a minefield where the slightest rejection, whether real or perceived, can send them into a painful emotional freefall, where self-injury and even suicide seem like reasonable options to unbearable suffering.

With borderline personality disorder, evidence-based psychotherapies, dialectic behavior therapy (DBT) in particular, have been specifically studied with people who have both a personality and substance use disorders. However, once we move away from borderline personality disorder there are few controlled studies that specifically address a particular personality disorder, and almost none that examine co-occurring substance use and personality disorders. As regards medications for personality disorders, at the time of this book's publication no treatments are FDA-approved for any of the personality disorders. This represents one of the many areas in working with people who have co-occurring disorders where what needs to occur clinically has not yet been validated experimentally.

While potentially daunting, this lack of research should not deter the clinician from constructing effective and integrated treatment for individuals with any of the personality disorders. As with all clients, it boils down to the individual and that person's goals around their mental health and substance use problems. Things to keep in mind are similar to those covered throughout this book:

- Conduct a thorough assessment. (Chapters 2–4)
- Based on the assessment, make recommendations for the appropriate level of care. (Chapter 7)
- Active safety concerns always come first (suicidality and/or homicidality, serious medical concerns, grave disability, dangerous withdrawal or intoxication states).
- Identify connections between the mental disorder and the substance use. Does someone with avoidant personality disorder turn to alcohol when confronted with a feared situation (liquid courage)? Does someone with schizotypal disorder use hallucinogens or cannabis to add support for their particular worldview? Does someone with antisocial disorder get into legal difficulties (commit crimes) when they are under the influence of alcohol or cocaine? Is that something they might want to address?

- Psychoeducation. Explore with clients what is known and how improving either the substance use or mental health problem will typically generate positive gain in the other problem.

- Use motivational strategies to help move people in the direction of wanted/desirable change.

- Employ cognitive-behavioral techniques to target specific distortions, and maladaptive behaviors.

    o For someone with avoidant personality disorder, this would include identifying the avoidant behaviors and corresponding thoughts and emotions, and then work to consistently, and safely, expose the individual to those things, people, and situations.

    o For someone with paranoid personality disorder, it will involve the identification of misperceptions and helping them to challenge their beliefs with objective data.

    o For someone with obsessive-compulsive personality disorder, it will be helping them challenge long-held beliefs about behavior, the need to be perfect and have others be perfect, and that there may indeed be multiple ways to get a job done.

- Treat other co-occurring mental disorders.

- Attend to active medical issues.

- Help develop and enhance daily wellness routines.

Dialectic Behavior Therapy

(DBT): Developed by Marsha Linehan, Ph.D., dialectic behavior therapy has been shown in more than 20 controlled studies to be an effective treatment for borderline personality disorder in terms of decreasing suicidal and non-suicidal self-injurious behavior, decreasing rates of hospitalization, and in improving quality of life. More recently, DBT has been shown to be effective in working with a broader range of individuals, including those with co-occurring substance use disorders. It has also been studied in people with antisocial personality disorder, including prison studies, and the results have been positive.

DBT is a manual-based therapy grounded on a triad of cognitive behavior therapy, mindfulness (founded in Zen and other contemplative practices), and dialectics (the recognition that there can be multiple and at times seemingly conflicting truths). The core dialectic in DBT is one of radical acceptance, while moving the person to change maladaptive and harmful behaviors and patterns of thought. An example of this core dialectic could include a statement such as, "It makes total sense you're feeling this way, <u>and</u> we need to help you find some way other than cutting yourself, or drinking till you pass out, to deal with phone calls from your mother."

DBT recognizes that people with borderline personality disorder have tremendous difficulty with emotion regulation, and can go from feeling okay to suicidal in the flash of a thought. DBT, through the use of CBT and behavioral chain analysis, helps the person tease apart what it is that triggers their emotions and problem behaviors. It then identifies skills the person needs to learn and practice that will help them manage not just painful feelings, but also how to successfully negotiate real-life situations, and relationships.

The structure of DBT as it has been most studied includes:

1. Weekly skills training groups, which last between one-and-a-half to two hours. These are structured to review material from the prior session, including homework, and then present the new session's material. There are four topical modules: mindfulness, interpersonal effectiveness, emotion regulation, and distress tolerance.

2. Individual (1:1) DBT therapy, which is typically weekly. The individual therapy utilizes a diary card, which the patient completes and brings to each session. There is a hierarchy to what will be discussed based on the presence, or absence, of suicidal thought or behavior, non-suicidal self-injury, therapy-interfering behaviors (missed appointments, excessive demands on the therapist's time, the therapist being unavailable), and quality of life–interfering behaviors, such as problem substance use.

3. Consultation team. The DBT team meets weekly to practice the therapy, provide case consultation, and enhance their skills, so that they can in turn teach the skills more effectively. It is not a business meeting, and in the DBT lingo is considered "therapy for the therapist."

4. Telephone consultation. The patient has the ability and is encouraged to contact the therapist between sessions when in need of skills coaching. Parameters around acceptable times and reasons to call are established early in the therapy.

5. Accessory services. These might include access to a prescribing physician or APRN, case management for some clients, family psychoeducation, mutual self-help, such as AA or NA, and structuring of the treatment environment/facility to support fidelity to the model. An example of structuring the treatment environment is ensuring that DBT clinicians have their schedules cleared consistently for the non-billable weekly consultation team.

Pharmacotherapy

As mentioned, there are no FDA approved medications, and so all prescribing for these disorders is "off label." Prescribing, therefore, is often used to target core symptoms and comorbid mental disorders, such as mood instability, irritability, depression, insomnia, anxiety, impulsivity, inattention, and so on. In addition, people with co-occurring personality and substance use disorders may benefit from medication-assisted therapies for tobacco, alcohol, and opioids (Chapters 16–18).

While it is common for individuals with borderline personality disorder to be prescribed multiple psychotropic medications—so-called drug cocktails, there is limited evidence to support the efficacy of such strategies for decreasing symptoms and improving outcomes. Where individuals with borderline personality disorder struggle with recurrent suicidality, overdoses are common, often with the psychiatric medications they have been prescribed. Therefore, any medication strategies need to include the relative safety of medications prescribed, as well as the quantity given at any time.

At present, there is some evidence to support the usefulness of mood stabilizers (lamotrigine/Lamictal, valproic acid/Depakote) and some of the second-generation antipsychotics (aripiprazole/Abilify, olanzapine/Zyprexa) for decreasing symptoms of impulsivity and mood instability. The anticonvulsant topiramate/Topamax may also have some benefit in decreasing impulsivity and mood instability. And some evidence supports the use of Omega-3 fatty acid supplementation.

Although antidepressants, including SSRIs, are widely prescribed for people with borderline personality disorders, recent studies have shown disappointing results with their use. There is some concern that these agents might actually worsen symptoms of irritability and mood instability, especially with people who may have co-occurring bipolar-spectrum disorders.

CASE STUDY: TRACEY RACE

Tracey Race is a 32-year-old, twice-divorced and now separated from her third husband, Caucasian woman. She is a mother of three, who initially states she is self-referred to get help for her substance use problems and "horrible mood swings," but then adds "I need to be in treatment, or my husband will use my drinking and the pills to take the kids." She currently shares custody with her estranged husband for her two daughters. Her son, born when Tracey was 16, was placed in a closed adoption. She works full time, mostly from home, as an insurance adjuster.

She says when she was a teenager and in college, she had several psychiatric assessments and brief trials of medication and therapy. "The meds either didn't work, made me gain weight, or made me worse."

Between the ages of 11 and 12, Tracey was sexually molested by an uncle. The abuse continued for more than a year, although she is unable to remember much about that time. "I don't think I want to remember." She states that when she reported the molestation to her mother, she wasn't believed. However, her uncle was no longer allowed into the home, and Tracey reports this situation created a rift in her mother's family for which her mother continues to blame Tracey. No charges were ever brought against the uncle. She admits to occasional nightmares related to the abuse, but no flashbacks. She speculates that the abuse may have something to do with her difficulty in trusting people, especially men.

She first started cutting herself with a razor or box cutter when she was in junior high. "It wasn't to try and kill myself, although that's what everyone kept thinking. It just relieves the stress." She admits to frequent (daily) suicidal thinking and says she's had it since she was 13. She has taken several overdoses in the past. She describes episodes where she becomes acutely upset and will impulsively take, "whatever I can get my hands on." She has had two psychiatric hospitalizations, both following overdoses. The first was after the adoption of her son, a decision she regrets deeply. "My mother talked me into it. Said she wouldn't pay for college if I didn't go through with the adoption." The second was when she was a sophomore in college and her boyfriend had broken up with her. She says her most recent overdose was about three months ago when her husband served her with divorce papers and revealed that he had been having an affair with a mutual friend. She took a combination of lorazepam/Ativan, OxyContin, and alcohol. She did not seek treatment, and slept for two days.

Her first use of alcohol and cannabis was at age 13, when her uncle would get her drunk. "I have mood swings like you can't believe and the booze and pot helped numb me out and calm the anxiety. It's the same thing with the pills (mostly opioids), at least it was in the beginning." She reports binge drinking of between half a pint to a pint of hard liquor, one to three times per week. She has never been in a detox program, she has never had a seizure, although she states her hands sometimes shake in the morning after a binge. She adds that she sometimes will go months without a drink, and her last drink was over a week prior to this evaluation. She smokes cannabis daily, and has been taking OxyContin, and recently heroin (snorted), up to 10 bags/day. She has never injected drugs. If she goes more than half a day without opioids she begins to experience withdrawal symptoms, which get severe after a day. She has purchased buprenorphine/Suboxone illicitly and is hoping to get it prescribed as a result of today's evaluation. She smokes a half-pack of cigarettes daily and has been smoking since she was 13. She denies habitual use of benzodiazepines or other sedatives.

Her family psychiatric history includes a sister with depression, a brother who is opioid dependent, and her mother who has been treated for anxiety and depression. Her father is in recovery from an alcohol use disorder.

Her medical history includes asthma, for which she has a rescue inhaler. She has had three live births, one miscarriage, and two abortions. She had a tubal ligation after her last child. She has no allergies. She is currently on no prescribed medications.

Tracey was born and raised in suburban New York. She is the middle of three children. Her parents divorced when she was nine. She describes her early years as being quite chaotic with frequent fights between her parents and witnessing her mother get hit by her father when he'd been drinking. She lived with her mother and had no contact with her father until she went to college.

She describes doing well in school, but dropped out as a sophomore in high school when she became pregnant. She subsequently completed high school and attended college where she achieved a B.A. in finance and an M.B.A. She has worked in the insurance industry since graduation. She describes her job as incredibly stressful, but well paying. She likes being able to work from home, but adds that she is socially isolated and can go for weeks on end with only having direct contact with her children and her drug dealer. She describes having no close friends and that in the past her intense mood swings and rage attacks have ended relationships.

She has been married three times. The first when she was 20, "we fought all the time." She reports the relationship turned physically abusive and ended after eight months. The second marriage was when she was 22 and lasted two years. "He was a worse drunk than I was." She remarried when she was 25 and has two daughters, Kayla and Erin (ages 6 and 4).

She comes to this evaluation dressed in a business suit and is neatly groomed. She describes her mood as depressed (9 out of 10, with 10 being the worst) and highly anxious, also a 9 out of 10. While describing intense depression and anxiety, she appears calm and pleasant. She denies experiencing any auditory or visual hallucinations, but states she can get paranoid, especially when she is under stress—like now. She admits to some thoughts of suicide, but adds she has no intention of acting upon them at this time. She also describes frequent urges to cut herself, but states she's not acted on these in several years.

Her vital signs are stable. She is not tremulous and does not appear to be in opioid withdrawal. A dipped urine sample is positive for cannabis and opioids. Her breathalyzer is negative.

Diagnostic Discussion: This case study, which includes multiple substance use problems—opioids, alcohol, cannabis, tobacco—and serious mood symptoms and problem behaviors, including suicidality and self-injury, is fairly typical for individuals with co-occurring substance use and borderline personality disorder. However, the history of trauma, transient paranoia, depression, and anxiety will need to be further explored to better assess for the presence, or absence, of other major diagnoses, such as a major depressive or bipolar-spectrum disorder, PTSD, substance-induced mood disorder, and so on.

Step One: Level of Care Determination

In this case, despite active suicidality, the client reports she is unlikely to act on these thoughts and has had them daily for many years. Also, while her use of alcohol is problematic, it has been a week since her last drink, and she has no history or objective findings of active withdrawal. Likewise, she is not actively dependent on benzodiazepines. Her stated goal is to get into treatment in an effort to retain shared custody of her children, and she also expresses a desire to be prescribed buprenorphine for opioid replacement therapy, which she views as her most pressing concern.

Taking all of these factors into account, reasonable levels of care would include:

- An intensive outpatient program (IOP) that includes opioid replacement therapy along with treatment for her other substance use problems and specialized treatment for her borderline personality disorder. An IOP that offers a dual-diagnosis DBT track could be ideal.

- Parallel outpatient treatment, where she receives opioid replacement in an office-based setting, along with treatment and monitoring of her other substance use problems, combined with admission to a comprehensive dialectic behavior therapy program, which includes a dual diagnosis focus.

- Integrated outpatient treatment, where she receives opioid replacement therapy and other substance use treatment, along with co-occurring comprehensive DBT therapy within the same practice setting.

Step Two: Constructing the Problem/Need List

Substance Use	Mental Health	Medical
Fears she'll lose custody of her children if not in treatment	Molested as a child by an uncle, which when reported was initially not believed and then not supported	Asthma as a child
Alcohol and cannabis use started at age 13	Several psychiatric assessments as a teen and in college	Three live births, one miscarriage, two terminations
Daily use of OxyContin and/or heroin (10 bags heroin)	Multiple unsuccessful medication trials	Tubal ligation
No intravenous drug use	Started cutting herself in junior high: still has urges to cut, but has not done so in years	Not tremulous
Experiences opioid withdrawal	Daily thoughts of suicide	Goes into opioid withdrawal within half a day of last use
Binge drinking multiple times per week	Multiple overdoses in the past	
Father with alcohol problem	Two inpatient admissions following overdoses	

No history of withdrawal seizures or delirium	Recent multidrug overdose in which she did not seek help	
Occasional shakiness after heavy drinking	Impulsivity	
Last drink over a week ago	Mood swings and rage attacks	
Has gone for extended periods without alcohol	Chaotic childhood	
Urine positive for opioids and cannabis	Witnessed domestic violence	
Use of benzodiazepines and other sedative hypnotics, but not currently	Parents divorced when patient was age 9	
Father with alcohol problem	Minimal contact with her father	
No history of withdrawal seizures or delirium.	Teenage pregnancy, child given up for adoption	
Smokes cannabis daily	Socially isolated	
Smokes half pack cigarettes/day	No close friends	
	Depressed and anxious	
	Transient stress-related paranoia	

Although this person's presenting problems/needs can be assessed in several ways, the following three-item list incorporates the majority of her symptoms and helps the clinician focus on what is emergent (frequent and current suicidality), urgent (high-risk drug use), as well as what will be the focus for longer-range treatment (long-standing problems with emotion regulation and mood swings).

1. **Suicidality** as evidenced by (AEB) daily thoughts of suicide, past history of overdose attempts, and recent overdose in which she did not seek help.
2. **Severe and active high-risk substance use problems** AEB daily opioid use, binge drinking, and daily cannabis and tobacco use. Experiences opioid withdrawal within half a day of last use.
3. **Severe mood swings,** with emotional lability, impulsivity, and high levels of depression and anxiety. History of self-injurious—but non-suicidal—self-harm.

Step Three: Establishing the Initial Goals/Objectives for Treatment

1. **Suicidality**
   - Short-term goals (with target dates):
     1) To establish and maintain a safety plan (at the time of this evaluation 8/12/2014, and to be reassessed at each session).
     2) To have no active suicidal behavior (currently 8/12/2014 and ongoing).
   - Long-term goal: To be free from suicidal thoughts and behaviors.

2. **Severe and active high-risk substance use problems** AEB daily opioid use, binge drinking, and daily cannabis and tobacco use. Experiences opioid withdrawal within half a day of last use.

   - Short-term goals (with target dates):

     1) To be evaluated for and, if appropriate, started on medication-assisted treatment for opioid dependence (by end of the week 8/15/2014).

     2) To eliminate binge drinking behavior and be in early abstinence for alcohol (immediately).

     3) To assess levels of motivation to decrease and/or eliminate cannabis and tobacco use (8/12/2014).

   - Long-term goals:

     1) To be abstinent from alcohol.

     2) To be on opioid replacement therapy.

     3) To be abstinent from tobacco.

     4) To be abstinent from cannabis.

     5) To be abstinent from benzodiazepines.

3. **Severe mood swings,** emotional lability and impulsivity, with high levels of depression and anxiety. History of self-injurious—but nonsuicidal—self-harm.

   - Short-term goals (with target dates):

     1) To have a 30 percent reduction in depressive and anxious symptoms as measured using a 10-point scale (one month from today 9/12/2014).

     2) To be free from stress-related paranoia and rage attacks (two months from today 10/12/2014).

     3) To practice, and document using her diary card, at least two DBT skills daily (one month from today 9/12/2014).

   - Long-term goals:

     1) To have a stable mood, as measured by self-report.

     2) To experience levels of depression and/or anxiety no greater than a 4 on a 10-point scale.

     3) To be free from thoughts and urges to self-harm.

TREATMENT/RECOVERY PLAN

> **Patient's Name:** Tracey Race
> **Date of Birth:** 12/2/1982
> **Medical Record #:** XXX-XX-XXXX

Level of Care: Outpatient Co-Occurring Dialectic Behavior Therapy with Medication Management

ICD-10 Codes	DSM-5 Diagnoses
F11.20	Opioid use disorder, moderate
F60.3	Borderline personality disorder
F32.9	Unspecified depressive disorder with anxious distress
F10.20	Alcohol use disorder, moderate
F17.200	Tobacco use disorder, moderate
F12.20	Cannabis use disorder, moderate
Z63.5	Disruption of family by separation or divorce

The individual's stated goal(s): "I want my mood to be stable. I want to be off all street drugs. I want to be a good mother. Eventually, but not yet, I'd like to stop smoking cigarettes."

---

1. Problem/Need Statement: Suicidality AEB daily thoughts of suicide, past history of overdose attempts, and recent multidrug overdose in which she did not seek help.

Long-Term Goal: To be free from suicidal thoughts and behaviors.

Short-Term Goals/Objectives (target date):

1. To establish and maintain a safety plan (at the time of this evaluation 8/12/2014, and to be reassessed at each session).

2. To have no active suicidal behavior (currently 8/12/2014 and ongoing).

---

2. Problem/Need Statement: Severe and active high-risk substance use problems AEB daily opioid use, binge drinking, and daily cannabis and tobacco use. Experiences opioid withdrawal within half a day of last use.

Long-Term Goal(s):

1. To be abstinent from alcohol.

2. To be on opioid replacement therapy.

3. To be abstinent from tobacco.

4. To be abstinent from cannabis.

5. To be abstinent from benzodiazepines.

Short-Term Goals/Objectives (target date):

1. To be evaluated for and, if appropriate, started on medication-assisted treatment for opioid dependence (by the end of the week 8/15/2014).

2. To eliminate binge drinking behavior and be in early abstinence for alcohol (immediately).

3. To assess levels of motivation to decrease and/or eliminate cannabis and tobacco use (8/12/2014).

---

3. Problem/Need Statement: Severe mood swings, with emotional lability and impulsivity, with high levels of depression and anxiety. History of self-injurious, but nonsuicidal, harm.

Long-Term Goal(s):

1. To have a stable mood, as measured by self-report.

2. To experience levels of depression and/or anxiety no greater than a 4 on a 10-point scale.

3. To be free from thoughts and urges to self-harm.

Short-Term Goals/Objectives (Target date):

1. To have a 30 percent reduction in depressive and anxious symptoms as measured using a 10-point scale (one month from today 9/12/2014).

2. To be free from stress-related paranoia and rage attacks (two months from today 10/12/2014).

3. To practice, and document using her diary card, at least two DBT skills daily (one month from today 9/12/2014).

Interventions					
Treatment Modality	**Specific Type**	**Frequency**	**Duration**	**Problem Number**	**Responsible Person(s)**
Medical	Complete diagnostic evaluation	Upon admission	Two hours	1,2,3	MD, RN, client
	Medication management to include opioid replacement therapy	At least monthly	20–30 minutes	1,2,3	MD and client
Individual Therapy	Dual diagnosis–focused dialectic behavior therapy	Weekly	One hour/ six months to one year	1,2,3	DBT therapist and client

Group Therapy	Dual diagnosis–focused DBT skills training	Weekly	Two hours/ six months to one year	1,2,3	DBT skills trainer and client
Laboratory	Routine blood work	Upon admission, and as needed	N/A	1,2,3	MD and client
	Drug screens	Upon admission, and at least monthly	For the duration of treatment	2	MD and client
Mutual Self-Help	AA/NA	At least two meetings/ week	Ongoing	2	Client

Identification of strengths: Intelligent and articulate. Motivated to work on both her substance use and emotional/behavioral difficulties. Has a strong work ethic, and finds her job to be an important source of self-respect and stability.

Peer/family/community supports to assist: Unable to identify any at this time, but the client is willing to explore mutual self-help groups in the community.

Barriers to treatment: Inability to stop using illicit opioids and alcohol.

Staff/client-identified education/teaching needs: To fully understand the risks/benefits of any recommended medications, including buprenorphine for opioid replacement therapy. To understand the principles and goals of dialectic behavior therapy.

Assessment of discharge needs/discharge planning: To be reassessed at six months, and as needed. When goals achieved can move toward less intensive level of treatment.

Completion of this treatment/recovery plan was a collaborative effort between the client and the following treatment team members:

SIGNATURES		Date/Time
Client	Tracey Race	8/12/2014 2:15pm
Physician	*Lenore Picano, MD*	8/12/2014 2:20pm
Primary Therapist		8/12/2014 2:22pm

Substance-Specific Topics and Treatments

CHAPTER 16

Alcohol

OVERVIEW

More than half of Americans over the age of 12 drink alcohol, and nearly one quarter report binge drinking in a given month. Heavy drinking—at least five episodes of binge drinking in a month—is reported by more than 17 million Americans (6.5%). Current alcohol use among youths, ages 12 to 17, is nearly 13 percent, with 7.2 percent reporting binge drinking and 1.5 percent heavy drinking.

Alcohol is one of the three leading causes of preventable death in the United States, where 18 million people meet criteria for alcohol use disorders. Rates of alcohol use disorder are roughly twice as high in men (10–12.4%) versus women (4.5–5%). The peak ages for developing alcohol use disorders are in the teens through the twenties, but they can occur at any age.

The negative health consequences of alcohol problems can range from mild to severe, with damage possible to most organ systems and tissues, including the nervous system. Serious health outcomes include alcohol-related dementias (alcohol is a neurotoxin and causes loss of both gray and white matter), liver failure, alcoholic hepatitis, cirrhosis, pancreatitis, ulcers, esophageal varices, and increased rates of stroke and certain cancers. Beyond the impact of

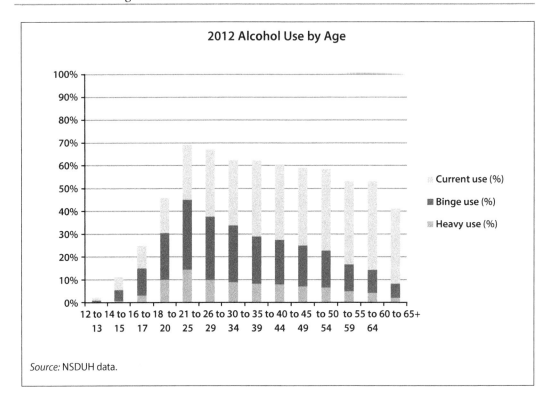

2012 Alcohol Use by Age

Legend:
- Current use (%)
- Binge use (%)
- Heavy use (%)

Source: NSDUH data.

alcohol on the body are deaths and injury associated with alcohol-related accidents and the finding that many homicides and suicides are committed while under the influence. In 2012, it was estimated that 11.2 percent of Americans over the age of 12 drove under the influence of alcohol at least once during the year. Finally, while the vast majority of unintentional fatal overdoses in the United States involve opioids, many of those fatalities involve the concomitant use of alcohol or other central nervous system depressants (benzodiazepines, barbiturates). The net result of these combinations is an increased risk for respiratory depression and death.

Rates of co-occurring alcohol use disorders are high among people with most mental disorders, with worse overall outcomes.

WOMEN AND ALCOHOL

While women have lower rates of alcohol use disorder, they achieve higher blood-alcohol levels when consuming the same amount as men. This is due to women, on average, weighing less than men and on women having a higher fat-to-water ratio—alcohol is dissolved in water. They are also more likely to develop serious physical complications from alcohol use, including increased rates of breast cancer. On average, women experience severe negative health outcomes of heavy alcohol use 10 years sooner than men, which is sometimes referred to as the telescoping effect.

Pregnant women who drink put their unborn children at increased risk for learning and behavioral problems, as well as fetal alcohol spectrum problems. Among pregnant women ages 15 to 44, 8.5 percent reported using alcohol, with 2.7 percent reporting binge drinking and

0.3 percent reporting heavy drinking. These numbers are much lower than for nonpregnant women in the same age range.

ASSESSMENT AND DIAGNOSTIC ISSUES

People with co-occurring disorders are frequently drawn to alcohol for the short-term benefits, such as decreased anxiety and enhanced social ease, but the longer-term effects of heavy use can lead to a broad range of clinical presentations. This becomes part of the challenge in working with co-occurring disorders as it's often unclear what role the substance use, in this case alcohol, plays in the overall clinical presentation. Alcohol-induced depressive disorders and anxiety disorders are often impossible to differentiate from their non-alcohol-related variants during the initial assessment process. It may be only over the course of treatment and sustained abstinence that you and your client will be able to clarify that in fact all, or most of the mental disorder, was in fact due to the alcohol. A careful history as part of the initial assessment may help clarify which came first, the mental disorder or the substance use problem.

Over time, problem alcohol use can manifest with a broad range of emotional, behavioral, physical, and cognitive problems. Some of these will resolve over the course of treatment, such as the hallucinosis that can occur with alcohol withdrawal delirium; others, such as alcohol-related dementia/alcohol neurocognitive disorder (Korsakoff's syndrome) may not go away.

While the assessment of an alcohol use disorder is incorporated into the overall comprehensive assessment (Chapters 2–4) there are some key findings that will help in both assessment and treatment.

Cognitive Examination

People with long-term alcohol use are at increased risk of cognitive impairment that is directly due to alcohol's damaging effects on the brain. These deficits and findings range from subtle to severe and may include:

- Problems with short-term memory
- Problems with learning new material
- Confabulation. This is where the individual makes up a plausible story to cover for what may be lapses in memory

Physical Findings

In addition to the physical symptoms of withdrawal states covered in the following sections, long-term drinkers may display a number of findings on routine or more-focused physical examination. These can include:

- An enlarged and/or tender liver
- Tremor
- Psoriasis (dry and flaky patches of skin)

- Broken capillaries on the nose and cheeks (spider veins)
- Red palms
- Jaundice (yellow cast to the skin, often first detected in the whites of the eyes, or the underside of the tongue)
- Presence of fluid in the belly (ascites—associated with liver failure and cirrhosis)
- An enlarged spleen
- Clubbing of the fingers

Lab Results

- Liver function tests (transaminases). These are enzymes made in the liver.
  - Gamma-glutamyl transferase (GGT/GGTP). This is the enzyme that is most closely associated with alcohol use, and will remain elevated for three to four weeks after heavy consumption has stopped. With abstinence it should return to normal levels.
  - Elevations in other liver enzymes, including Alkaline phosphatase.
- Elevated mean corpuscular volume. This is a measure of the size of the red blood cells, and is often elevated in people who have had long-standing alcohol use disorders.
- Other abnormal labs may include:
  - Increased bilirubin
  - Decreased albumin (a protein associated with liver health and nutritional status)
  - Decreased magnesium
  - Decreased potassium
  - Increased serum prothrombin time (a measure of the blood's ability to clot)

MODERATE VERSUS HEAVY DRINKING

Based on current dietary guidelines, the amount of alcohol a person can consume and be considered a moderate drinker is:

- Women on average no more than one standard drink/day or seven drinks/week.
- Men on average no more than two standard drinks/day or fourteen drinks/week.

Alcohol consumption in excess of these amounts is considered heavy. The current definitions of a standard drink are:
- Five ounces of wine
- Twelve ounces of beer
- One-and-a-half ounces of an eighty proof liquor, such as vodka, rum, gin, or whiskey

Binge drinking/use is defined as the rapid consumption of alcohol (within 2 hours), in which the blood alcohol level meets or exceeds 0.08 grams/deciliter. For men, this is typically five or more standard drinks, and for women, four or more drinks.

Heavy drinking/use is defined as five or more drinks on five or more days within a 30-day period.

MILD, MODERATE, AND SEVERE ALCOHOL USE DISORDERS

Alcohol use disorders (formerly alcohol abuse and dependence) are defined by the DSM-5 according to the number of symptoms a person experiences. These criteria address craving, continued use despite negative consequences (health, occupational, legal, and/or social), unsuccessful attempts to cut down, dangerous activity while intoxicated, and experiencing symptoms of tolerance and withdrawal. The number of symptoms, combined with the clinical impression, is used to rate the disorder as mild (two to three symptoms), moderate (four to five), or severe (more than six symptoms).

As with all substance use disorders in the DSM-5, if withdrawal symptoms are present, the disorder is considered to be at least moderate. Other modifiers/specifiers are then added, such as in early remission (3–12 months) or late remission (more than 12 months). These same time frames are used for all of the substance use disorders.

THE ASSESSMENT OF ALCOHOL WITHDRAWAL

The majority of people who are dependent on alcohol are able to safely withdraw with minimal intervention; for others alcohol withdrawal can be severe and include withdrawal seizures, cognitive disturbances (hallucinations and confusion), and dangerous elevations in blood pressure and pulse rate. The most serious and potentially fatal manifestation of alcohol withdrawal is delirium tremens (DTs). People at the greatest risk for complicated withdrawal syndromes include:

- People with histories of prior complicated withdrawals (i.e., withdrawal seizures, delirium, hallucinations)
- People with comorbid medical conditions, including heart, liver, and lung diseases
- Poor nutritional status

Alcohol withdrawal delirium/delirium tremens is a hyperadrenergic state characterized by confusion, hallucinations (often visual), elevated temperature, sweating, rapid pulse, and elevated blood pressure. It can be rapidly progressive and in heavy drinkers can begin within hours to two–four days after the last drink. Withdrawal from alcohol can last up to a week and in some cases longer.

Alcohol withdrawal delirium is a medical emergency that requires inpatient medical stabilization, which will likely include the use of intravenous benzodiazepines, careful monitoring of electrolytes, repletion of vitamins (thiamine and folic acid), and stabilization of blood pressure and pulse.

THE CLINICAL INSTITUTE WITHDRAWAL ASSESSMENT (CIWA-AR)

The Clinical Institute Withdrawal Assessment (CIWA-Ar) is the most widely used tool to assess severity of alcohol withdrawal. A modified version, the CIWA-B, addresses benzodiazepine withdrawal.

The CIWA is completed by a nurse or other trained clinical observer and incorporates blood pressure and pulse with the following 10 symptom domains:

1. Sweating
2. Anxiety
3. Tremor
4. Auditory disturbances
5. Visual disturbances
6. Agitation
7. Nausea
8. Tactile disturbances
9. Headache
10. Orientation and clouding of sensorium

The maximum score possible is a 67. Many facilities that perform detoxification will use protocols and/or guidelines that connect the CIWA to the use of medication. The CIWA-Ar is not copyrighted and may be used freely. A score of 15 or greater is associated with an increased risk of serious withdrawal. The higher the score, the greater the risk.

In working with individuals who have co-occurring mental disorders and alcohol withdrawal, clinicians may encounter complicating factors when using the CIWA.

- Is the anxiety from withdrawal or an underlying anxiety disorder?
- Are the visual or auditory disturbances withdrawal or core symptoms of a schizophrenia-spectrum disorder?
- Is the tremor new or is it a side of effect of lithium or an antipsychotic medication?

One approach that can help clarify what symptoms are secondary to withdrawal and what are related to an underlying mental disorder is to ask:

- Are these symptoms new or old?
- Have they changed or worsened in the setting of not drinking (since your last drink)?

Regardless, because of the potential seriousness of alcohol withdrawal, when in doubt go ahead and treat what might be symptoms of withdrawal.

CLINICAL INSTITUTE WITHDRAWAL ASSESSMENT FOR ALCOHOL (CIWA-Ar)

Patient_____ Date_____ Time_____

Pulse or heart rate taken for one minute_____ Blood Pressure ___/___

Nausea and Vomiting—Ask "Do you feel sick to your stomach? Have you vomited?" Observation:	Tactile Disturbances—Ask "Have you any itching, pins and needles sensations, any burning, any numbness, or do you feel bugs crawling on or under your skin?" Observation:
0 no nausea and vomiting	0 none
1 mild nausea and vomiting	1 very mild itching, pins and needles, burning or numbness
2	2 mild itching, pins and needles, burning or numbness
3	
4 intermittent nausea with dry heaves	3 moderate itching, pins and needles, burning or numbness
5	
6	4 moderately severe hallucinations
7 constant nausea, frequent dry heaves and vomiting	5 severe hallucinations
	6 extremely severe hallucinations
	7 continuous hallucinations
Tremor—Arms extended and fingers spread apart. Observation:	**Auditory Disturbances**—Ask "Are you more aware of sounds around you? Are they harsh? Do they frighten you? Are you hearing anything that is disturbing to you? Are you hearing things you know are not there?" Observation:
0 no tremor	0 not present
1 not visible, but can be felt fingertip to fingertip	1 very mild harshness or ability to frighten
2	2 mild harshness or ability to frighten
3	3 moderate harshness or ability to frighten
4 moderate, with patient's arms extended	4 moderately severe hallucinations
5	5 severe hallucinations
6	6 extremely severe hallucinations
7 severe, even with arms not extended	7 continuous hallucinations

Paroxysmal Sweats—Observation	**Visual Disturbances**—Ask "Does the light appear to be too bright? Is its color different? Does it hurt your eyes? Are you seeing anything that is disturbing to you? Are you seeing things you know are not there?" Observation:
0 no sweat visible	0 not present
1 barely perceptible sweating, palms moist	1 very mild sensitivity
2	2 mild sensitivity
3	3 moderate sensitivity
4 beads of sweat obvious on forehead	4 moderately severe hallucinations
5	5 severe hallucinations
6	6 extremely severe hallucinations
7 drenching sweats	7 continuous hallucinations
Anxiety—Ask "Do you feel nervous?" Observation:	**Headache, Fullness in Head**—Ask "Does your head feel different? Does it feel like there is a band around your head?" Do not rate for dizziness or lightheadedness. Otherwise, rate severity:
0 no anxiety, at ease	0 not present
1 mildly anxious	1 very mild
2	2 mild
3	3 moderate
4 moderately anxious or guarded, so anxiety is inferred	4 moderately severe
5	5 severe
6	6 very severe
7 equivalent to acute panic states as seen in severe delirium or acute schizophrenic reactions	7 extremely severe
Agitation—Observation:	**Orientation and Clouding of Sensorium**—Ask, "What day is this? Where are you? Who am I?"
0 normal activity	0 oriented and can do serial additions
1 somewhat more than normal activity	1 cannot do serial additions or is uncertain about date
2	2 disoriented for date by no more than two calendar days
3	
4 moderately fidgety and restless	3 disoriented for date by more than two calendar days
5	
6	4 disoriented for place and/or person
7 paces back and for during most of the interview, or constantly thrashes about	
	Total CIWA-Ar Score* _____ **Rater's Initials** _____ ***Maximum possible score 67**
This scale is not copyrighted and can be reproduced freely.	**Source: Sullivan et al., 1989**

The Treatment of Alcohol Withdrawal

Facilities that treat alcohol withdrawal typically do so following written protocols or guidelines, combined with clinical judgment. Medically supervised detoxification will likely involve:

- The use of benzodiazepines to prevent seizures and decrease the autonomic excitability and risk for seizures associated with withdrawal. These may be long-acting agents, such as diazepam/Valium or chlordiazepoxide/Librium, or medications with shorter half-lives such as oxazepam/Serax or lorazepam/Ativan. While typically taken by mouth, in more serious withdrawal syndromes these medications will be delivered intravenously, and in doses large enough to control symptoms.

- Repletion of thiamine (Vitamin B1). This needs to be done prior to the administration of any carbohydrates to prevent the development of a serious complication—Wernicke's encephalopathy, which is characterized by visual disturbances, unsteady gait, and confusion/delirium.

- Repletion of folic acid.

- Use of medications, such as beta-blockers, to help control elevations in blood pressure and pulse.

- Some protocols may also allow for the use of other anticonvulsants to help prevent seizures.

Pharmacotherapy

There are currently three FDA approved medications for the treatment of alcohol use disorder: Naltrexone, which is available as a daily medication (Revia) and long-acting injection (Vivitrol), acamprosate/Campral, and the behavioral aversive disulfiram/Antabuse.

- Acamprosate/Campral is generally well tolerated and has been shown to diminish cravings for alcohol as well as the number of drinks consumed when someone does lapse. It is safe and could be considered for people on psychiatric medications. It has few side effects, the most common being upset stomach, a feeling of bloating or gassiness. Adherence may be difficult as it requires three times a day dosing.

- Naltrexone (Revia, Vivitrol) is an opioid blocker that has been shown to decrease cravings for alcohol as well as for the amount consumed. It is generally safe, but individuals on the longer-acting form should consider wearing a medic alert bracelet, should they require emergency analgesia. Because they are on an opioid blocker, the amounts of medication used should they need emergency pain relief could be considerable and place them at risk for respiratory depression.

- Disulfiram/Antabuse is a behavioral aversive that works by preventing the breakdown of alcohol in the body through the inhibition of the enzyme, acetaldehyde dehydrogenase. As a result, acetaldehyde, which is noxious in high concentrations, accumulates and the person experiences unpleasant reactions—nausea, vomiting, flushing, accelerated heart rate, headache, and confusion. Disulfiram's use should be limited to individuals who are highly motivated for total abstinence. It's best avoided in people with poor impulse control, especially if they also have underlying medical problems, as there have been deaths from respiratory and cardiac complications associated with drinking alcohol when on disulfiram.

CHAPTER 17

Tobacco

> **Overview**
> **Treatment of Tobacco Use Disorders**
> Psychosocial Treatments
> Pharmacological Treatments

OVERVIEW

Tobacco use is the number one cause of preventable death in the United States (more than 400,000 annually). It is the leading cause of cancer deaths and greatly increases a person's risk for heart attack, stroke, and chronic obstructive pulmonary disease (COPD). On average, people who smoke die 10 years younger than the general population.

The good news is that overall rates of smoking in the United States have diminished from more than 40 percent of the adult population in 1965 to about 20 percent in 2011 (69.5 million people).

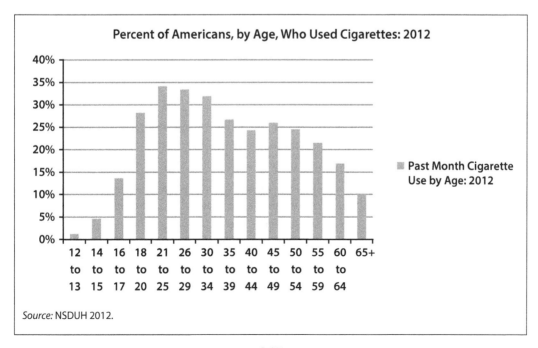

Source: NSDUH 2012.

However, according to SAMHSA's National Survey on Drug Use and Health (NSDUH), rates of daily tobacco use are higher among people with any mental illness than the general population (36.1% vs. 21.4%), as is the number of cigarettes smoked in a month (331 vs. 310). Men of all ages have higher rates of tobacco use than women. Quit rates among people with mental illness are lower than the general population.

The Centers for Disease Control (CDC) report worse statistics, finding that people with mental illness are twice as likely to smoke and currently represent about one-third of smokers. They project that, based on current trends, people with mental illness will become the majority of cigarette smokers in the United States.

The National Comorbidity Study, which broke down data by specific diagnoses, reported elevated rates of lifetime smoking among all mental illnesses, with the highest rates found in people with bipolar disorder (68.8%), substance use disorders (49%), schizophrenia (49.4%), generalized anxiety disorder (46%), and PTSD (46.3%). Quit rates are much lower among people with mental illnesses, when compared to the general population.

Tobacco control programs, which include education, regulation and taxation of tobacco products, efforts to decrease exposure to secondhand smoke, establishment of smoke-free environments, QUIT LINES, and so forth, have shown success in the general population, but have had poor outcomes with people who have mental illness. This finding has led to a growing interest into integrating tobacco cessation efforts into mental health and substance use services.

TREATMENT OF TOBACCO USE DISORDERS

There are effective treatments for tobacco cessation, yet studies find these are underutilized in people with mental illness. These include a variety of therapeutic strategies, medications, and decisions made at a governmental or organizational level to increase the likelihood that someone will be able to quit. Additionally, there is a misperception that people with mental illness are not as interested in quitting as those without.

For smokers with mental illness, a number of factors need to be addressed to enhance their chances of quitting.

1. At an organizational level, providers need to make smoking cessation a priority. This will include:

   • Everyone is assessed for tobacco use.

   • Everyone who smokes or uses tobacco is asked about their thoughts/plans for quitting. This question is posed both upon admission and throughout the course of treatment.

   • Everyone who wishes to quit will be offered treatment to help in achieving that goal.

2. Cigarette smoking (not the nicotine) through interactions in the liver can significantly lower the blood levels of many psychiatric medications, including several of the first- and second-generation antipsychotics. For some individuals this lowering of medication levels may be associated with a worsening of psychiatric symptoms, a decrease in medication side effects, or both.

3. Development of smoke-free environments has greatly limited the availability of places where people can smoke. Smoke-free zones include mental health clinics, hospitals, social clubs, and mutual-support settings, such as 12-step groups.

Psychosocial Treatments

There is a wealth of information and support to help people quit smoking. This includes websites and government-sponsored programs (some of which are funded by tobacco-settlement money).

- Smokefree.gov is a well-organized website that provides education, along with free resources.
- 1-800-QUIT-NOW is a federal/state initiative that provides free counseling and, in some states, free nicotine patches (and possibly other forms of nicotine replacement such as gum or lozenges) to help people stop smoking.

Nonpharmacologic strategies to help people quit smoking are similar to those used for other problem substance use behaviors, and include:

- Education
  - An honest look at smoking's effect on the mind and the body: 10 years of lost life, greatly increased risks for heart attack, stroke, and cancer, and increased levels of depression.
  - Educate around potential withdrawal associated with tobacco cessation (may last a few weeks), including increased irritability, increased anxiety and depression, and increased appetite.
- Motivational enhancement
  - Weighing the pros and cons of smoking: "It calms me down, but I can't stand the way it makes my clothes smell, and my car is like a giant ashtray." Have the client put their pros and cons into writing and carry them in their purse or wallet. Instruct them that whenever they want to light up, they should first read their pros and cons list.
  - Increasing the discomfort around smoking.
  - Encouraging change talk: "It sounds like you're really thinking about quitting; that's awesome. Do you have a quit plan?"
  - Creating a written quit plan, which includes a date and telling friends and family about it.
- Cognitive-behavioral approaches. This can include group, individual, and self-directed strategies
  - Identify triggers for smoking.
  - Introduce a "delay" before lighting up. This is where a certain time period, starts short and then is made longer, is introduced before each cigarette. This delay increases an awareness of the act of smoking and decreases the automatic patterns. "Before you light up, wait fifteen seconds. You can still have the cigarette, but you have to wait. Then when you're doing that consistently increase to thirty seconds, then a minute, two minutes, and so forth."
  - Create rules around smoking, such as no smoking in the house and in the car.
  - Create a reward system whereby money saved from not smoking goes to something else.
  - When the quit plan goes into effect, make certain all tobacco products are out of the house. Avoid situations and people who are actively smoking, at least initially.

- Mindfulness training
  - o Observe the urge to smoke and let it pass.
  - o When you light up, smoke with complete attention.

Pharmacological Treatments

Several FDA-approved treatments are currently available to help with smoking cessation. They include various forms of nicotine replacement (patches, gum, lozenges, vapor), as well as the medications varenicline/Chantix and bupropion/Zyban (a low dose of the antidepressant bupropion/Wellbutrin). The selection of a medication to help people with co-occurring mental disorders quit will be influenced by their underlying mental disorder and the potential risks/benefits of the particular medication.

In general tobacco replacement is considered safe, but make certain that the person understands how the particular medication is to be used and the potential risks should they continue to smoke while on replacement therapy (palpitations, flushing, nausea). There is also growing controversy around e-cigarettes (vaporized nicotine), as it appears these may, especially for younger people, be creating nicotine dependence and subsequent smoking. These are not currently regulated by the Food and Drug Administration (FDA), and it is not clear what is contained in the vapor.

The medication varenicline/Chantix, which carries the highest quit rate of all available medications, also has the highest rate of adverse reactions. These can include everything from intense and unpleasant dreams, to an increase in suicidal and even homicidal thinking; its use needs to be carefully weighed, especially in individuals who are already struggling with emotional instability. One recent study has shown promise with individuals with schizophrenia whose psychiatric symptoms were stable.

Bupropion (Zyban, Wellbutrin) may also be of benefit in smoking cessation. But as with any antidepressant, its potential for manic switching in susceptible individuals needs to be considered.

CHAPTER 18

Opioids

OVERVIEW

The past 30 years have seen a dramatic rise in the number of Americans with opioid use disorders, currently at more than 2 million people. A recent Youth Risk Behavior Survey of high school students reported nearly 3 percent of students had tried heroin in the past year and 20 percent had taken prescription drugs, including opioids, without a prescription. And it is estimated that 1 percent of pregnant women use illicit opioids.

This increase in opioid use has been accompanied by a fourfold rise in the number of people seeking treatment for opioid use disorders since 1998. Most concerning is the 400 percent increase in opioid-related deaths since the late 1990s, the highest rates being found with women.

Currently opioids are implicated in more than 90 percent of unintentional fatal overdoses in the United States. Many of these deaths involve poly-pharmacy with opioids combined with other central nervous system depressants such as alcohol or benzodiazepines (diazepam/Valium-type drugs).

Reasons for this marked increase in opioid use include the tremendous rise in prescriptions for narcotic pain medications, as well as the relative low cost and easy access to heroin. The 2012 National Survey on Drug Use and Health (NSDUH) showed that 54 percent of nonmedical pain-killer users obtained the opioids for free from friends and relatives, most of whom had prescriptions.

Intravenous use of opioids, as well as other drugs, adds a layer of serious and potentially life-threatening health risks, which include infectious diseases such as HIV/AIDs, Hepatitis C, cellulitis, bacterial endocarditis (infections on the leaflets of the heart valves), and septicemia (blood infections).

Once dependent on opioids, people become trapped in a cycle of needing to obtain an adequate supply to prevent them from going into withdrawal (jonesing, dope sickness). Depending on the availability and their choice of opioid, they may need to dose themselves from once a day (methadone, buprenorphine) to every four to six hours (heroin, oxycodone/ OxyContin, Vicodin).

The ways in which people become addicted to opioids vary. For some it starts with medications prescribed for pain, that they are unable or unwilling to stop. Others enjoy the euphoric effects of opioids, and some, with co-occurring mood and anxiety problems, find a temporary relief from painful and negative emotions.

For people with chronic pain conditions, who grow tolerant to the effects of their medications, this can lead to overusing their prescriptions and then running out. To prevent a return of symptoms, which have now been complicated by withdrawal syndromes, people are faced with difficult choices, such as buying medication illicitly, finding additional prescribers who are unaware that the patient is already prescribed opioids—so-called doctor shopping—or diverting medications from others who have been given legitimate prescriptions. If people are unable to obtain prescription medications they may turn to heroin to relieve both their pain and to prevent withdrawal.

A common pattern of usage starts with trying a pain pill or two orally, then snorting them. First experiences with heroin usually involve snorting, but in time many people want to experience the more intense high from injecting the drug. Heroin can also be smoked (chasing the dragon).

The array of available opioids is vast, and it is common for people to not understand that the medication they are taking is in fact an opioid and can be habit forming. This may be especially true for some of the newer pain medications, which bind to opioid receptors in the brain and are habit forming, tramadol/Ultram being one example.

Types of Opioids

When discussing opioids and treatment of opioid use disorders, it is useful to understand differences between the various agents. These include the relative half-lives of the different compounds (how long they stay in the body and how frequently people need to be dosed), as well as their overall effect on the body. The following terms help describe how particular substances work at the opioid receptors in the brain and body.

- Agonist/Pure agonist—These substances, when taken in higher quantities, have no ceiling effect. In the case of opioids it means that when a pure agonist is taken in a great enough dose the person will eventually experience respiratory arrest and stop breathing. Examples include heroin, methadone, fentanyl, and morphine.

- Antagonist (blocker)—These substances bind to the opiate receptor and block it from being available to other substances, and include naltrexone (Revia) and naloxone (Narcan). These are not opioids, although naloxone is combined with the opioid buprenorphine to make the medications Suboxone, Zubsolv, and available generics.

- Partial agonist—This substance provides some of the typical opioid effect (pain relief, prevention of withdrawal symptoms), but when taken in higher doses it has a ceiling effect and will not lead to respiratory depression unless combined with other central nervous system depressants. Buprenorphine, whether alone or in combination with Naloxone (Suboxone, Subutex, Zubsolv) is the most widely used partial agonist. Clients and clinicians need to know that it is in fact an opioid.

Opioids

Substance	How Used	Dosing Frequency	Type
Buprenorphine (Subutex)	Sublingual (under the tongue)	Once or twice daily, more frequently if used for pain	Partial agonist
Buprenorphine/naloxone (Suboxone, Subsolv)	Sublingual	Once or twice daily, more frequently if used for pain	Partial agonist combined with an antagonist
Codeine (Darvon)	Oral	Every 3–6 hours	Pure agonist
Fentanyl	Transdermal/patch, oral (lozenge), injection	• Oral unclear • Injection every 4 hours • Patch every 72 hours	Pure agonist
Heroin	Snorted, injected, smoked	Every 4–8 hours	Pure agonist
Hydrocodone (Vicodin, Lortab, Lorcet)	Oral	Every 4–6 hours	Pure agonist
Hydromorphone (Dilaudid)	Oral, rectal (suppository), Intravenous	Every 3–4 hours	Pure agonist
Methadone (Dolophine, Amidone, Methadose)	Oral	Once a day	Pure agonist
Meperidine (Demerol)	Oral, Intravenous	Every 2–3 hours	Pure agonist
Morphine	Oral, intravenous	• Immediate release every 3–4 hours • Slow release every 8–12 hours	Pure agonist
Opium	Smoked	Every 4–6 hours	Pure agonist
Oxycodone (OxyContin, Roxicodone, Percocet, Percodan, etc.)	Oral	• Immediate release every 3–4 hours • Sustained release (OxyContin) every 8–12 hours	Pure agonist
Propoxyphene (Darvocet)	Oral	Every 3–4 hours	Pure agonist
Sufentanil	Intravenous	Every 2–4 hours	Pure agonist

OPIOID WITHDRAWAL

Opioid withdrawal states create intense physical and psychological symptoms that perpetuate the cycle of drug seeking and addiction. For many people with long-standing opioid habits, it is no longer about experiencing the euphoric highs, but much of their day is focused on doing whatever it takes to stay out of withdrawal.

Depending on the substance used, withdrawal symptoms can start within a few hours of the last dose. Symptoms can be divided between those that are physically and psychologically distressing. Acute withdrawal symptoms can last from a few days to more than two weeks. Physical symptoms of withdrawal may include:

- Diarrhea
- Cramping (muscles, stomach)
- Achiness (bones, muscles)
- Muscle twitches
- Pupil dilation (midriasis)
- Yawning
- Runny nose
- Tearing
- Nausea and vomiting
- Hot and cold flashes, sweating
- Gooseflesh (piloerection)

Psychological symptoms of opioid withdrawal include the following:

- Anxiety
- Intense cravings to use
- Irritability
- Depression
- Restlessness

ASSESSMENT TOOLS

There are a number of tools used to quantify the severity of withdrawal syndromes. Two that are often used, and at times used together, are the Clinical Opiate Withdrawal Scale (COWS) and Subjective Opiate Withdrawal Scale (SOWS).

Clinical Opiate Withdrawal Scale

The Clinical Opiate Withdrawal Scale (COWS) is an 11-item assessment completed by a clinician that assesses the severity of changes in pulse rate, sweating, pupil size, restlessness, degree of cramping and achiness, stomach upset/nausea and vomiting, tremors, anxiety and irritability, gooseflesh, and yawning/tearing. It can be performed at intervals to assess improvement. Downloadable copies of the COWS are available on a number of websites, including a flow sheet that allows symptoms to be tracked over time: www.csam-asam.org/sites/default/files/pdf/misc/COWS_induction_flow_sheet.doc.

The Subjective Opiate Withdrawal Scale

Similar to the COWS, the Subjective Opiate Withdrawal Scale (SOWS) is a 16–item Likert-based tool completed by the client. It can be informative to complete both of these instruments and then compare the results. Do they show a relatively similar severity of withdrawal, or is one significantly higher than the other? A downloadable version of the SOWS is available at www.ncbi.nlm.nih.gov/books/NBK143183/bin/annex10-fm2.pdf.

TREATMENT OF OPIOID USE DISORDERS

In working with people who have opioid use disorders, especially those that are moderate and severe, it is crucial to assess and address this problem directly and promptly. What does the client want? Do they want to be opiate free? If so, what timeframe are they looking at? Or, are they looking to get on some form of opioid replacement therapy?

For those who are committed to detoxifying from opioids there are various taper strategies that can be used, and certain medications, such as the alpha-agonist Clonidine, can be used off-label to help decrease some of the physical symptoms of withdrawal. Some inpatient facilities do a rapid (one to two weeks) taper using the medication buprenorphine/naloxone (Suboxone/Zubsolv), although long-term results from such rapid tapers are not encouraging. Other detox protocols use the long-acting opioid methadone. Because both methadone and buprenorphine have long half-lives, it is common for people to be discharged from inpatient detox units while they are still in the midst of the withdrawal process. This approach places them at tremendous risk for relapse.

For many individuals who have been using opioids for extended periods, abstinence may not be realistic or might not be realistic right now. It is important to acknowledge the person's long-term goal of being completely free of opioids, but to set a more immediate goal of getting them off street drugs or illicitly obtained prescriptions, and pursuing a course of opioid replacement therapy.

And finally, for people who have achieved abstinence from opioids, the risk of relapse is high, especially during the first year. Psychological, and possibly pharmacological, strategies along with wellness routines can be used to help with relapse prevention.

Opioid Replacement Therapy

In the United States there are currently two standard forms of opioid replacement therapy—methadone and buprenorphine

Methadone. Synthesized in 1939 by German scientists, methadone was brought to the United States in 1947 for the treatment of narcotic dependency. It is a DEA schedule II controlled substance and is a pure opioid agonist with a half-life of 24–36 hours. On account of the long and variable half-life, withdrawal from methadone can be protracted and last from several days to several weeks.

As replacement treatment for opioid use disorders, methadone can only be prescribed through opioid treatment programs (OTP) that are state licensed and approved by SAMHSA. There are approximately 2,000 of these licensed centers that operate nationwide.

The side effects of methadone are similar to other opioids—sedation, nodding, constipation, dry mouth, urinary retention. Methadone comes with a black box warning for QT prolongation—dose dependent—and a pretreatment electrocardiogram (ECG) is recommended. Because of this, it's best to avoid other medications that cause cardiac conduction delays as this adverse reaction can be additive and lead to a dangerous arrhythmia, heart failure, and sudden death.

Recent studies using doses of 120–150 mg per day showed reduced use of illicit opioids and were found to be safe. The current consensus is that 60–100 mg per day is safe and effective. Less than 60 mg per day is associated with increased relapse rates.

Methadone can be dangerous and potentially lethal in overdose or when combined with other sedatives, such as benzodiazepines, or alcohol.

Most clinics require daily attendance and include some form(s) of therapy and psychiatric consultation. A list of local opioid treatment programs maintained by SAMHSA can be accessed at dpt2.samhsa.gov/treatment/directory.aspx.

Buprenorphine. Buprenorphine (Subutex) is a partial opioid agonist/antagonist that is typically combined with the opioid blocker naloxone (Narcan) under the trade names Suboxone and Zubsolv. By occupying the opioid receptor site, buprenorphine blocks the effects of other opioids, so if a person were to use heroin or most narcotic pain medication while taking buprenorphine, that person would not get the euphoric effect of the other drug. Buprenorphine is less sedating and does not have "the high" of other opioids, although some people do report a general feeling of well-being, especially when they first start using the medication.

Buprenorphine is taken under the tongue (sublingually) as either a strip or a dissolving tablet. Taken in this manner the naloxone (Narcan) component is inactive; however, should the medication be misused and snorted or injected, the naloxone (Narcan) would precipitate symptoms of withdrawal. Even so, some people have reported snorting the pill form of this medication, and experienced a euphoric high.

Prior to starting buprenorphine, patients should be in active opioid withdrawal in order to prevent the medication from precipitating a withdrawal when it displaces the other opioid the patient has been using from the receptors.

Unlike methadone, buprenorphine does not have to be prescribed through a SAMHSA-designated opioid treatment program. Physicians (MDs and DOs) who wish to prescribe buprenorphine for the treatment of opioid use disorders must receive additional education and obtain a special DEA waiver, "the X," which involves one day of training and completion of an application. Strict guidelines limit the number of patients a prescribing physician can see. Initially it can be as many as 30, and then after a year, if the prescriber meets certain requirements, this number can be increased to 100.

Credentialed physicians are able to prescribe buprenorphine as opioid replacement therapy through a typical office practice or through a substance use or co-occurring program. Initially, patients receive a small prescription for the medication, but when stable they may receive monthly prescriptions. Typical doses for opioid replacement therapy are 8–16 mg per day of the buprenorphine component. Higher doses are associated with a greater risk of medication diversion.

Other Medication-Assisted Treatment for Opioid Use Disorders

Also FDA-approved for the treatment of opioid use disorders is the opioid antagonist, naltrexone. As opposed to methadone and buprenorphine (opioid replacement therapies), naltrexone is for individuals who are completely opioid free (at least 7–10 days, possibly longer for longer-acting opioids such as methadone or buprenorphine). Using naltrexone while still on an opioid will precipitate withdrawal symptoms.

Naltrexone is available as both a long-acting (once a month) injection or as a daily medication. Unlike buprenorphine and methadone, it does not carry a risk of dependence or diversion. No special licensure is required to prescribe naltrexone.

People wishing to be on this medication need to be informed that should they use opioids while on naltrexone, they will not get the euphoric feeling or pain relief associated with opioids. It is possible for patients to fatally overdose with opioids while on naltrexone, most commonly this occurs when patients miss doses of oral naltrexone, are at the end of the injection period for the long-acting form, or attempt to override the effects of naltrexone with large doses of opioids.

Adverse reactions reported with naltrexone include liver toxicity, fatigue, loss of appetite, injection site reactions (long-acting formulation), and an allergic pneumonia, which has also been reported with the injectable form.

It is recommended that patients on the long-acting injectable naltrexone wear a medical alert bracelet to alert emergency personnel in the event they are unconscious. If opioids are required for acute pain management, such as might be needed after an accident, this might not be possible, especially outside of a supervised medical setting, for an individual on naltrexone.

OVERDOSE RESCUE KITS

On account of the nearly 400 percent increase in overdose deaths involving opioids, many states have passed legislation to allow prescribers to write prescriptions for injectable and/or inhalable naloxone/Narcan. These overdose rescue kits can be prescribed for the identified patient or for a family member or significant other.

Naloxone/Narcan is a potent opioid antagonist that when injected into a muscle (IM) or blood vessel (IV) or inhaled can rapidly reverse the effects of an opioid overdose. Naloxone/Narcan is also short acting, and if the person overdosed with a long-acting opioid, such as methadone, a second dose may be required while waiting for emergency services to arrive.

PREGNANCY, BREAST FEEDING, AND OPIOID USE DISORDERS

Opioid use disorders occur most frequently in adolescents and young adults. As a result, it is important to understand some basics on how to help a woman who is opioid dependent manage a pregnancy and postpartum period.

Although it is completely understandable for a pregnant woman to want to be off of all drugs and medication throughout her pregnancy and while breast feeding, it is not always realistic. For women who are opioid dependent and discover they are pregnant, it is vitally important to ascertain the woman's goals around her drug usage. If she is committed to being opioid free throughout the pregnancy and postpartum period, then a realistic and gentle taper should be initiated. Abrupt discontinuation of opioids should be avoided as this is associated with miscarriage, preterm labor, and fetal distress.

The risk for relapse is quite high, and research shows that pregnancy outcomes (more miscarriages, premature delivery, lower birth weights) are worse for women who go on and off opioids through the course of their pregnancy. This makes sense as not only is the woman going in and out of withdrawal, so too is her unborn child. Where muscle cramps are a typical feature of opioid withdrawal, it is easy to see how unwanted uterine cramping could have an overall deleterious effect on the fetus, including preterm labor and miscarriage.

Opioid Replacement Therapy During Pregnancy

For many women with moderate or severe opioid use disorders, one practical approach is to remain on, or get on, some form of opioid replacement therapy. There is a large literature on managing pregnancy for women on methadone, and also considerable evidence to support maintaining women on buprenorphine through the course of their pregnancy.

Advantages to opioid replacement therapy during pregnancy include decreased relapse rates, lower rates of HIV and hepatitis infections, better obstetrical care, reduced fetal mortality, increased fetal growth, and an increased likelihood that the infant will go home with the mother.

An emerging literature also indicates that women on buprenorphine, versus methadone, have a decreased rate of preterm labor, and the infants have generally less severe withdrawal symptoms after birth.

General guidelines for pregnant women on opioid replacement therapy include:

- If a woman is already on opioid replacement therapy, it is best to leave her on that agent (either methadone or buprenorphine—typically if a woman is on buprenorphine/naloxone, she will be switched to a buprenorphine-only medication).

- Frequent and regular clinical contacts are important between the pregnant woman and the clinical program through which she receives the opioid replacement therapy.

- An ongoing liaison should occur between the prescriber of the opioid replacement therapy and the obstetrician.

- The woman's partner should be included in the treatment process and receive education about the risks and benefits of opioid replacement therapy. If the partner is actively using illicit substances and/or alcohol, this needs to be addressed, as it may well trigger the pregnant woman to relapse.

- The woman should understand all the risks related to both being on opioid replacement therapy through pregnancy, as well as the risks of tapering off, including a greatly increased risk for relapse with illicit narcotics.

  o The woman should understand that her baby will be at risk for a neonatal abstinence syndrome (a withdrawal syndrome, which may require medical management following delivery).

o The woman should be aware that children born to women who are opioid dependent are at an increased risk for sudden infant death syndrome and that close pediatric supervision is recommended.

Opioid Replacement Therapy During Breast Feeding (Lactation)

Both methadone and buprenorphine are detected in breast milk, although in low concentrations. The current recommendation is that if a woman wishes to breast feed, the benefits of doing so outweigh the risks.

CHAPTER 19

Selected Topics for Other Substances

OVERVIEW

SAMHSA's 2012 National Survey on Drug Use and Health found that nearly 24 million Americans had used one or more illicit drugs within a given month (9.2% of the population older than age 12). This number represents an increase from the period between 2002 to 2008 (7.9% to 8.3%). The most commonly used substance was cannabis, where it's reported there are currently over seven million habitual users (greater than twenty days in a month) in the United States.

Significant trends in the use of illicit substances include:

- The number of heroin users increased from 373,000 (2007) to 669,000 (2012).

- A reported 2.6 percent of the population used nonprescribed psychotherapeutic medications (stimulants, pain killers, tranquilizers, sedatives).

    o 4.9 million used pain relievers (1.9%)

o 1.2 million used stimulants (0.5%)

o 440,000 methamphetamine users (0.2%)—down from 731,000 users in 2006

- The rate of current illicit drug use has increased markedly in those ages 50–64 (baby boomers).

- Approximately 10.3 million people ages 12 and up reported having driven under the influence of illicit drugs in 2012.

- Although less than the rate for nonpregnant women in this age range (10.7%), 5.9 percent of pregnant women, ages 15 to 44, were current users of illicit drugs in 2011–2012.

Past-Month Use of Illicit Drugs

Substance	All Ages	Ages 12–17	Ages 18–25	Adults Older Than 25
All illicit drugs	9.2%	9.5%	21.3%	7.0%
Marijuana (including hashish)	7.3%	7.2%	18.7%	5.3%
Inhalants	n/a	0.8%	n/a	0.1%
Psychotherapeutics*	2.6%	2.8%	5.3%	2.1%
Hallucinogens**	0.4%	0.6%	1.7%	0.2%
Cocaine	0.6%	Less than 0.2%	1.1%	0.6%

(*Source:* 2012 National Survey on Drug Use and Health)

* Psychotherapeutics include prescription pain killers, tranquilizers, sedatives, and stimulants (includes methamphetamine).

** Hallucinogens in this survey include LSD, PCP, Ecstasy (MDMA) and related compounds, Peyote, mescaline, and psilocybin mushrooms.

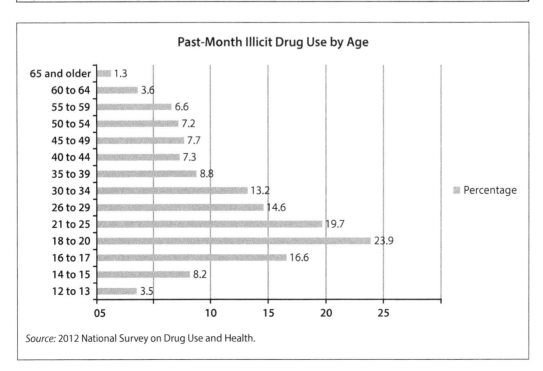

Past-Month Illicit Drug Use by Age

Age	Percentage
65 and older	1.3
60 to 64	3.6
55 to 59	6.6
50 to 54	7.2
45 to 49	7.7
40 to 44	7.3
35 to 39	8.8
30 to 34	13.2
26 to 29	14.6
21 to 25	19.7
18 to 20	23.9
16 to 17	16.6
14 to 15	8.2
12 to 13	3.5

Source: 2012 National Survey on Drug Use and Health.

COCAINE

Cocaine, derived from the leaves of the coca plant, can be taken orally, snorted, smoked (crack, freebase), and injected. It is highly habit forming due to its strong effects on the brain's reward system. Earlier studies on primates dramatically demonstrated this when monkeys, given the choice between food and cocaine, consistently pushed the bar for cocaine and ignored the food.

Cocaine is a central nervous system stimulant that increases heart rate, suppresses appetite, and provides the user with feelings of increased energy, euphoria, and confidence. The effects of cocaine are short acting, 15 minutes to an hour.

Negative health outcomes from cocaine include damage to the heart (myocardial ischemia) from vasospasm combined with increased heart rate and elevated blood pressure (cardiac workload). These effects are especially notable when alcohol is combined with cocaine, where it forms cocaethlyene, which is associated with increased cardiac toxicity. With heavy use, cocaine is associated with sudden cardiac death and stroke.

The method of cocaine use also carries specific risks, from bloody noses, to destruction of nasal cartilage from inhaling, to abscesses, increased rates of HIV/AIDs and Hepatitis B and C with intravenous use, to burns, shortness of breath, chest pain, and lung spasm with smoked (crack, freebase) cocaine.

Cocaine Withdrawal/Crash

Users of cocaine, after a binge, often experience a "crash" or come down. This crash is characterized by:

- Tiredness
- Vivid dreams
- Sleep disturbance (too much or too little)
- Increased appetite
- Depressed and/or anxious mood (can be severe)
- Suicidality

Pharmacological Treatments

At the time of this book's publication there are no FDA approved treatments for cocaine use disorders. However, a number of studies have been conducted, with people who have both cocaine use disorders and a co-occurring mental disorder. What these studies show when taken together is that when the mental disorder is well controlled, such as with the use of antipsychotic medications in people with schizophrenia, the severity and frequency of cocaine use diminishes.

In addition, a number of medications are being assessed for their potential benefits in diminishing cravings and relapses. Although not FDA approved, their off-label use could be considered when working with individuals who are struggling to achieve abstinence from cocaine. These agents include:

- topiramate/Topamax
- gabapentin/Neurontin

- diclofenac/Baclofen
- amantadine/Symmetrel

STIMULANTS, INCLUDING "BATH SALTS"

Stimulants (psychostimulants), other than cocaine and caffeine, include prescription medications for ADHD (methylphenidate/Ritalin/Concerta and amphetamines and mixed amphetamine salts/Adderall/Vyvanse), and a large number of synthetic compounds, which go by a variety of names, including "bath salts" and "plant food." Typical effects of stimulants may include:

- Increased energy
- Diminished appetite
- Decreased sleep
- Increased alertness
- Increased concentration
- Increased heart rate and blood pressure
- Increased anxiety
- Increased irritability

With heavy use or in high dosages, additional symptoms of paranoia and psychosis are possible.

Issues Specific to "Bath Salts" and Related Compounds

The past several years have seen a marked rise in the use of stimulants sold over the counter and through the Internet. Many of these compounds contain the stimulant 3,4-methlymethcathinone/MDPV (mephedrone). Despite legislative attempts to ban these substances, they continue to be sold and used. Their availability has created significant issues in emergency rooms and hospitals, where users are appearing with symptoms of agitation, confusion, psychosis (at times persistent), elevations in blood pressure and pulse, dilated pupils (mydriasis), tremors, seizures, and organ failure (liver and kidney). Deaths due to MDPV toxicity have been reported.

Treatment for MDPV toxicity is supportive and includes the use of sedatives, including intravenous administration of diazepam/Valium-type drugs to help manage the confusional delirium. This is similar to treatment for alcohol and benzodiazepine withdrawal. If psychotic features are prominent, there are reports of using tranquilizers, as well.

The withdrawal syndrome from stimulants, if any, is similar to that seen with cocaine. It can include dysphoria, tiredness, excessive sleepiness, vivid dreams, and cravings to use.

CANNABIS

Second to alcohol, cannabis is the most commonly used mind-altering drug in the United States, both in the general population and with people who have co-occurring mental disorders. It is associated with increased psychotic symptoms in people with schizophrenia, as well as an increased frequency of mania, psychosis, suicide attempts, and overall illness severity in people who have bipolar disorder. Significant evidence now indicates that marijuana use may precipitate psychosis in susceptible individuals. In multiple large studies, use of cannabis has been associated with much greater (sevenfold) rates of psychotic disorders, as well as earlier onset. It appears that this relationship between cannabis and schizophrenia may have a genetic underpinning (a gene that codes for an enzyme involved in dopamine synthesis). Conceptually, it's as if marijuana in these vulnerable individuals switches on the illness. What is not known is whether cessation of cannabis in these same people might eventually lead to symptom resolution.

Attitudes and policies toward cannabis are undergoing significant change with more than 20 states having legalized medical marijuana, and Colorado and Washington having legalized recreational use for people over the age of 21. In contrast, the federal government and the Drug Enforcement Agency continue to consider cannabis an illegal substance.

Pharmacological Treatments

To date there are no FDA approved medications for the treatment of cannabis use disorders.

Synthetic Cannabis (Incense, Spice, K-2)

Sold under a variety of names, and typically marked, "not for human consumption" there has been a tremendous growth in the use of synthetic intoxicating drugs. While many of these have been designated illegal/banned, they continue to be popular, especially among teens and young adults. In addition to the relative availability of these substances (purchased over the Internet, at gas stations and head shops), many are drawn to them because they pass undetected on most standard drug screens. Special tests are available, and one study that looked at urine samples from juvenile probation departments showed positive rates of synthetic cannabis of more than 30 percent.

Synthetic cannabis is a mixture of plant material with laboratory-produced chemicals. It acts on the cannabinoid receptors in the brain. However, unlike natural cannabis, which contains tetrahydrocannabinol (THC), the synthetic compounds are more potent (100–800 times) and are full agonists that can create a much more dramatic drug effect. Effects can include:

- Euphoria, relaxation
- Agitation
- Confusion, and changes in perception; altered sense of time
- Anxiety
- Depression
- Nausea and vomiting
- Increased pulse and blood pressure
- Hallucinations, including command auditory hallucinations, as well as visual and tactile hallucinations
- Paranoia
- Red eyes
- Seizures (rarely reported)

Treatment of Synthetic Cannabis Toxicity

Over the past several years, emergency rooms have seen a marked rise in people admitted in psychotic and agitated states, having used synthetic cannabis, often combined with alcohol and other substances. The diagnostic picture is often complicated because synthetic cannabis does not show up on most routine drug screens.

Treatment is supportive and may involve the use of sedatives and possibly tranquilizers (neuroleptics/antipsychotics) to help manage symptoms of agitation and psychosis.

HALLUCINOGENS

Hallucinogens are compounds that cause changes in perception to where the user experiences phenomenon beyond the range of what is considered normal consciousness. The intoxicating effects of hallucinogens vary widely with some more associated with psychedelic experiences (tripping), and others more leading to out-of-body/dissociative or confusional/delirious states. Some substances, such as the "club drug" MDMA (3,4-methylenedioxy-*N*-methylamphetamine)—aka ecstasy, XTC—have both stimulant and hallucinogenic properties, as well as providing users with a sense of increased connectivity to others (empathogenic). Negative consequences from stimulant use most frequently are related to the acute intoxication stage when judgment may be impaired. Persistent psychotic states can also be associated with hallucinogens, some of these lasting on the order of weeks, months, or even longer, especially with PCP. Commonly used hallucinogens include:

- Lysergic acid (LSD)
- Psilocybin mushrooms (magic mushrooms)
- Peyote
- Mescaline
- Ayahuasca (a combination of plants used in some South American religious and shamanistic traditions, including the Church of Santo Daime)
- MDMA (3,4-methylenedioxy-*N*-methylamphetamine) ecstasy/XTC/Molly/Mandy
- Phencyclidine (PCP)
- Datura stramonium (Jimson weed/the devil's cucumber)
- Ketamine
- Salvia divinorum

OVER-THE-COUNTER MEDICATIONS

Clinicians need to be aware that a large number of substances found in over-the-counter cold/flu and sleeping medications, as well as nutritional supplements, can be misused as intoxicants. Among these are:

Dextromethorphan

(DXM): Found in numerous cold and cough preparations, dextromethorphan is typically combined with acetaminophen. At normal doses this compound has minimal psychoactive properties. However, in higher doses it creates a dissociated hallucinogenic effect, often referred to as "robo-tripping" because of its association with the over-the-counter medication Robitussin®. Because dextromethorphan is typically combined with other ingredients, acetaminophen in particular, significant risk for liver and kidney toxicity occurs when people take hallucinogenic doses of DXM. Habitual users report withdrawal symptoms, which can include lethargy, fatigue, nightmares, insomnia, and depression. Some states have restricted the sale of dextromethorphan-containing compounds, but it is not currently a controlled substance in the United States.

Diphenhydramine

Diphenhydramine, which is found in some cold preparations and over-the-counter sleep aids, has been used recreationally for its sedative and, in much higher than recommended doses, hallucinatory properties. Because of its strong anticholinergic properties, typical side effects include:

- Dry mouth
- Blurry vision
- Constipation
- Urinary retention
- Drowsiness
  In higher doses, symptoms of diphenhydramine toxicity can include:
- Hallucinations
- Agitation
- Palpitations
- Bowel obstruction
- Seizure
- Coma
- Death

Ephedrine and Pseudoephedrine

Ephedrine, which is found in the traditional Chinese Medicinal herb Ma huang (Ephedra sinica), is included in many cold, asthma, and flu medications. Because ephedrine can be used in the manufacture of methamphetamine, legislation has limited the use of ephedrine and requires the recording of information identifying all individuals who purchase ephedrine-containing compounds. Once sold over-the-counter, ephedrine-containing compounds must now be specifically requested.

INTERNET ISSUES

Clinicians need to be aware that many clients research and obtain mind-altering substances through the Internet. Numerous websites and blogs are devoted to specific drugs and to the cultures of "tripping" and to being a "hallucinaut." If one searches for ways to fool/pass a drug test, there are over four million hits. Just entering the term "robotripping" into a search engine brings up over half a million hits.

Clinically, this plays out in a number of ways, as people obtain substances through the Internet:

- Substances that are controlled in this country but are sold over-the-counter in other countries such as Canada, Mexico, Japan, India, and Russia.
- Substances that are not on the market in this country. Here the list is vast, as there are many medications used in the world that are not FDA approved for use in this country. These include tranquilizers, sedatives, and pain killers, many of which have tremendous potential for misuse, abuse, and physiologic dependence and associated withdrawal symptoms and syndromes.
- Substances that are incorrectly labeled. Here it is the ultimate case of "buyer beware"; the Internet purchaser must rely on the seller's honesty regarding the substance they are purchasing.
- Substances of uncertain strength and purity.
- Substances that have been specifically banned in this country, such as flunitrazepam (Rohypnol/Roofies), an ultra-fast-acting benzodiazepine and amnestic agent that has been associated with date rape.
- Component ingredients for substances, such as plants used in the production of the hallucinogen Ayahuasca.
- Faking drug tests: The Internet has a seemingly limitless array of products, blogs, and websites devoted to passing drug tests. These sites often include the sale of compounds used to confound tests, as well as techniques to slip clean, warm urine into the cup when giving a test.

When faced with the dizzying number of substances available through the Internet and varying points of view being expressed, it is important for clinicians to maintain an openness and willingness to learn about whatever over-the-counter, nutritional, and/or Internet-purchased substances their client has obtained. This starts in the assessment process and continues over the course of treatment.

One approach, when faced with an unknown substance, is to start with an Internet search. Here it is helpful to obtain multiple resources, which include:

- Consumer-driven sites
  - o Ask your clients which ones they use.
  - o See which sites have the most hits for the topic you have searched.
  - o See what has been written about the substance on Wikipedia.org and erowid.org. These sources often includes a treasure trove of links to related articles, websites, and blogs.
- Professional websites
  - o WebMD (webmd.com)
  - o PubMed (pubmed.org)
- Governmental websites
  - o Substance Abuse and Mental Health Service Administration (SAMHSA.gov)

State by State Guide to Mental Health Agencies and Prescription Monitoring Programs

(Including District of Columbia and Puerto Rico)

State Mental Health Agency	Prescription Monitoring Programs (PMPs)
Alabama Department of Mental Health www.mh.alabama.gov/ Phone: 800-367-0955	Alabama Department of Public Health www.adph.org/PDMP/Default.asp?id=1229 E-mail: link on website Phone: 877-703-9869
Alaska Department of Health and Human Services Division of Behavioral Health dhss.alaska.gov/dbh/Pages/default.aspx	Alaska's Prescription Drug Monitoring Program (provided through Health Information Design, LLC) www.alaskapdmp.com/ E-mail: akpdmp-info@hidinc.com Phone: 855-263-6404
Arizona Department of Health Services Division of Behavioral Health Services www.azdhs.gov/bhs/ Phone: 602-364-4558	Arizona State Board of Pharmacy www.azpharmacy.gov/CS-Rx_Monitoring/default.asp E-mail: dwright@azpharmacy.gove Phone: 602-771-2744 Fax: 602-771-2748
Arkansas Department of Human Services Division of Behavioral Health Services http://humanservices.arkansas.gov/dbhs/Pages/default.aspx Phone: 501-686-9164	Arkansas Department of Health http://arkansaspmp.com/ E-mail: denise.robertson@arkansas.gov Phone: 501-683-3960 Fax: 501-661-2769

(Continued)

(Continued)

State Mental Health Agency	Prescription Monitoring Programs (PMPs)
California Department of Healthcare Services Mental Health Services Division www.dhcs.ca.gov/services/Pages/MentalHealthPrograms-Svcs.aspx	State of California Department of Justice (CURES program) https://pmp.doj.ca.gov/pmpreg/RegistrationType_input.action
Colorado Department of Human Services Community Behavioral Health www.colorado.gov/cs/Satellite/CDHS-BehavioralHealth/CBON/1251581077594	Colorado State Board of Pharmacy (PDMP) (overseen by Health Information Designs) www.hidinc.com/copdmp E-mail: pdmpinqr@ state.co.us. Help desk: 855-263-6403
Connecticut Department of Mental Health and Addiction Services www.ct.gov/dmhas/site/default.asp Phone: 860-418-7000	Connecticut Prescription Monitoring Program https://www.ctpmp.com/Login.aspx?ReturnUrl=%2fdefault.aspx E-mail: DCP.Prescriptions@ct.gov Phone: 860-713-6073
Delaware Health and Social Services Division of Substance Abuse and Mental Health http://dhss.delaware.gov/dsamh/	Office of Controlled Substances http://dpr.delaware.gov/boards/controlledsubstances/pmp/ E-mail: depmp-info@hidinc.com Phone: 855-263-6401
District of Columbia Department of Behavioral Health http://dmh.dc.gov/ Phone: 202- 673-7440	None, but implementation is in process.
Florida Department of Children and Families Mental Health www.myflfamilies.com/service-programs/mental-health Phone: 866-762-2237	Florida Prescription Drug Monitoring Program (E-FORCSE)/Electronic Florida Online Reporting of Controlled Substance Evaluation www.hidinc.com/flpdmp Phone: 850-245-4797
Georgia Department of Behavioral Health and Developmental Disabilities http://dbhdd.georgia.gov/ Phone: 877-715-4225	Overseen by Health Information Designs www.hidinc.com/gapdmp E-mail: gapdmp-info@hidinc.com Phone: 855-729-8919
Hawaii Department of Health Adult Mental Health Division http://health.hawaii.gov/amhd/ Phone: 808-586-4400	Department of Public Safety (overseen by Relay Health) http://pmp.relayhealth.com/HI/ E-mail: HIPMP@relayhealth.com Phone: 800-892-0333

Idaho Department of Health and Welfare Mental Health Services www.healthandwelfare.idaho.gov/?TabId=103	Idaho Board of Pharmacy/Prescription Monitoring Program http://ipmp.bop.idaho.gov/ E-mail: pmp@bop.idaho.gov Phone: 208-334-2356
Illinois Department of Human Services Division of Mental Health www.dhs.state.il.us/page.aspx?item=29728	Illinois Prescription Monitoring Program www.ilpmp.org/ E-mail: dhs.pmp@illinois.gov Phone: 217-524-2158
Indiana Family and Social Services Administration Division of Mental Health and Addiction www.in.gov/fssa/dmha/4521.htm	Indiana Scheduled Prescription Electronic Collection and Tracking Program (INSPECT) www.in.gov/pla/2943.htm E-mail: inspect@pla.IN.gov Phone: 317-234-4458
Iowa Department of Human Services Division of Mental Health and Disability Services www.dhs.state.ia.us/mhdd/	Iowa Board of Pharmacy Prescription Monitoring Program https://pmp.iowa.gov/IAPMPWebCenter/Login.aspx?ReturnUrl=%2fIAPMPWebCenter%2fdefault.aspx Phone: 515-281-5944
Kansas Department for Aging and Disability Services Kansas Behavioral Health Services www.kansasbehavioralhealthservices.org/bhs1.0/ Phone: 785-296-3471	Kansas Board of Pharmacy www.kansas.gov/pharmacy/KSPMP.htm E-mail: pmpadmin@pharmacy.ks.gov Phone: 785-296-6547
Kentucky Cabinet for Health and Human Services Department for Behavioral Health, Developmental and Intellectual Disabilities http://dbhdid.ky.gov/kdbhdid/default.aspx Phone: 502-564-4527	Kentucky All Schedule Prescription Electronic Reporting (KASPER) www.chfs.ky.gov/os/oig/KASPER.htm E-mail: ekasperhelp@ky.gov Phone: 502-564-2703
Louisiana Department of Health and Hospitals Office of Behavioral Health www.dhh.louisiana.gov/index.cfm/page/97/n/116	Louisiana Board of Pharmacy Prescription Drug Monitoring www.labp.com/index.cfm?md=pagebuilder&tmp=home&pid=5&pn Phone: 225-925-6496
Maine Department of Health and Human Services Substance Abuse and Mental Health Services www.maine.gov/dhhs/samhs/mentalhealth/ Phone: 207-287-2595	Substance Abuse and Mental Health Services www.maine.gov/dhhs/samhs/osa/data/pmp/index.htm Phone: 866-792-3149

(Continued)

(Continued)

State Mental Health Agency	Prescription Monitoring Programs (PMPs)
Maryland Department of Health and Mental Hygiene http://dhmh.maryland.gov/SitePages/Home.aspx Phone: 410-767-6500	Maryland Prescription Drug Monitoring (overseen by Health Information Designs) www.hidinc.com/mdpdmp.html E-mail: mdpdmp-info@hidinc.com Phone: 855-729-8920
Massachusetts Health and Human Services Department of Mental Health www.mass.gov/eohhs/gov/departments/dmh/ Phone: 800-221-0053	Massachusetts Online Prescription Monitoring Program www.mass.gov/dph/dcp/onlinepmp
Michigan Department of Community Health Behavioral Health and Developmental Disabilities Administration www.michigan.gov/mdch/0,4612,7-132-2941---,00.html	Michigan Automated Prescription System (MAPS) www.michigan.gov/lara/0,4601,7-154-35299_63294_63303_55478-232708--,00.html
Minnesota Department of Human Services Adult Mental Health www.dhs.state.mn.us/main/idcplg?IdcService=GET_DYNAMIC_CONVERSION&RevisionSelectionMethod=LatestReleased&dDocName=id_000085 Phone: 651-431-2225	Minnesota Prescription Monitoring Program http://pmp.pharmacy.state.mn.us/ E-mail: mnpdm-info@hidinc.com Phone: 866-792-3149
Mississippi Department of Mental Health www.dmh.ms.gov/ Phone: 877-210-8513	Mississippi Prescription Monitoring Program http://pmp.relayhealth.com/MS/ E-mail: MSPMP@relayhealth.com Phone: 800-892-0333
Missouri Department of Mental Health http://dmh.mo.gov/ Phone: 800-364-9687	None
Montana Department of Public Health and Human Services Addictive and Mental Disorders Division www.dphhs.mt.gov/mentalhealth/ Phone: 406-444-3964	Department of Labor and Industry Montana Prescription Drug Registry (MPDR) http://bsd.dli.mt.gov/license/bsd_boards/pha_board/mpdr/MPDR_info.asp
Nebraska Department of Health and Human Services Division of Behavioral Health http://dhhs.ne.gov/behavioral_health/Pages/behavioral_health_index.aspx	Nebraska Department of Health and Human Services Prescription Drug Monitoring Program http://dhhs.ne.gov/publichealth/Pages/crlMailServPrescDrugMonProgram.aspx

Nevada Department of Health and Human Services Division of Public and Behavioral Health http://mhds.state.nv.us/	Nevada Prescription Monitoring Program http://pmp.relayhealth.com/NV/ E-mail: ladams@pharmacy.nv.gov Phone: 775-687-5694
New Hampshire Department of Health and Human Services Bureau of Behavioral Health www.dhhs.state.nh.us/dcbcs/bbh/	Board of Pharmacy Prescription Drug Monitoring Program www.nh.gov/pharmacy/prescription-monitoring/ E-mail: pharmacy.board@nh.gov Phone: 603-271-2350
New Jersey Department of Human Services Division of Mental Health Services www.state.nj.us/humanservices/dmhs/home/index.html Phone: 800-382-6717	New Jersey Division of Consumer Affairs Prescription Monitoring Program www.njconsumeraffairs.gov/pmp/
New Mexico Human Services Department Behavioral Health Services Division www.hsd.state.nm.us/bhsd/ Phone: 505-476-9277	New Mexico Regulation and Licensing Department: Prescription Monitoring Program www.rld.state.nm.us/boards/Pharmacy_Prescription_Monitoring_Program.aspx Phone: 505-222-9837
New York Office of Mental Health www.omh.ny.gov/	Internet System for Tracking Over-Prescribing-Prescription Monitoring Program (I-STOP/PMP) www.health.ny.gov/professionals/narcotic/prescription_monitoring/ Phone: 866-529-1890
North Carolina Division of Mental Health, Developmental Disabilities, and Substance Abuse Services www.ncdhhs.gov/mhddsas/	North Carolina Controlled Substance Reporting System www.ncdhhs.gov/MHDDSAS/controlledsubstance/
North Dakota Department of Human Services Mental Health and Substance Abuse Services Division www.nd.gov/dhs/services/mentalhealth/ Phone: 701-328-8920 Toll free ND only: 800-755-2719	North Dakota Board of Pharmacy Prescription Drug Monitoring Program https://www.nodakpharmacy.com/PDMP-index.asp
Ohio Department of Mental Health and Addiction Services http://mha.ohio.gov/ Phone: 877-275-6364	Ohio Automated Rx Reporting System www.ohiopmp.gov/Portal/Default.aspx

(*Continued*)

(Continued)

State Mental Health Agency	Prescription Monitoring Programs (PMPs)
Oklahoma Department of Mental Health and Substance Abuse Services http://ok.gov/odmhsas/ Phone: 405-522-3908	Oklahoma Bureau of Narcotics & Dangerous Drugs Control: Prescription Monitoring Program http://ok.gov/odmhsas/ E-mail: pmpadmin@obn.state.ok.us Phone: 877-627-2674
Oregon Addictions and Mental Health Services Division www.oregon.gov/oha/amh/Pages/index.aspx	Oregon Prescription Drug Monitoring Program www.orpdmp.com/ E-mail: pdmp.health@state.or.us Phone: 971-673-0741
Pennsylvania Department of Public Welfare Office of Mental Health and Substance Abuse Services www.dpw.state.pa.us/dpworganization/officeofmentalhealthandsubstanceabuseservices/	Commonwealth of Pennsylvania Prescription Monitoring Program www.attorneygeneral.gov/drugs.aspx?id=5946
Puerto Rico www.assmca.gobierno.pr/ (website is in Spanish)	
Rhode Island Department of Behavioral Healthcare, Developmental Disabilities, and Hospitals www.bhddh.ri.gov/	Rhode Island Department of Health Prescription Monitoring Program www.health.ri.gov/programs/prescriptionmonitoring/ E-mail: Optimum Technology rirxreport@otech.com Phone: 866-683-3246
South Carolina Department of Mental Health www.state.sc.us/dmh/ Phone: 803-898-8581	South Carolina Department of Health and Environmental Control-Prescription Monitoring Program (SCRIPTS) www.scdhec.gov/administration/drugcontrol/pmp.htm E-mail: SCRIPTS@dhec.sc.gov Phone: 803- 896-0688
South Dakota Department of Social Services Behavioral Health Services http://dss.sd.gov/behavioralhealthservices/community/ Phone: 605-773-7076	South Dakota Board of Pharmacy Prescription Drug Monitoring Program http://doh.sd.gov/boards/pharmacy/pdmp.aspx
Tennessee Department of Mental Health and Substance Abuse Services www.tn.gov/mental/	Tennessee Department of Health Controlled Substance Monitoring Program http://health.state.tn.us/boards/ControlledSubstance/index.shtml\

Texas Department of State Health Services Mental Health and Substance Abuse Division www.dshs.state.tx.us/mentalhealth.shtm	Texas Department of Public Safety Texas Prescription Program www.txdps.state.tx.us/RegulatoryServices/ prescription_program/
Utah Department of Human Services Division of Substance Abuse and Mental Health www.dsamh.utah.gov/	Utah Controlled Substance Database Program www.csd.*utah*.gov E-mail: msim@utah.gov
Vermont Department of Mental Health http://mentalhealth.vermont.gov/	Department of Health: Prescription Monitoring Program http://healthvermont.gov/adap/Vpms.aspx E-mail: vpms-info@hidinc.com Phone: 800-225-6998
Virginia Department of Behavioral Health and Developmental Services www.dbhds.virginia.gov/	Virginia Department of Health Professions www.dhp.virginia.gov/dhp_programs/pmp/ default.asp E-mail pmp@dhp.virginia.gov Phone: 804-367-4566
Washington Department of Social and Health Services Division of Behavioral Health www.dshs.wa.gov/dbhr/mh_information.shtml	Washington State Department of Health Prescription Monitoring Program www.doh.wa.gov/ PublicHealthandHealthcareProviders/ HealthcareProfessionsandFacilities/ PrescriptionMonitoringProgramPMP.aspx E-mail: prescriptionmonitoring@doh.wa.gov Phone: 360-236-4806
West Virginia Department of Health and Human Resources Bureau for Behavioral Health and Health Facilities www.dhhr.wv.gov/bhhf/Pages/default.aspx	West Virginia Board of Pharmacy Controlled Substance Monitoring Program www.csapp.wv.gov/Account/Login. aspx?ReturnUrl=%2f
Wisconsin Department of Health Services Mental Health Programs www.dhs.wisconsin.gov/mentalhealth/	Department of Safety and Professional Services Prescription Drug Monitoring Program http://dsps.wi.gov/pdmp/
Wyoming Department of Health Behavioral Health Division (Mental Health and Substance Abuse Services) http://health.wyo.gov/mhsa/index.html Phone: 800-535-4006 307-777-6494	Wyoming State Board of Pharmacy Prescription Drug Monitoring Program http://pharmacyboard.state.wy.us/pdmp.aspx E-mail: bop@wyo.gov

References and Resources

RESOURCES

1. **The American Psychiatric Association/DSM-5.** The DSM-5 is the current psychiatric diagnostic manual in the United States. Updates and corrections, as well as free downloadable assessment measures and articles related to the DSM-5 are available on this site.

   www.DSM5.org

2. **American Society of Addiction Medicine (ASAM).** This professional organization is comprised of physicians and other addiction specialists. They support research and education around substance use disorders, treatment, and prevention.

   www.asam.org

3. **The Food and Drug Administration (FDA).** This organization approves and oversees pharmaceutical medications in the United States. Copies of all package inserts, warnings, prescribing updates, and so on are available through this site.

   www.fda.gov

4. **The National Alliance on Mental Illness (NAMI).** The largest advocacy organization for families of people with mental illness offers up-to-date information, peer and family support, and clear and concise articles on a broad range of topics, mostly related to mental health and psychiatric disorders, and some pertaining to co-occurring and substance use disorders as well.

   www.nami.org

5. **The National Committee for Quality Assurance (NCQA).** This private nonprofit organization is focused on improving the quality of health care. They accredit health plans and other organizations and promote continuous quality improvement practices.

   www.ncqa.org

6. **The Substance Abuse and Mental Health Service Administration (SAMHSA).** SAMHSA is the governmental agency tasked with overseeing the public health efforts to address mental health and substance abuse in the United States. They are part of the Department of Health and Human Services. Their vision statement is recovery-based and focuses on prevention, treatment, and overall well-being.

The SAMHSA website is easy to search and contains a wealth of publications, which include treatment guidelines, DVDs, and materials for people in recovery, as well as for family members. Most of the SAMHSA publication can be downloaded or ordered for free. They also maintain a mailing list where all new publications are announced and offered to the public.

www.samhsa.gov

- **The National Registry of Evidence-Based Programs and Practices (NREPP):** This is SAMHSA's easily searchable database with hundreds of evidence-based interventions. www.nrepp.samhsa.gov/Index.aspx

- **The National Survey on Drug use and Health:** This survey provides national and state date on tobacco, alcohol, and drug use. https://nsduhweb.rti.org/

7. **U.S. Department of Health and Human Services: Agency for Healthcare Research and Quality (AHRQ)**

- **National Guideline Clearinghouse (NGC):** The NGC is a public resource for evidence-based practice guidelines. It is easily searchable and includes guidelines for medical, mental, and substance use disorders. www.guideline.gov/

- **Patient-Centered Medical Home Resource Center:** www.pcmh.ahrq.gov

8. **The World Health Organization (WHO).**

www.who.org

References

1. American Psychiatric Association. *Diagnostic and Statistical Manual of Mental Disorders*, 4th ed. American Psychiatric Publishing, 2000.

2. American Psychiatric Association. *Diagnostic and Statistical Manual of Mental Disorders*, 5th ed. American Psychiatric Publishing, 2013.

3. Center for Substance Abuse Treatment. *Substance Abuse Treatment for Persons with Co-Occurring Disorders.* Treatment Improvement Protocol (TIP) Series 42. DHHS Publication No. (SMA) 05-3992. Rockville, MD: Substance Abuse and Mental Health Services Administration, 2005.

4. Croghan, T. W., and Brown, J. D. *Integrating Mental Health Treatment into the Patient-Centered Medical Home.* (Prepared by Mathematica Policy Research under Contract No. HHSA290200900019I TO2.) AHRQ Publication No. 10-0084-EF. Rockville, MD: Agency for Healthcare Research and Quality, 2010.

5. Drake, R. et al. Dual diagnosis: 15 years of progress. *Psychiatric Services.* September 2000;51(9):1126–1129.

6. Drake, R. et al. Implementing dual diagnosis services for clients with severe mental illness. *Psychiatric Services.* 2001;52(4):469–476.

7. Brunton, L., Chabner, B., and Knollman, B. *Goodman & Gilman's The Pharmacological Basis of Therapeutics*, 12th ed. McGraw-Hill, 2011.

8. Minkoff, K. Best practices: Developing standards of care for individuals with co-occurring psychiatric and substance use disorders. *Psychiatric Services*. 2001;52:597–599.

9. The National Council for Community Behavioral Healthcare. *Behavioral Health/Primary Care Integration and the Person-Centered Healthcare Home*. April 2009. Available at www. allhealth.org/BriefingMaterials/BehavioralHealthandPrimaryCareIntegrationandthePers on-CenteredHealthcareHome-1547.pdf.

10. O'Brien, C. P. et al. Priority actions to improve the care of persons with co-occurring substance abuse and other mental disorders: A call to action. *Biological Psychiatry*. 2004;56:703–713.

11. SAMHSA: SAMHSA's working definition of Recovery: 10 Guiding Principles of Recovery. 2013. Available at http://store.samhsa.gov/shin/content/PEP12-RECDEF/PEP12-RECDEF.pdf.

Chapters 2 through 6: The Comprehensive Assessment of Co-Occurring Substance Use and Mental Disorders, Creating Problem/Need Lists, Setting Goals and Objectives, and Developing Treatment and Recovery Plans

RESOURCES

1. Macarthur Research Network on Mental Health and the Law. *The Macarthur Violence Risk Assessment Study*. http://macarthur.virginia.edu/risk.html.

REFERENCES

1. American Psychiatric Association. *The DSM-5*. American Psychiatric Publishing, 2013.

2. American Psychiatric Association. *The DSM-IV-TR™*. American Psychiatric Publishing, 2000.

3. Babor, T. F. et al. *AUDIT: The Alcohol Use Disorders Identification Test*, 2nd ed. World Health Organization Department of Mental Health and Substance Dependence, 2001. WHO/MSD/MSB/016a. http://whqlibdoc.who.int/hq/2001/WHO_MSD_MSB_01.6a. pdf?ua=1.

4. Ewing, John A. Detecting alcoholism: The CAGE Questionnaire. *JAMA*. 1984;252:1905–1907.

5. Joint Commission. *A Practical Guide to Documentation in Behavioral Health Care*, 4th edition. Joint Commission Resources, 2013.

6. Joint Commission. *2012 Behavioral Health Care Requirements*.

7. Kitchens, J. M. Does this patient have an alcohol problem? *JAMA*. 1994;272(22): 1782–7.

8. Scott, C. et al. Evaluating psychotic patients' risk of violence: A practical guide. *Current Psychiatry*. May 2013;12(5):29–32.

Chapter 7: Levels of Care

RESOURCES

1. The American Society of Addiction Medicine (ASAM). www.asam.org.

2. General Service Office of Alcoholics Anonymous. A.A. Fact File. Copyright 1956. http://aa.org.

3. Information about Narcotics Anonymous. Copyright 2006–2012. http://na.org.

REFERENCES

1. ASAM/Mee-Lee, D., ed. *The ASAM Criteria: Treatment Criteria for Addictive, Substance-Related, and Co-Occurring Conditions*, 3rd ed. Carson City, NV: The Change Companies; 2013.

2. Bond, G.R. et al. An update on randomized controlled trials of evidence-based supported employment. *Psychiatric Rehabilitation Journal*. 2008;31:280–290.

3. Bond, G. R. et al. Assertive community treatment for people with severe mental illness: Critical ingredients and impact on patients. *Disability Management, Health Outcomes*. 2001;9:141–159.

4. Copeland, M. E. *Wellness Recovery Action Plan*. Dummerston, VT: Peach Press, 1997.

5. Davidson, L. et al. Creating a recovery-oriented system of behavioral healthcare: Moving from concept to reality. *Psychiatric Rehabilitation Journal*. 2007;31:23–31.

6. Kidd, S. A. et al. Fidelity and recovery-orientation in assertive community treatment. *Community Mental Health*. 2010;46:342–350.

7. Kolsky, G. Current Sate AOD Agency Practices Regarding the use of Patient Placement Criteria (PPC) and Update. Available at www.asam.org/docs/publications/survey_of_state_use_of_ppc_nasadad-2006.pdf?Status=Master&sfvrsn=2.

8. Mueser, K. T. et al. Illness management and recovery: A review of the research. *Psychiatric Services*. 2002;53:1272–1284.

9. Randall, G. E. et al. Fidelity to assertive community treatment program standards: A regional survey of adherence to standards. *Community Mental Health*. 2012;48:138–149.

10. Teague, G. B. et al. Program fidelity in assertive community treatment: Development and use of a measure. *American Journal of Orthopsychiatry*. 1998;68(2):216–232.

11. U.S. Department of Health and Human Services. Definitions and Terms Relating to Co-Occurring Disorders. 2006; DHHS Publication No 06-4163.

12. Watts, J. et al. A phenomenological account of users' experiences of assertive community treatment. *Bioethics*. 2002;16:339–454.

13. Wholey, D. R. et al. The teamwork in assertive community treatment (TACT) scale: Development and validation. *Psychiatric Services*. 2012;63(11):1108–117.

Chapter 8: Key Psychotherapies, Mutual Self-Help, and Natural and Peer Supports

REFERENCES

1. Beck, J. *Cognitive Behavioral Therapy: Basics and Beyond*, 2nd ed. New York, NY: The Guilford Press;2011.

2. Davis, M. et al. *The Relaxation and Stress Reduction Workbook*. New Harbinger Press, 2008.

3. Hanh, Tich Nhat. The *Miracle of Mindfulness: An Introduction to the Practice of Meditation*. Beacon Press, 1999.

4. Kabat-Zinn, J. *Wherever You Go, There You Are*. Hyperion, 2005.

5. Kabat-Zinn, J. *Full Catastrophe Living: Using the Wisdom of Your Body and Mind to Face Stress, Pain, and Illness*. Delta, 1990.

6. Marlatt, A. *Harm Reduction: Pragmatic Strategies for Managing High-Risk Behaviors*. Guilford Press, 1998.

7. McKay, M. et al. *Thoughts and Feelings: Taking Control of Your Mood and Your Life: A Workbook of Cognitive Behavioral Techniques*. New Harbinger Publications, 1997.

8. Miller, W. R. and Rollnick, S. *Motivational Interviewing: Preparing People for Change*, 2nd ed. Guilford Press, 2002.

Chapter 9: Co-Occurring Attention Deficit Hyperactivity Disorder and Related Disorders

RESOURCES

1. Attention Deficit Resources (ADD-Resources) is a nonprofit that maintains an excellent website geared toward parents, people with ADHD, and clinicians. It includes information and links to downloadable screening tools, including the SNAP-IV. addresources.org

2. Adult ADHD Self-Report Scale-V1.1 (ASRS-V1.1) downloadable files for both the six-item screening tool and full 18-question symptom checklist. Through Harvard's web page for the National Comorbidity Survey: www.hcp.med.harvard.edu/ncs/asrs.php

References

1. Blix, O. et al. Treatment of opioid dependence and ADHD/ADD with opioid maintenance and central stimulants. *Heroin Addiction and Related Clinical Problems*. 2009;11:5–14.

2. Carpentier, P. J. et al. Influence of attention deficit hyperactivity disorder and conduct disorder on opioid dependence severity and psychiatric comorbidity in chronic methadone-maintained patients. *European Addiction Research*. 2011;17:10–20.

3. Charach, A. et al. Childhood attention-deficit/hyperactivity disorder and future substance use disorders: Comparative meta-analysis. *Journal of the American Academy of Child and Adolescent Psychiatry*. 2011;50(1):9–21.

4. Daigre, C. et al. Adult ADHD Self-Report Scale (ASRS-v1.1) symptom checklist in patients with substance use disorders. *Actas Españolas Psiquiatria* 2009;37(6):299–305.

5. Dakwar, E. et al. The utility of attention-deficit/hyperactivity disorder screening instruments in individuals seeking treatment for substance use disorders. *Journal of Clinical Psychiatry.* 2012;73(11):1372–1378.

6. Faraone, S. V. et al. Substance use among ADHD adults: Implications of late onset and subthreshold diagnoses. *American Journal of Addiction.* 2007;16 Supplement 1:24.

7. Kessler, R. C. et al. The prevalence and correlates of adult ADHD in the United States: Results from the National Comorbidity Survey Replication. *American Journal of Psychiatry.* 2006;163:716.

8. Knop, J. et al. Childhood ADHD and conduct disorder as independent predictors of male alcohol dependence at age 40. *Journal of Studies on Alcohol and Drugs.* 2009;70(2):169–177.

9. Kooij, S. et al. Reliability, validity, and utility of instruments or self-report and informant report concerning symptoms of ADHD in adult patients. *Journal of Attention Disorders.* 2008;11:445–458.

10. Levin, F. R. et al. Treatment of methadone-maintained patients with adult ADHD: Double-blind comparison of methylphenidate, bupropion, and placebo. *Drug Alcohol Dependence.* 2006;81:137–148.

11. McAweeney, M. et al. Symptom prevalence of ADHD in a community residential substance abuse treatment program. *Journal of Attention Disorders.* 2010;13(6):601–608.

12. The MTA Cooperative Group. A 14-month randomized clinical trial of treatment strategies for attention-deficit/hyperactivity disorder. Multimodal treatment study of children with ADHD. *Archives of General Psychiatry.* 1999;56:1073.

13. Murphy, P. et al. Use of self-ratings in the assessment of symptoms of attention deficit hyperactivity disorder in adults. *American Journal of Psychiatry.* 2000;157:1156.

14. Roy, A. The relationships between attention-deficit/hyperactive disorder, conduct disorder and problematic drug use. *Drugs Education Prevention Policy.* 2008;15:55–75.

15. Safren, S. A. et al. Cognitive-behavioral therapy for ADHD in medication-treated adults with continued symptoms. *Behaviour Research and Therapy.* 2005;43:831.

16. Schubiner, H. et al. Prevalence of attention-deficit/hyperactivity disorder and conduct disorder among substance abusers. *Journal of Clinical Psychiatry.* 2000;61:244–251.

17. Sepulveda, D. R. et al. Misuse of prescribed stimulant medication for ADHD and associated patterns of substance use: Preliminary analysis among college students. *Journal of Pharmacy Practice.* 2011;24(6): 551–560.

18. Solanto, M. V. et al. Efficacy of meta-cognitive therapy for adult ADHD. *American Journal of Psychiatry.* 2010;167:958.

19. Warden, D. et al. Major depression and treatment response in adolescents with ADHD and substance use disorder. *Drug and Alcohol Dependence.* 2012;120:214–219.

20. Wilens, T. E. et al. Does ADHD predict substance-use disorders? A 10-year follow-up study of young adults with ADHD. *Journal of the American Academy of Child and Adolescent Psychiatry.* 2011;50(6):543–553.

21. Wilens, T. E. et al. The intersection of attention-deficit/hyperactivity disorder and substance abuse. *Current Opinions in Psychiatry.* 2011;24:280–285.

22. Winhusen, T. M. et al. Subjective effects, misuse, and adverse effects of osmotic-release methylpenidate treatment in adolescent substance abusers with attention-deficit/hyperactivity disorder. *Journal of Child and Adolescent Psychopharmacology.* 2011;21(5): 455–463.

Chapter 10: Depressive Disorders and Co-Occurring Substance Use Disorders

REFERENCES

1. Blanco, C. et al. Differences among major depressive disorder with and without co-occurring substance use disorders and substance-induced depressive disorder: Results from the National Epidemiologic Survey on Alcohol and Related condition. *Journal of Clinical Psychiatry.* 2012;73(6):865–873.

2. Brewer, J. A. et al. Mindfulness-based treatment for co-occurring depression and substance use disorders: What can we learn from the brain? *Addiction.* 2010;105(10):1698–1706.

3. Delgadilo, J. et al. Depression, anxiety and comorbid substance use: Association patterns in outpatient addictions treatment. *Mental Health and Substance Use.* 2013;6(1):59–75.

4. Hides, L. et al. Cognitive behavior therapy (CBT) for the treatment of co-occurring depression and substance use: current evidence and directions for future research. *Drug Alcohol Rev.* 2010;29(5):508–517.

5. Hides, L. et al. Outcomes of an integrated cognitive behavior therapy (CBT) treatment program for co-occurring depression and substance misuse in young people. *Journal of Affective Disorders.* 2009;121(1–2):169–174.

6. Hunter, S. B. et al. Treating depression and substance use: A randomized controlled trial. *Journal of Substance Abuse Treatment.* 2012;43(2):137–151.

7. Ioveino, N. et al. Antidepressants for major depressive disorder and dysthymic disorder in patients with comorbid alcohol use disorders: A meta-analysis of placebo-controlled randomized trials. *Journal of Clinical Psychiatry.* 2011;72(8):1144–1151.

8. Langas, A. M. et al. Independent versus substance-induced major depressive disorders in first-admission patients with substance use disorders: An exploratory study. *Journal of Affective Disorders.* 2013;144(3):279–283.

9. Lydecker, K. P. et al. Clinical outcomes of an integrated treatment for depression and substance use disorders. *Psychology of Addictive Behaviors.* 2010;24(3):453–465.

10. Lyness, J. M. *Clinical Manifestations and Diagnosis of Depression. UpToDate.* Wolters Kluwer. 2013

11. Marmorstein, N. R. Associations between subtypes of major depressive episodes and substance use disorders. *Psychiatry Research*. 2011;186(2–3):248–253.

12. National Guideline Clearinghouse: Practice guideline for the treatment of patients with major depressive disorder, 3rd edition. 2013. Available at www.guideline.gov/popups/printView.aspx?id=24158.

13. Osilla, K.C. et al. Developing an integrated treatment for substance use and depression using cognitive-behavioral therapy. *Journal of Substance Abuse Treatment*. 2009;27(4):412–420.

14. Pettinati, H. M. et al. Current status of co-occurring mood and substance use disorders: A new therapeutic target. *American Journal of Psychiatry*. 2013;170(1):23–30.

15. Schukit, M. A. et al. Relationships among independent major depressions, alcohol use, and other substance use and related problems over 30 years in 397 families. *Journal of Studies on Alcohol and Drugs*. 2013;74(2):271–279.

Chapter 11: Bipolar Disorder and Co-Occurring Substance Use Disorders

RESOURCES

1. The Depression and Bipolar Support Alliance. This is a peer-directed not-for-profit organization for people with mood disorders. www.dbsalliance.org

References

1. Atkins, C. *The Bipolar Disorder Answer Book*. Sourcebooks, 2007.

2. Brown, E. S. et al. A randomized, double-blind, placebo-controlled pilot study of naltrexone in outpatients with bipolar disorder and alcohol dependence. *Alcoholism Clinical and Experimental Research*. 2009;33:1863–1869.

3. Duffy, A. et al. Adolescent substance use disorder during the early stages of bipolar disorder: A prospective high-risk study. *Journal of Affective Disorders*. 2012;142:57–64.

4. Farren, C. K. et al. Bipolar disorder and alcohol use disorder: A review. *Current Psychiatry Reports*. 2012;14:659–666.

5. Farren, C. K. et al. Predictive factors for relapse after an integrated inpatient treatment program for unipolar depressed and bipolar alcoholics. *Alcohol*. 2010;45:527–533.

6. Frank, E. et al. Two-year outcomes for interpersonal and social rhythm therapy in individuals with bipolar I disorder. *Archives of General Psychiatry*. 2005;62:996–1004.

7. Lam, D. H. et al. A randomized controlled study of cognitive therapy for relapse prevention for bipolar affective disorder: outcome of the first year. *Archives of General Psychiatry*. 2003;60:145–152.

8. Large, M. et al. Cannabis use and earlier onset of psychosis: A systematic meta-analysis. *Archives of General Psychiatry*. 2011;68(6):555–561.

9. McGorry, P. Transition to adulthood: The critical period for pre-emptive disease-modifying care for schizophrenia and related disorders. *Schizophrenia Bulletin.* 2011;37(3):523–530.

10. Miklowitz, D. J. et al. A randomized study of family-focused psychoeducation and pharmacotherapy in the outpatient management of bipolar disorder. *Archives of General Psychiatry.* 2003;60:904–912.

11. Salloum, I. M. et al. Impact of substance abuse on the course and treatment of bipolar disorder. *Bipolar Disorders.* 2000;2(3):269–280.

12. Salloum, I. M. et al. Efficacy of valproate maintenance in patients with bipolar disorder and alcoholism: A double-blind placebo-controlled study. *Archives of General Psychiatry.* 2005;62:37–45.

13. Schimmelmann, B. G. et al. Prevalence and impact of cannabis use disorders in adolescents with early onset first episode psychosis. *European Psychiatry.* 2012;27:463–469.

14. Swann, A. C. The strong relationship between bipolar and substance-use disorder. *Annals of the New York Academy of Science.* 2010;1187:276–293.

15. Tolliver, B. K. et al. Implications and Strategies for Clinical Management of Co-occurring Substance Use in Bipolar Disorder. *Psychiatric Annals.* May 2012;42(5): 190-197.

16. Tolliver, B. K. et al. A randomized, double-blind, placebo-controlled trial of acamprosate in alcohol-dependent individuals with bipolar disorder: A preliminary report. *Bipolar Disorder.* 2012;14:54–63.

17. Weiss, R. D. et al. A "community friendly" version of integrated group therapy for patients with bipolar disorder and substance dependence: A randomized controlled trial. *Drug and Alcohol Dependence.* 2009;104:212–219.

Chapter 12: Anxiety Disorders and Co-Occurring Substance Use Disorders

REFERENCES

1. Baker, A. L. et al. Psychological interventions for alcohol misuse among people with co-occurring depression or anxiety disorders: A systematic review. *Journal of Affective Disorders.* 2012;139:217–229.

2. Fatséas, M. et al. Relationship between anxiety disorders and opiate dependence—A systematic review of the literature: Implications for diagnosis and treatment. *Journal of Substance Abuse Treatment.* 2010;38:220–230.

3. Magidson, J. F. et al. Comparison of the course of substance use disorders among individuals with and without generalized anxiety disorder in a nationally representative sample. *Journal of Psychiatric Research.* 2012;46:659–666.

4. Marmorstein, N. R. Anxiety disorders and substance use disorders: Different associations by anxiety disorder. *Journal of Anxiety Disorders.* 2012;26:88–94.

5. Merikangas, K. R. et al. *Comorbidity in Anxiety Disorders. Current Topics in Behavioral Neuroscience.* Springer-Verlag, 2009.

6. Reedy, A. R. et al. Treatment issues with substance use disorder clients who have mood or anxiety disorders. *Mental Health and Substance Use: Dual Diagnosis.* 2008;1(1).44–53.

7. Smith, J. P. et al. Comorbidity of generalized anxiety disorder and alcohol use disorders among individuals seeking outpatient substance abuse treatment. *Addictive Behaviors.* 2010;35:42–45.

8. Watkins, K. E. et al. Review of treatment recommendations for person with a co-occurring affective or anxiety and substance sue disorder. *Psychiatric Services.* 2005;56:913–926.

9. Watkins K. E. et al. Prevalence and characteristics of clients with co-occurring disorders in outpatient substance abuse treatment. *American Journal of Drug and Alcohol Abuse.* 2004;30:749–764.

10. Wolitzky-Taylor, K. et al. Longitudinal investigation of the impact of anxiety and mood disorders in adolescence on subsequent substance use disorder onset and vice versa. *Addictive Behaviors.* 2012;37:982–985.

Chapter 13: Posttraumatic Stress Disorder and Co-occurring Substance Use Disorders

RESOURCES

1. International Society for Traumatic Stress Studies (ISTSS). istss.org

2. The National Center for PTSD (U.S. Department of Veterans Affairs). This rich resource provides access to free online trainings, many of which offer continuing education (CE) and continuing medical education (CME) credits. www.ptsd.va.gov/index.asp.

References:

1. Benish, S. et al. The relative efficacy of bona fide psychotherapies for treating post-traumatic stress disorder: A meta-analysis of direct comparisons. *Clinical Psychology Review.* 2008;28;5:746–758.

2. Berenz, E. C. et al. Treatment of co-occurring posttraumatic stress disorder and substance use disorders. *Current Psychiatry Reports.* 2012;14:469–477.

3. Bisson, J. et al. Psychological treatment of post-traumatic stress disorder (PTSD). *Cochrane Database of Systematic Reviews.* 2007;3:CD003388.

4. Bliese, P. D. et al. Validating the primary care posttraumatic stress disorder screen and the posttraumatic stress disorder checklist with soldiers returning from combat. *Journal of Consulting and Clinical Psychology.* 2008;76:272–281.

5. Bradley, R. et al. A multidimensional meta-analysis of psychotherapy for PTSD. *American Journal of Psychiatry.* 2005;162(2):214–227.

6. Brady, K. T. et al. Substance abuse and posttraumatic stress disorder. *Current Directions in Psychological Science.* 2004;13:206–209.

7. Breslau, N. et al. Short screening scale for DSM-IV post-traumatic stress disorder. *American Journal of Psychiatry.* 1999;156:908–911.

8. Brewin, C. R. Systematic review of screening instruments for adults at risk of PTSD. *Journal of Traumatic Stress.* 2005;18:53–62.

9. Coffey, S. F. et al. Changes in PTSD symptomatology during acute and protracted alcohol and cocaine abstinence. *Drug and Alcohol Dependence.* 2007;87:241–248.

10. Donovan, B. et al. "Transcend": Initial outcomes from a posttraumatic stress disorder/substance abuse treatment program. *Journal of Traumatic Stress.* 2001;14:757–772.

11. Eftekhan, A. et al. Effectiveness of national implementation of prolonged exposure therapy in Veterans Affairs care. *JAMA Psychiatry.* 2013;70:949–955.

12. Ferri, M. et al. Alcoholics Anonymous and other 12-step programs for alcohol dependence. Cochrane database of systematic reviews. 2006. Article Number: CD005032, doi:10.1002/14651858.CD005032.pub2.

13. Foa, E. B. et al. *Effective Treatments for PTSD: Practice Guidelines from the International Society for Traumatic Stress Studies,* 2nd ed. New York: Guilford Press, 2008.

14. Foa, E. B., Keane, T. M., & Friedman, M. J. *Effective Treatments for PTSD: Practice Guidelines from the International Society for Traumatic Stress Studies (1–388).* New York: Guilford, 2009.

15. Greyber, L. et al. Eye movement desensitization reprocessing, posttraumatic stress disorder, and trauma: A review of randomized controlled trials with children and adolescents. *Child Adolescent Social Work Journal.* 2012;29(5):409–425.

16. Harrington, T. et al. The psychometric utility of two self-report measures of PTSD among women substance users. *Addictive Behaviors.* 2007;32:2788–2798.

17. Johnson, B. A. et al. Topiramate for treating alcohol dependence—a randomized controlled trial. *JAMA.* 2007. 298:1641–1651.

18. Johnson, B. A. et al. Update on neuropharmacological treatments for alcoholism: Scientific basis and clinical findings. *Biochemical Pharmacology.* 2008;75:34–35.

19. Kessler, R. C. et al. Prevalence, severity, and comorbidity of 12-month DSM-IV disorder in the National Comorbidity Survey Replication. *Archives of General Psychiatry.* 2005;62:617–627.

20. Killeen, T. et al. Adverse events in an integrated trauma-focused intervention for women in community substance abuse treatment. *Journal of Substance Abuse Treatment.* 2008;35:304–311.

21. Killeen, T. et al. The use of exposure-based treatment among individuals with PTSD and co-occurring substance use disorders: Clinical considerations. *Journal of Dual Diagnosis.* 2011;7(4):194–206.

22. Krystal, J. H. et al. Noradrenergic and serotonergic mechanisms in the neurobiology of posttraumatic stress disorder and resilience. *Brain Research.* 2009;1293:13–23.

23. Monson, C. M. et al. Cognitive processing therapy for veterans with military-related posttraumatic stress disorder. *Journal of Consulting and Clinical Psychology.* 2006;74:898–907.

24. Najavits, L. M. et al. "Seeking Safety" outcome of a new cognitive-behavioral psychotherapy for women with posttraumatic stress disorder and substance dependence. *Journal of Trauma Stress.* 1998,11:437–456.

25. Najavits, L. M. *Seeking Safety: A Treatment Manual for PTSD and Substance Abuse.* New York: Guilford Press; 2002

26. Norman, S. B. et al. Review of biological mechanisms and pharmacological treatments of comorbid PTSD and substance use disorder. *Neuropharmacology.* 2012;62:542–551.

27. Pae, C. U. et al. The atypical antipsychotics olanzapine and risperidone in the treatment of posttraumatic stress disorder: A meta-analysis of randomized double-blind placebo-controlled clinical trials. *International Clinical Psychopharmacology.* 2008;23:1–8.

28. Power, M. B. et al. A meta-analytic review of prolonged exposure for posttraumatic stress disorder. *Clinical Psychology Review.* 2010;30:635–641.

29. Ravindran, L. N. et al. Pharmacotherapy of PTSD: Premises, principles, and priorities. *Brain Research.* 2009;1293:24–39.

30. Resick, P. A. et al. Cognitive processing therapy for rape victims: A treatment manual. Newbury Park, CA: Sage, 1996.

31. Simpson, T. L. et al. Symptoms of posttraumatic stress predict craving among alcohol treatment seekers: results of a daily monitoring study. *Psychology of Addictive Behaviors.* 2012. doi: 10.1037/a0027169.

32. Southwick, S. et al. *Resilience: The Science of Mastering Life's Greatest Challenges.* Cambridge University Press. 2012

33. Torchalla, I. et al. Integrated treatment programs for individuals with concurrent substance use disorders and trauma experiences: A systematic review and meta-analysis. *Journal of Substance Abuse Treatment.* 2012;42:65–77.

34. van Dam, D. et al. Psychological treatments for concurrent posttraumatic stress disorder and substance abuse disorder: A systematic review. *Clinical Psychology Review.* 2012;32:202–215.

35. Veteran's Administration and Department of Defense. Clinical Practice Guideline for the Management of Post-Traumatic Stress Disorder. 2010. Available at www.healthquality.va.gov/ptsd/cpg_PTSD-FULL-201011612.pdf.

Chapter 14: Schizophrenia, Other Psychotic Disorders, and Co-Occurring Substance Use Disorders

REFERENCES

1. Andreasson, S. et al. Cannabis and schizophrenia. A longitudinal study of Swedish conscripts. *Lancet.* 1987;2:1483–1486.

2. Batkin, S. I. et al. Medical comorbidity in patients with schizophrenia and alcohol dependence. *Schizophrenia Research.* 2009;107(2–3):139–146.

3. Beebe, L. H. et al. Motivational intervention increases exercise in schizophrenia and co-occurring substance use disorders. *Schizophrenia Research.* 2012;135(1–3):204–205.

4. Bellack, A. S. et al. Behavioral treatment for substance abuse in people with serious and persistent mental illness: A handbook for mental health professionals. New York: Routledge, 2007.

5. Bellack, A. S. et al. A randomized clinical trial of a new behavioral treatment for drug abuse in people with severe and persistent mental illness. *Archives of General Psychiatry.* 2006;63:426–432.

6. Bruentte, M. F. et al. Implementation of integrated dual disorders treatment: A qualitative analysis of facilitators and barriers. *Psychiatric Services.* 2008;59(9):989–995.

7. Drake, R. E. et al. Dual Diagnosis: 15 years of progress. *Psychiatric Services.* 2000;51(9): 1126–1129.

8. Drake, R. E. et al. Implementing dual diagnosis services for clients with severe mental illness. *Psychiatric Services.* 2001;52(4):476–496.

9. Drake, R. E. et al. A systematic review of treatments of psychosocial research on psychosocial interventions for people with co-occurring substance use disorders: A review of specific interventions. *Journal of Substance Abuse Treatment.* 2008;34:123–138.

10. Drake, R. E. et al. A review of treatments for people with severe mental illnesses and co-occurring substance use disorders. *Psychiatric Rehabilitation Journal.* 2004;27:360–374.

11. Drake, R. E. et al. Assertive community treatment for patients with co-occurring severe mental illness and substance use disorder: A clinical trial. *American Journal of Orthopsychiatry.* 1998;68:201–215.

12. Fergusson, D. M. et al. Tests of causal linkages between cannabis use and psychotic symptoms. *Addiction.* 2005;100:354–366.

13. Hasnain, M. et al. Clinical monitoring and management of the metabolic syndrome in patients receiving atypical antipsychotic medications. Primary Care Diabetes. 2008. doi:10.1016/j.pcd.2008.10.005.

14. Hawthorne, W. B. et al. Incarceration among adults who are in the public mental health system: Rates, risk factors, and short-term outcomes. *Psychiatric Services.* 2012;63(1): 26–32.

15. Himelhoch, S. et al. Understanding associations between serious mental illness and hepatitis C virus among veterans: A national multivariate analysis. *Psychosomatics.* 2009;50(1): 30–37.

16. Horsfall, J. et al. Psychosocial treatments for people with co-occurring severe mental illnesses and substance use disorders(dual diagnosis): A review of the empirical evidence. *Harvard Review of Psychiatry.* 2009;17(1):24–34.

17. Kay, S. R. et al. The positive and negative syndrome scale (PANSS) for schizophrenia. *Schizophrenia Bulletin.* 1987;13(2):261–276.

18. Koola, M. M. et al. Alcohol and cannabis use and mortality in people with schizophrenia and related psychotic disorders. *Journal of Psychiatric Research.* 2012;46(8):987–993.

19. Lybrand, J. et al. Management of schizophrenia with substance use disorders. *Psychiatric Clinics of North America.* 2009;32(4):821–833.

20. Magura, S. Effectiveness of dual focus mutual aid for co-occurring substance use and mental health disorders: A review and synthesis of the "Double Trouble" in Recovery evaluation. *Substance Use Misuse.* 2008;43(12–13):1904–1926.

21. Matusow, H. et al. Consumers' experiences in dual focus mutual aid for co-occurring substance use and mental health disorders. *Substance Abuse Research and Treatment.* 2013;7:39–47.

22. McHugo, G. J. et al. A 10-year study of steady employment and non-vocational outcomes among people with serious mental illness and co-occurring substance use disorders. *Schizophrenia Research.* 2012;138(2–3):233–239.

23. Mueser, K. T. et al. Family intervention for co-occurring substance use and severe psychiatric disorders: Participant characteristics and correlates of initial engagement and more extended exposure in a randomized controlled trial. *Addictive Behavior.* 2009;34(10):867–877.

24. Muesser, K. T. et al. Psychosocial interventions for adults with severe mental illnesses and co-occurring substance use disorders: a review of specific interventions. *Journal of Dual Diagnosis.* 2005;1:57–82.

25. Overall, J. E. et al. The Brief Psychiatric Rating Scale (BPRS). *Psychological Reports.* 1962;10:799–812.

26. Ross, S. et al. Co-occurring psychotic and addictive disorders: Neurobiology and diagnosis. *Clinical Neuropharmacology.* 2012;35(5):235–243.

27. Schmidt, L. M. et al. The impact of substance use disorders on the course of schizophrenia—A 15-year follow-up study: Dual Diagnosis over 15 years. *Schizophrenia Research.* 2011;130(1–3):228–233.

28. Smelson, D. A. et al. Pharmacological treatment of schizophrenia and co-occurring substance use disorders. *CNS Drugs.* 2008;22(11)903–916.

29. Tehhula, W. N. et al. Behavioral treatment of substance abuse in schizophrenia. *Journal of Clinical Psychology.* 2009;65(8):831–841.

30. Tiet, Q. Q. et al. Treatments for patients with dual diagnosis: A review. *Alcoholism Clinical and Experimental Research.* 2007;31:513–536.

31. Tsai, J. et al. Housing preferences and choices among adults with mental illness and substance use disorders: A qualitative study. *Community Mental Health.* 2010;46(4):381–388.

32. Vincent, P. C. et al. Validation of the revised Problems Assessment for Substance Using Psychiatric Patients. *Addictive Behavior.* 2011;36(5):494–501.

33. Vogel, H. S. et al. Double Trouble in Recovery: Self-help for people with dual diagnoses. *Psychiatric Rehabilitation Journal.* 1998;21(4):356–364.

34. Ziedonis, D. M. et al. Improving the care of individuals with schizophrenia and substance use disorders: Consensus recommendations. *Journal of Psychiatric Practice.* 2005;11: 315–339.

Chapter 15: Personality Disorders and Co-Occurring Substance Use Disorders

RESOURCES

1. Behavioral Tech, LLC. http://behavioraltech.org

2. DBT Self-Help (A consumer-owned and -operated site). dbtselfhelp.com

3. National Education Alliance for Borderline Personality Disorder (NEABPD). www.borderlinepersonalitydisorder.com

4. Treatment and Research Advancements National Association for Personality Disorders (TARA NAPD)—advocacy and support for families and people with BPD. www.tara4bpd.org.

REFERENCES

1. American Psychiatric Association. Practice guideline for the treatment of patients with borderline personality disorder. *American Journal of Psychiatry.* 2001;158:1–52.

2. Dimeff, L. et al. *Dialectical Behavior Therapy in Clinical Practice: Applications across Disorders and Settings.* The Guilford Press, 2007.

3. Gunderson J. Borderline personality disorder. *New England Journal of Medicine.* 2011;2037–2042.

4. Ingenhoven, T. et al. Effectiveness of pharmacotherapy for severe personality disorders: Meta-analyses of randomized controlled trials. *Journal of Clinical Psychiatry.* 2010;71(1):14–25.

5. Koerner, K. *Doing Dialectical Behavior Therapy: A Practical Guide.* Guilford Press, 2011.

6. Lenzenweger, M. F. al. DSM-IV personality disorders in the National Comorbidity Survey Replication. *Biological Psychiatry.* 2007; 62(6):553–564.

7. Lieb, K. et al. Pharmacotherapy for borderline personality disorder: Cochrane systematic review of randomised trials. *British Journal of Psychiatry.* 2010;196:4–12.

8. Linehan, M. *Skills Training Manual for Treating Borderline Personality Disorder.* The Guilford Press, 1993.

9. Linehan, M. *Cognitive-Behavioral Treatment of Borderline Personality Disorder.* The Guilford Press, 1993.

10. Linehan, M. et al. Dialectical behavior therapy versus comprehensive validation therapy plus 12-step for the treatment of opioid dependent women meeting criteria for borderline personality disorder. *Drug and Alcohol Dependence* 2002;67:13–26.

11. Linehan, M. et al. Dialectical behavior therapy for patients with borderline personality disorder and drug-dependence. *American Journal of Addictions.* 1999;8:279–292.

12. McKay, M. et al. *Dialectical Behavior Therapy Skills Workbook: Practical DBT Exercises for Learning Mindfulness, Interpersonal Effectiveness, Emotion Regulation, and Distress Tolerance.* New Harbinger Publications, 2007.

13. Oldham, J. M. Guideline Watch: Practice guideline for the treatment of borderline personality disorder. APA Practice Guidelines, 2005.

14. Trull, T. J. et al. Research on borderline personality disorder an update. *Current Opinion in Psychiatry*. 2003;16:77–82.

Chapter 16: Alcohol

RESOURCES

1. Adult Children of Alcoholics. Mutual self-help for people who grew up in alcoholic and otherwise dysfunctional households. Utilizes a 12-step approach. www.adultchildren.org/

2. Al-anon and Alateen. Mutual self-help for friends and families of problem drinkers. Utilizes a 12-step approach. www.al-anon.alateen.org/

3. Alcoholics Anonymous. aa.org

4. National Institute on Alcohol Abuse and Alcoholism. www.niaaa.nih.gov/

5. SMART Recovery. A non-12-step mutual self-help organization that emphasizes empowerment. www.smartrecovery.org/

6. U.S. Department of Agriculture and U.S. Department of Health and Human Services. In *Dietary Guidelines for Americans*, Chapter 3—Foods and Food Components to Reduce . 7th ed, Washington, DC: U.S. Government Printing Office, 2010, pp. 30–32.

References

1. ASAM: Addiction Medicine Essentials: Clinical Institute Withdrawal Assessment of Alcohol Scale, Revised (CIWA-Ar). *Supplement of ASAM News*. 2001;16(1).

2. Busto, U. E. et al. A clinical scale to assess benzodiazepine withdrawal. *Journal of Clinical Psychopharmacology*. 1989;9(6):412–416.

3. Foy, A. et al. Use of an objective clinical scale in the assessment and management of alcohol withdrawal in a large general hospital. *Alcoholism: Clinical and Experimental Research*. 1988;12:360–364.

4. Mayo-Smith, M. F. et al. Management of alcohol withdrawal delirium: An evidence-based practice guideline. *Archives of Internal Medicine*. 2004;164:1405–1412.

5. Skinner, H. A. et al. Reliability of alcohol use indices. The Lifetime Drinking History and the MAST. *Journal of Studies on Alcohol and Drugs*. 1982;43:1157–1170.

6. Sullivan, J. T. et al. Assessment of alcohol withdrawal. The revised Clinical Institute Withdrawal Assessment for Alcohol scale (CIWA-AR). *British Journal of Addiction*. 1989;84:1353–1357.

Chapter 17: Tobacco

RESOURCES

1. Centers for Disease Control and Prevention: Vital Signs Telebriefing on Cigarette Smoking among Adults with Mental Illness. www.cdc.gov/media/releases/2013/t0205_smoking_mentally_ill.html

2. Smokefree.gov: This well-organized website provides a wealth of information, along with free resources.

3. 1-800-QUIT-NOW. This federal/state initiative provides free counseling and, in some states, free nicotine patches to help people stop smoking.

References:

1. Lasser, K. et al. Smoking and mental illness: A population-based prevalence study. *JAMA*. 2000;284(20):2606–2610.

2. SAMHSA: Smoking and Mental Illness. *The NSDUH Report*. February 6, 2013.

3. Williams, J. M. et al. Viewpoint: Partnership between tobacco control programs and offices of mental health needed to reduce smoking rates in the United States. *JAMA Psychiatry*. October 30, 2013.

Chapter 18: Opioids

REFERENCES

1. Agency for Healthcare Research and Quality (AHRQ). Naltrexone for the management of opioid dependence (Guideline Summary NGC-5507) (Jan. 2007).

2. American College of Obstetricians and Gynecologists (ACOG) Committee Opinion No. 524: Opioid abuse, dependence, and addiction in pregnancy. *Obstetrics and Gynecology*. 2012;119(5):1070–1076.

3. Back, S. E. et al. Gender and prescription opioids: Findings from the National Survey on Drug Use and Health. *Addictive Behavior*. 2010;35(11):1001–1007.

4. Back, S. E. et al. Characteristics and correlates of men and women with prescription opioid dependence. *Addictive Behaviors*. 2011;36(8):829–834.

5. Brady, K. T. et al. *Women and Addiction: A Comprehensive Handbook*. New York: Guilford Press, 2009.

6. The Cochrane Collaboration. *Maintenance Agonist Treatments for Opiate Dependent Pregnant Women (Review)*. Wiley, 2011.

7. De Maeyer, J. et al. Quality of life among opiate-dependent individuals: A review of the literature. *International Journal of Drug Policy*. 2010;21(5):364–380.

8. Fareed, A. et al. Methadone maintenance dosing guideline for opioid dependence: A literature review. *Journal of Addictive Diseases*. 2010; 29(1):1–14.

9. Hall, A. J. et al. Patterns of abuse among unintentional pharmaceutical overdose fatalities. *JAMA*. 2008;300(22):2613–2620.

10. Jones, H. E. et al. Neonatal abstinence syndrome after methadone or buprenorphine exposure. *New England Journal of Medicine*. 2010;363(24):2320–2331.

11. Jones, H. E. et al. Treating the partners of opioid-dependent pregnant patients: Feasibility and efficacy. *American Journal of Drug and Alcohol Abuse*. 2011;37(3):170–178.

12. Kakko, J. et al. Buprenorphine and methadone treatment of opiate dependence during pregnancy: Comparison of fetal growth and neonatal outcomes in two consecutive case series. *Drug and Alcohol Dependence.* 2008;96(1–2):69–78.

13. Krupitsky, E. et al. Injectable extended-release naltrexone for opioid dependence: A double-blind, placebo-controlled, multicenter randomized trial. *Lancet.* 2011;377: 1506–1513.

14. Lacroix, I. et al. Buprenorphine versus methadone in pregnant opioid-dependent women: A prospective multicenter study. *European Journal of Clinical Pharmacology.* 2011;67(10):1053–1059.

15. McLellan, A. T. et al. Prescription opioids, overdose deaths, and physician responsibility. *JAMA.* 2008;300(22):2672–2673.

16. SAMHSA Advisory. An introduction to extended-release injectable naltrexone for the treatment of people with opioid dependence. 2012; DHHS Publication No. (SMA) 12-4682.

17. SAMHSA TIP 40. Clinical Guidelines for the use of buprenorphine in the treatment of opioid addiction. 2004. DHHS Publication No. (SMA) 06-4218.

18. Trafton, J. A. et al. Consistent adherence to guidelines to improve opioid dependent patients' first year outcomes. *Journal of Behavioral Health Services and Research.* 2007;34(3):260–271.

19. Unger, A. et al. Gender issues in the pharmacotherapy of opioid-addicted women: Buprenorphine. *Journal of Addictive Disorders.* 2010;29(2):217–230.

20. Wesson, D. R. et al. The Clinical Opiate Withdrawal Scale (COWS). *Journal of Psychoactive Drugs.* 2003;35(2):253–259.

Chapter 19: Selected Topics for Other Substances

REFERENCES

1. Agrawal, A. et al. Cannabis involvement in individuals with bipolar disorder. *Psychiatry Research.* 2011;185:459–61.

2. Benotsch, E. G. et al. Intentional misuse of over-the-counter medications, mental health, and polysubstance use in young adults. *Journal of Community Health.* 2013.

3. The Centers for Disease Control. Emergency department visits after use of a drug sold as "bath salts"—Michigan, November 13, 2010–March 31, 2011. *Morbidity and Mortality Weekly.* 2011;60.

4. Eden Evins, A. et al. The effect of marijuana use on the risk for schizophrenia. *Journal of Clinical Psychiatry.* 2012;73(11):1463–1468.

5. Fergusson, D. M. et al. Tests of causal linkages between cannabis use and psychotic symptoms. *Addiction.* 2005;100:354–366.

6. Jerry, J. et al. Synthetic legal intoxicating drugs: The emerging "incense" and "bath salt" phenomenon. *Cleveland Clinic Journal of Medicine.* 2012;79(4):258–264.

7. Large, M. et al. Cannabis use and earlier onset of psychosis. *Archives of General Psychiatry.* 2011;68(6):555–561.

8. Loeffler, G. et al. "Bath salt" induced agitated paranoia: A case series. *Journal of Studies on Alcohol and Drugs.* 2012;73(4):706.

9. Murphy, C. M. et al. "Bath salts" and "plant food" products: The experience of one regional U.S. poison center. *Journal of Medical Toxicology.* 2013;9(1):42–48.

10. Pierre, J. M.: Cannabis, synthetic cannabinoids, and psychosis risk: What the evidence says. *Current Psychiatry.* 2011;10(9):49–58.

11. Prosser, J. M. et al. The toxicology of bath salts: A review of synthetic cathinones. *Journal of Medical Toxicology.* 2012;8(1):33–42.

12. Ross, E. A. et al. "Bath salts" intoxication with methylenedioxypyrovalerone. *American Journal of Medicine.* 2012. doi.org/10.1016/j.amjmed.2012.02.019.

13. Ross, E. A. et al. "Bath Salts" intoxications. *New England Journal of Medicine.* 2011;365(10):967–968.

14. Salloum, I. M. et al. Patient characteristics and treatment implications of marijuana abuse among bipolar alcoholics: Results from a double blind, placebo-controlled study. *Addictive Behaviors.* 2005;30:1702–1708.

15. van Rossum, I. et al. Does cannabis use affect treatment outcome in bipolar disorder? A longitudinal analysis. *Journal of Nervous and Mental Disease.* 2009;197(1):35–40.

16. Williams, J. F. et al. Abuse of proprietary (over-the-counter) drugs. *Adolescent Medical Clinics.* 2006;17(3):733–750.

17. Wilson, B. et al. Synthetic cannabinoids, synthetic cathinones, and other emerging drugs of abuse. *Psychiatric Annals.* 2013;43(12):558–564.

Index